658.3124

The
Coaching
Manual

Books that make you better

Books that make you better. That make you *be* better, *do* better, *feel* better. Whether you want to upgrade your personal skills or change your job, whether you want to improve your managerial style, become a more powerful communicator, or be stimulated and inspired as you work.

Prentice Hall Business is leading the field with a new breed of skills, careers and development books. Books that are a cut above the mainstream – in topic, content and delivery – with an edge and verve that will make you better, with less effort.

Books that are as sharp and smart as you are.

Prentice Hall Business.
We work harder – so you don't have to.

For more details on products, and to contact us, visit
www.pearsoned.co.uk

The
Coaching
Manual

The definitive guide to the process, principles and skills of personal coaching

Third edition

Julie Starr

**Prentice Hall
Business
is an imprint of**

Harlow, England • London • New York • Boston • San Francisco • Toronto • Sydney • Singapore • Hong Kong
Tokyo • Seoul • Taipei • New Delhi • Cape Town • Madrid • Mexico City • Amsterdam • Munich • Paris • Milan

PEARSON EDUCATION LIMITED

Edinburgh Gate
Harlow CM20 2JE
Tel: +44 (0)1279 623623
Fax: +44 (0)1279 431059
Website: www.pearsoned.co.uk

First published in Great Britain in 2002
Second edition published 2008
Third edition 2011

© Pearson Education Limited 2008, 2011

The right of Julie Starr to be identified as author of this work has been asserted by her in accordance with the Copyright, Designs and Patents Act 1988.

ISBN: 978-0-273-74058-2

British Library Cataloguing-in-Publication Data
A catalogue record for this book is available from the British Library

Library of Congress Cataloging-in-Publication Data
Starr, Julie.
   The coaching manual : the definitive guide to the process, principles and skills of personal coaching / Julie Starr. – 3rd ed.
      p. cm.
   Includes index.
   ISBN 978-0-273-74058-2 (pbk.)
   1. Personal coaching – Handbooks, manuals, etc. I. Title.
   BF637.P36S73 2011
   158'.3–dc22

                                                                    2010037614

10 9 8 7 6 5 4 3 2
14 13 12 11

Typeset in Palatino LT Std 10/15pt by Fakenham Photosetting Ltd, Fakenham, Norfolk

Printed by Ashford Colour Press Ltd., Gosport

Contents

Acknowledgements

There are many people who have contributed to the development of the ideas and thoughts in the book and I hope I've remembered to acknowledge most of them. So I would like to express gratitude for the work of the following people: Anthony Robbins, Stephen Covey, John Grinder, Richard Bandler, Deepak Chopra, M. Scott Peck, Landmark Education, Brian Tracey, Frank Daniels, Brandon Bays and Milton H. Erickson.

I'd also like to thank Dr Xanthe Wells, Scott Downing, Mike Fryer, Bob Janes, Joss Kang, Richard Watts, Julia Whiteley, Marcia Yudkin and Rachael Stock for their challenges, thoughts and ideas in preparation of the text.

chapter

1

Introduction

Welcome to the third edition of *The Coaching Manual*. Since the book was first written, I have watched as the awareness of and appetite for coaching continue to emerge. Professionally, coaching is firmly established and that's positive, for at the heart of coaching is an awareness of our basic interdependency as people, and there is much good that can come from that simple truth.

The Coaching Manual has been translated into several languages and now supports the practice and development of coaching far and wide. Since the publication of the first edition I have continued to work and study within the field of personal development and, in particular, personal coaching. In this edition, we have made the manual more practical, by adding a Toolkit that offers 'instant access' to some useful routines and processes that will help you develop your skills immediately. The purpose of this edition is to build on the base of the first two, by offering further insights and guidance for anyone involved in coaching, in any situation. I hope you enjoy this book and find it supports the work that you do.

* * * *

I wonder why you are reading this book?

Maybe you want to learn more about coaching, or begin coaching others. Perhaps you're already coaching and are ready to develop your knowledge and skills further. Maybe you work in the field of learning, development or therapy and are interested in what coaching has to offer. Or perhaps you're considering engaging a coach and want to know what you're 'getting into'. Whatever your reasons, I'm optimistic that you've come to the right place.

Coaching people is a highly rewarding thing to do. It is about enabling people to create change through learning. Coaching is also about people being more, doing more, achieving more and, above all, contributing more. In our constant quest for success, happiness and fulfilment, coaching provides a way by which one person can truly support the progress of another.

So, whoever you are, I'll say welcome. Your interest benefits us all. The field of coaching needs more of us to constantly develop our own learning, and so improve general standards of coaching everywhere.

The purpose of this book

This book explains the principles and approaches of personal coaching and shows you how to apply them in any coaching situation: from business coaching for performance, to more holistic life coaching. For those already coaching, the manual offers new insights and fresh ideas. For the new coach, the manual is a practical guide to begin and support your learning. For the busy manager, the manual provides techniques to use with your team.

The Coaching Manual covers the principles and beliefs that underpin coaching, describes the actual coaching process stage by stage, and gives fresh perspectives on the skills you need to develop. There is also the structure of a typical coaching conversation, to help you navigate through the first 'hello' to a typical 'farewell'. Plus, you'll get practical guidance on what works and what may simply get in the way of great coaching. When you're ready to leap into action, the Toolkit will help give you even more confidence to get started.

If you're interested in enlisting the services of a coach, either for yourself or others, you'll gain insight into coaching practices that will support you as a client.

Counsellors, or those thinking of going into counselling, will find relevant information and guidance. Many of our building blocks and skills are the same: principles of integrity and a person's responsibility for their actions are common to both. Skills of listening, questioning and establishing relationships are also key within both professions.

A manual that helps you to learn

This book is designed to provide you with a practical, enjoyable way to learn while you read. You'll find clearly marked sections, together with exercises and examples that will help you develop the skills, perspectives and beliefs of a good coach. Whether you're new to coaching, or have been coaching forever – this book will help you develop further. Some exercises are easy, while others are a real challenge. I invite you to discover which ones most benefit your learning.

The exercises and learning routines can be done in your normal, everyday circumstances – so you don't have to be coaching in order to learn coaching!

Some exercises can be done alone, others in the company of colleagues or friends. Often, you can try out the new behaviours or routines without people knowing that you're actually learning while you're with them.

There are also routines and language that you can use in coaching sessions, to help you to be really effective in those conversations. Once you've finished reading, you can use the book as an ongoing point of reference, to help you plan your coaching, brush up on your skills and stay on a path of progress.

What is personal coaching?

Going back to early forms of transportation, i.e. stagecoach or rail coach, the word 'coaching' literally means to transport someone from one place to another. In today's context, one thing that all forms of coaching seem to have in common is that people are using it to help them move forward or create change.

Put simply, coaching is a conversation, or series of conversations, that one person has with another. The person who is the coach intends to produce a conversation that will benefit the other person (the coachee) in a way that relates to the coachee's learning and progress. Coaching conversation might happen in many different ways and in many different environments.

Put simply, coaching is a conversation, or series of conversations, one person has with another.

Coaching has many different forms or expressions, within many different areas of human activity. There are sports coaches, music coaches, relationship coaches, voice coaches, writing coaches and time-management coaches, to name but a few. It appears that whatever you might be doing, there's a coach out there to help you do it!

The person who decides whether a conversation was a coaching conversation or not is normally the person who is being coached. If someone acknowledges the following to be true after a conversation, then they would probably accept that it was coaching:

➡ The focus of the conversation was primarily themselves and their circumstances.

➡ Their thinking, actions and learning benefited significantly from the conversation.

➡ They were unlikely to have had those benefits in thinking or learning within that time frame if the conversation hadn't happened.

So when we apply these simple principles, we realize we've been coaching each other forever. For generations, whether it's over the garden wall, a cup of tea or a beer in the pub, we've talked about what happens in our lives. We share our troubles and our dreams. We listen to each other and we advise each other. This process normally helps. Maybe we realize a solution, make a decision, or perhaps the conversation simply makes us feel better.

Try it yourself   **Where are you already coaching?**

Of the following, which do you do regularly?

➡ Give friends or colleagues advice.

➡ Listen to others' problems, to help and support them.

➡ Explain to other people how to do something better.

➡ Train others in new knowledge or skills.

➡ Manage the work of others.

➡ Give other people feedback or observations of their behaviour so that they can get better at something.

➡ Conduct job appraisals or assessments of people's work performance.

➡ Provide counselling for others.

➡ Perform personal coaching on a 1:1 basis.

If you do any of the above activities, you are already influencing others through some form of coaching. Whether your coaching conversations are planned or not, this book gives you support and practical guidance so that those conversations create great results.

Where does coaching come from?

In spite of the growth of coaching in business, the most recognized forms of coaching come from the sporting world. Having evolved over thousands of years, the figure of a sports coach working alongside top athletes is accepted without question. However, there may seem to be a contradiction in having someone who can't do what you can do, as well as you can do it, to help you to improve. Roger Federer's coach can't play tennis like Federer does and yet he plays a vital role in improving Federer's game. So why does Federer get help from a lesser player?

The reason is simple: because coaching is proven to work. It improves the results an individual is creating. A tennis coach needs coaching skills more than they need to be a good tennis player themselves. By applying principles of observation and feedback, sports coaches can make the difference between a world champion and an also-ran.

Strangely, when someone has all the skills needed to produce a result themselves, they can't always help someone else to do it. For example, a world-class football player might have real difficulty in coaching someone else to the same standard. This is because the perspectives and skills of a coach are essentially different from those of a football player. If a football player wants to become a great coach, they must begin to focus on developing coaching behaviours and skills. It's not enough to be able to 'do' – you have to be able to coach.

The same principle applies in business. Coaches work alongside individuals to help improve their performance at work, regardless of whether or not they could do that work themselves. What a coach can do is help someone see opportunities for improvement, as well as practical ways forward.

Coaching as an industry

The coaching industry is firmly established and still growing: Google 'life coaching' and you'll get over 11.5 million results; search for 'business coaching' and the results increase to over 12.5 million.

Within the business sector, the Chartered Institute of Personnel and Development (CIPD) found the following in their 2009 annual survey:

➡ Coaching is the most effective talent management activity used by organizations.

➡ 57 per cent agreed that being a coachee is encouraged by their organization.

➡ 55 per cent of respondents said that coaching was part of their organization's management development initiatives.

For more information visit www.cipd.co.uk.

The benefits of coaching are also widely acknowledged; in a survey by the Association Resources Centre and PricewaterhouseCoopers*, 2165 coaching clients from 64 countries reported improvements in:

Self esteem/self confidence	(80%)
Communication skills	(72%)
Interpersonal skills	(71%)
Work performance	(70%)
Relationships	(73%)
Work/life balance	(63%)

So whether you're interested in being a coach or coachee, the opportunities are already good and continue to increase.

How does personal coaching happen?

A personal coach normally works within arranged coaching sessions. The coach will usually use a blend of observation, talking, listening, questioning and reflecting back to the individual they are working with. If the situation or circumstances are suitable, a coach might also use other media to conduct a coaching session, such as telephone or e-mail.

Coaching might consist of two people talking in a room about things the coachee wants to change. This is sometimes called 'off-line' coaching. Alternatively, it might be a coach observing someone doing something, e.g. talking to customers or colleagues, then discussing that with them. This can be called 'on-line' coaching, as the action is actually happening.

Other coaching conversations might easily happen outside a formal coaching session. For example, a casual discussion around a challenging

*Survey on behalf of the International Coach Federation (ICF), www.coachfederation.org

situation or goal may easily produce a conversation in which the individual receives coaching.

Whether coaching happens in the workplace or outside, the two activities can easily merge into the same thing. It's often impossible to separate work from life anyway. People's lives don't package themselves into neat little bundles – job, home, money, health, etc. Our lives seem to contain themes that run through them like common-coloured thread. If you're not happy at work, that's likely to show up somewhere else. If you're not feeling healthy or full of energy, then that's likely to be mirrored elsewhere, e.g. in your relationships or social life.

The coaching relationship

The role of coach provides a kind of support distinct from any other. A coach will focus solely on an individual's situation with the kind of attention and commitment that the individual will rarely experience elsewhere.

If you imagine yourself being coached, you will perhaps appreciate why so many people engage the services of a coach. This person, your coach, will listen to you, with a curiosity to understand who you are, what you think and generally how you experience the world. Your coach will reflect back to you, with the kind of objective view that creates real clarity. During conversations, your coach will encourage you to rise to challenges, overcome obstacles and move into action.

What's most important during that conversation is you, your success, happiness and ultimate fulfilment. Having worked to establish exactly what you want to achieve from coaching, those goals and objectives become the focus for the conversation. As a consequence, the only agenda happening in the conversation is your agenda, which your coach will often guard more closely than you do. When you're ready to quit, no longer care that you want to get that promotion, get better at something, or change your lifestyle, your coach stays committed to those goals.

> What's most important during that conversation is you, your success, happiness and ultimate fulfilment.

When things don't go well, your coach supports you. When you experience success, your coach celebrates your achievements. Your coach will also help you to pinpoint exactly what you did that worked so well, so that you can do it again. A coaching relationship is like no other, simply because of its combination of objective detachment and commitment to the goals of the individual.

Little wonder then that so many people are finding that coaching relationships can help them develop and learn in ways that enable them to have or achieve what they really want.

Learn to coach by being coached

One of the best ways to learn how to be a good coach is to be coached. This way, you will experience what it feels like to be a coachee. You will understand what works and what doesn't, what feels right and what feels wrong. Surprisingly, that might not always be what you expect. For example, as a coach, silence can be uncomfortable, while for a coachee, the same silence can feel wonderful. A sense of rapid progress during a conversation can feel great for the coach, and yet turbulent for the coachee. So, if you're serious about developing your coaching skills, I recommend you have some sort of coaching as part of your development. As well as helping you develop as a coach, you'll probably find there are other benefits for your personal goals as well!

Coaching in business

Coaching is now big in business. Organizations now realize that they can improve both the performance and motivation of their people through coaching. Increasingly, a 'coaching' style of management is preferred to the more traditional approaches of 'command and control'. Instead of managers directing people, giving detailed instructions of what to do and when to do it, they focus more on encouraging people to think for themselves. We sometimes call that 'showing a hungry man how to fish' (rather than simply giving him a fish). When problems arise, coaching managers don't automatically jump in and solve them. Instead, they challenge others to resolve situations. Coaching managers provide support, challenge, feedback and guidance – but rarely answers.

Managers who coach often place as much importance on the development of people reporting to them as on the tasks those people are performing. For the manager, this means fewer queues of people at their desk asking what to do next (and much less worry if the manager wants a vacation). More of the manager's focus is on establishing conditions in which people can perform independently of the manager. Creating these conditions means more time is spent on activities such as objective setting, one-to-one meetings and team briefings. One-to-one meetings can now become coaching sessions, as the manager adopts a more supportive, challenging and developmental approach.

During team meetings, the manager can use the coaching skills of listening, questioning and goal setting to encourage the group to take responsibility for situations. Over time, colleagues learn more, perform better, and are generally more motivated by this nurturing style of leadership. As they become used to the manager's expectations of them, they begin to respond automatically to situations with more responsibility and empowerment.

Managers who coach improve productivity, morale and job satisfaction for their colleagues. Such managers, in turn, find that people are less dependent upon them, which often reduces pressure, or frees up time to concentrate on other priorities. As more businesses go multi-site or even global, the distance between managers and their teams widens. Here, a coaching style is essential for both sanity and success. As coaching managers increase people's independence, they directly reduce the dependency on themselves to be on-site, directing events.

Executive coaching

Organizations are now willing to invest in personal coaching for their senior managers and executives. By improving the performance of the most influential people in an organization, coaches are able to improve results across a broad area. In short, we create a positive influence on people who have influence. Senior managers encourage typical behaviours and ways of being within the rest of their organization. What they say and how they behave establish similar standards for people who work for them. If you are interested in coaching as a style of managing in the workplace, please see my book, *Brilliant Coaching*, which focuses on this topic directly.

Executive coaching is often done by coaches operating from outside the organization, whose services are requested for an agreed duration or number of coaching sessions. Increasingly, personal coaches are also being trained internally, as organizations realize the opportunity this presents. Internal coaches normally cost less, and can operate very effectively because of their knowledge of the operation. Unfortunately, senior staff can be wary of using internals, perceiving them to lack independence or credibility. The challenge for internal coaches is to prove that they can coach with real impact while maintaining a position of objectivity and trust. It's a worthwhile challenge, surely.

Within business, situations that benefit from personal coaching might include the following:

⇒ A manager with potential has been promoted and is having difficulty performing in the new role.

⇒ An individual is being groomed for senior management and needs to gain skills or experience before they can make that move.

⇒ An individual has relationship issues that are creating problems at an organizational level.

⇒ An organization has decided to align management behaviours to a set of core values, e.g. integrity, collaboration or innovation. Some managers will need coaching in these specific areas.

For example, during coaching a marketing director realizes that he acts competitively against the sales director. Owing to the competition he feels, he encourages his own department to withhold support and information from the sales department. This causes him problems. Last year he mistimed the launch of a range of sports gear – bringing it out on exactly the same day as the main competitors. Sales could have told him this was a mistake, but they heard about the launch too late. During coaching, the marketing director improves his relationship with the sales director, and encourages his department to adopt a more collaborative style. This results in marketing telling sales more about their plans for the year and what kind of products they're thinking of launching. As the flow and exchange of information improves, so does the quality of products and sales campaigns.

Businesses – harnessing the concept of interdependence

Coaching rests on the principle that as people we are interdependent: as human beings we acknowledge the simple truth of our connection and influence upon each other. This is different from operating from ideas of dependence, co-dependence or independence. When we operate from a belief that we are *dependent* on others, we are less able to influence them. That's because we have given our power to someone else: I depend on you to do something – and you are out of my control. When we build relationships of *co-dependence*, we have built a two-way reliance, i.e. you depend on me and I depend on you. We are both limited by our reliance on each other. *Independence* is the idea that we 'go it alone' or operate 'solo'. Being independent is generally perceived as a positive attribute, and preferable to dependency. For example, when someone acts independently, they are generally viewed as being unbiased or objective. It is also an indication of apparent confidence, e.g. 'Oh, he'll find his way there, he's a really independent character'. But independence is also a limit; an isolated position, summed up in the phrase 'no man is an island'.

Interdependence recognizes that we are part of a system and our ability to thrive and prosper will be affected by our ability to operate as part of that system. We realize that the 'go it alone' perspective of independence will only get us so far and that to truly prosper, both as individuals and as communities, we must foster behaviours that acknowledge our basic connections. For example, if you want to succeed in your work (whatever you might do) there are likely to be other people that help or hinder your progress. When people recommend you, you prosper; if people choose to engage your services, you will succeed. Even your ability to perform your work well is influenced by those around you; whether that's someone passing on your telephone message, giving you directions when you're lost, or making sure you get paid. Even if your work involves you spending lots of time alone, you're still connected. Through e-mail, telephone, the internet, your connection to others runs through your day like invisible threads.

Within business, building awareness of interdependency makes lots of sense. Our basic commercial goals and objectives (win customer, serve customer and reap reward) can only be achieved by the team operating together, and being aware of its connections and influence on overall results.

For organizations to truly succeed, this principle of interdependence must be woven throughout the fabric of the organization.

One of the reasons coaching is being used to enable better performance in the workplace is the simple link to interdependence. Coaching builds on this premise of interdependency by having one person support the success of another, whether that's managers coaching subordinates, or the other way round. To coach someone else increases your connection to them. Over time we realize the potential of creating results together.

Personal coaching: life/lifestyle

Coaching outside the workplace is now becoming common. This type of personal coaching is increasingly viewed as an acceptable form of support to anyone seeking to improve specific areas of their life, or simply their quality of life in general. Personal fulfilment, health, fitness, relationships, financial freedom are all common subjects for this type of coaching.

Why do people choose life coaching?

Coaching makes a valuable contribution to the process of helping people to experience life the way they want to experience it. For some people, coaching can literally change their lives for the better. With the support of a coach, people can make clearer judgements about situations, learn more from experiences, make better choices and take more effective decisions or actions.

For some people coaching can literally change their lives for the better.

For lots of us, life can be difficult. We place tremendous pressure on ourselves to have a lot, do a lot, and be generally successful in those areas of life we consider important. That might be having a great job, a great relationship, financial freedom – generally living a fabulous life.

I'm not going to debate whether that's right or wrong, but I do believe that coaching is a valuable counterbalance to that pressure. By engaging the services of a coach, we can begin to focus on what really is important to us and begin to shape what we need to do to align with that.

A comparison of coaching and therapy

There are obvious similarities between coaches and therapists. Both do a lot of talking and listening, both deal with people's problems. However, while coaching and therapy work in similar areas, they are not the same thing. Coaching supports general life situations, improving our performance and creating desirable results. Therapy normally focuses on specific, significant problems, e.g. trauma, mental illness, etc.

For example, coaching would be appropriate in the following situations:

➡ Putting together a life plan, understanding our aims and goals.

➡ Finding ways to reduce stress in our lives, or free up more time.

➡ Building a life/work balance that fulfils us.

➡ Improving our ability to relate to others.

➡ Improving our awareness of ourselves.

➡ Improving our self-discipline and motivation.

➡ Improving our health and well-being routines, e.g. diet, exercise.

There are obviously many more. What you'll notice from the above is that they are all goal-based objectives. That is, we want something we don't currently have and might use a coach to support us in attaining that. In addition, the problems associated with the goal might be making us unhappy, or even sick. For example, you're working 12-hour days on top of a 2-hour train journey and your relationship is in serious trouble because of that. In such situations, coaching is now an option where, before, therapy might have seemed to provide the only available support.

When coaching isn't the answer

It is important that a coach recognizes inappropriate situations for coaching. Where someone has issues that would be better addressed by a therapist, the coach should understand their own limitations. The skills and experience of the coach must be taken into account. As a guide, a coach with no relevant, specialist skills should avoid the following situations:

→ Ongoing dependency on class 'A' drugs, e.g. heroin, crack, cocaine.

→ Significant alcohol issues, e.g. someone who drinks to get through the day.

→ Where someone has experienced violent or sexual abuse and needs further support to deal with that.

→ Where someone is abusing others, either physically or sexually.

→ Mental illness, e.g. extreme and violent mood swings, ongoing depression, etc.

The skills of a therapist are often specialized to their area of therapy, e.g. addiction, abuse, mental illness, etc. To support individuals with extreme conditions or situations, a therapist will undergo specific training and development. They will normally have a relevant model, processes and ter- minology to deal with that situation. For example, Alcoholics Anonymous has a proven 12-step process that assists people to give up drinking, and psychiatrists study relevant theory in depth to be able to deal with more complex issues relating to mental health.

You will also notice that there is more emphasis on the 'problem' within the above situations. Often, the focus of coaching is more on 'solutions', e.g. 'What do you want instead?' The focus during therapy, however, tends to be more about the original, underlying problem; e.g. 'What causes you to avoid relationships?' A therapist may decide that an in-depth assessment, analysis and diagnosis of someone's problem is appropriate before the individual can progress. While self-awareness is also valuable in coaching, coaching doesn't rely upon an in-depth level of self-analysis in order to create results.

In summary, if a coach doesn't feel equipped to cope, they should refer the individual to a relevant specialist. If a coach does want to work in one of the above areas, then I would encourage them to seek the relevant training and support to do that.

Chapter summary **Introduction**

Coaching has been around forever. In more recent years, we've developed it into a profession. This profession focuses on techniques and methods that we understand make a difference to the results someone else is getting. Coaching is now firmly established as a way of supporting others in their quest to have what they really want, whether that is a specific goal or simply a lifestyle they want to create. Learning to coach others is both rewarding and fulfilling. And in a world where so many of us face complex life circumstances and decisions, coaching has a valuable contribution to make.

2

Collaborative
coaching

COACHEE: I guess I should.

COACH: Well there's a number of different ways you could do that. I'd suggest that initially you sit down and make a list of exactly what needs to be done, and make really firm commitments about when you intend to do them. I can help with that.

COACHEE: (hesitates) Oka-ay ...

You will notice from the dialogue that most of the talking is coming from the coach, who is clearly in control of the conversation. The ideas or solutions are also coming from the coach, and the coachee is expected to comply.

A collaborative style accepts that an individual often has their own answers and simply needs support for their own learning process.

For example, someone who constantly procrastinates or delays important tasks usually knows enough about themselves and their tendencies to be able to create improvement. Collaborative coaches will focus the individual/coachee on the relevant areas of their situation in order to surface ideas or insights needed to create progress. This style might sound like:

Non-directive conversation

COACH: What kind of things are you procrastinating about?

COACHEE: Well, I guess you'd call it administration, I mean generally. I don't like paperwork, you know, filling forms out, sending stuff off – I've a desk full of paper, its getting out of control.

COACH: What kind of problems does this cause you?

COACHEE: All sorts, from minor embarrassments when I have to apologize, to real dilemmas. I once had three credit cards in a row refused simply because I'd not sent off the payments, I was left standing in Rome airport with no way to pay for my return flight home.

COACH: How else does not dealing with this stuff affect you?

COACHEE: Well, to be honest, it makes me feel a bit of a mess. I mean, an adult who can't even send off a form when I said I would, and then have to request another because I've lost the original – I make myself look pretty stupid.

COACH: OK, we've talked a bit about consequences; let's look in a different direction – what stops you from getting this stuff done?

COACHEE: You know I could say I don't have time, but I don't think that's strictly true. I think it's more to do with the fact that I just begrudge doing it.

COACH: What is it about the paperwork that you don't like?

COACHEE: It's like being controlled, like someone else is making me do homework or something, when I'd rather be doing something else.

COACH: That's interesting isn't it? Is that true?

COACHEE: Well no, of course not, in actual fact, the reverse is probably true. If I got this stuff cleared I'd probably feel a whole lot freer and 10 pounds lighter – I could go and do whatever I wanted with a clear conscience.

Notice the coachee coming to their own learning, gaining their own insights and new perspectives on the situation. Also notice that the coach influences the focus and attention of the coachee, without telling them what to think.

In practice, an individual will feel like they've surfaced their own answers by exploring their own thoughts and ideas in a focused way. This will also feel more fulfilling for them as they reveal more of their inner resources.

Directive language – advantages

It's important to acknowledge that a directive style has its uses and can be what's needed. An example might be the case of basic skill transfer. If I can work a food blender and you can't, you might not respond well to me exploring your thoughts or feelings about that. You simply want to know what button on the blender does what and in what order.

Where an individual has little or no knowledge of a desired skill and simply needs to acquire basic knowledge quickly, directive language can work best. For the individual, this looks and feels more like instruction than coaching.

Within personal coaching, adopting a more directive style may sometimes be appropriate. For example, a simple piece of direct feedback may be more powerful for an individual than lots of indirect observations. Consider an individual who constantly goes off at tangents in conversation, appearing unwilling to focus on the topic they say they want to work on.

Examples of direct responses or requests might include:

> 'I notice that you often switch subjects, Jack, and I really need you to stay focused on our original topic of how you're feeling about this.'

> 'Jack, what he thinks isn't so important to me – simply tell me more about what *you* think.'

Obviously for the above responses to be fully effective, the coach's relationship with Jack must be based on trust and mutual respect. Jack is then more likely to view the above responses as helpful, rather than aggressive.

Directive language – disadvantages

Within coaching, a directive style has many disadvantages, namely:

➡ The coach assumes they have the best answers for the individual and they often don't.

➡ The coachee may feel dominated or controlled, as the coach assumes a position of 'knowing better'.

➡ The focus is mostly on the thoughts of the coach – which reduces the ability of the coachee to deepen their own learning in the conversation.

➡ The coach can experience unhealthy pressure in the conversation to know everything and be able to fix everything.

➡ The coach's focus is on 'I must find the right answer' instead of 'How can the coachee find their answer?' – this can result in valuable information or clues being overlooked.

➡ For the assignment to be successful, the coachee needs to engage with the ideas raised in the session, which they may do less often when the ideas are pressed upon them by the coach.

➡ The solutions from the coach might not have relevance for the coachee, and so they become meaningless advice. This can reduce the credibility of the coach.

➡ If the coachee has a tendency to avoid responsibility generally, they might actually enjoy the coach being in control and a directive style reinforces this.

Non-directive language – advantages

By creating learning for the individual *from* the individual, we experience the following benefits:

➡ The coachee experiences being truly listened to and appreciates the effort the coach makes to understand them.

➡ The relationship is based on equality, encouraging openness and trust. The coach is not claiming to have all the answers and the coachee feels their contribution is worthwhile.

➡ Insights, perspectives and ideas are highly relevant to the coachee and they relate to them with both ownership and responsibility.

➡ As most ideas and actions come from the coachee, so does the responsibility for their action and results.

➡ Solutions are developed from the understanding of the person experiencing the situation, so they are normally of much higher relevance and effectiveness.

➡ Thoughts and ideas provoke ongoing learning in the mind of the coachee. As if the conversation is a pebble being thrown into a pond, questions are the catalyst that begins a reaction. The ripples of a coaching conversation often reach beyond the actual conversation itself.

➡ If an idea doesn't get the result the coachee wanted, the coachee still feels ownership of the idea and so will be more willing to persist and get a better result.

Great coach	Not-so-great coach
Holds someone to account, in order to create a constant focus on the coachee's objectives, e.g. 'OK, again you said by the time we next met you'd have had the salary conversation with your manager – let's look at what's stopping you from having it.'	Allows themselves to be 'fobbed off' or sidetracked from issues of broken commitment, perhaps in order to maintain rapport. For example, 'Well, that's ok, you're really busy, can you do it when things calm down a bit?'
Is happier to achieve lasting results over time, than fast results that don't last.	Feels like they've failed if they don't see immediate results from the coaching.
Uses words and phrases that influence the individual positively, e.g. 'So imagine yourself speaking to an audience and this time you really enjoyed it – what would that feel like?'	Uses words clumsily and causes the coachee to feel negative or uncomfortable, e.g. 'Yes, your lack of confidence does seem to be a problem'.
Leads by example, e.g. shows up on time, calls when they said they would, keeps any commitments made, or makes amends when they don't.	Displays double standards, e.g. shows up late, uses weak excuses, isn't prepared for the session, etc.

Now that's obviously not an exhaustive list, although it does give you an idea of how a good coach can be distinguished from one who isn't so good.

A great coach is able to make the process of coaching look almost effortless.

A great coach is able to make the process of coaching look almost effortless.

To recap, the attributes of a good coach can be highlighted in three key areas:

➡ Principles or beliefs a coach operates from, e.g. 'we are equal in this conversation', or 'I need to understand first'.

➡ What a coach is able to do – their skills and knowledge.

➡ What a coach actually does, i.e. their actual behaviour.

From the outside, a great coach is able to make the process of coaching look almost effortless, like an easy, natural conversation. Partly that's because they are comfortable during the coaching process, but mostly it's because they've learned to coach effectively.

Chapter summary Collaborative coaching

Collaborative coaching is a wonderful coaching style because of its supportive, less directive approach. While directive styles can be effective, they demand a coach to be very confident about both the coaching relationship and also their own expertise and knowledge. In collaborative coaching, the coachee is encouraged to surface thoughts, insights and ideas, which they often experience as incredibly liberating. For any coach, to be a less directive coach is challenging and highly skilful when done effectively. For the individual being coached, it is often a profound experience that can literally change their life.

Coaching principles or beliefs

Operating principles for coaches

There are certain principles of perspective and belief that support collaborative coaching. A room may be full of fabulous coaches who all look different, sound different and appear different. However, when they coach, they are operating from a common set of beliefs. For example, they all believe in the power of coaching and they all believe that they can coach. These assumptions and beliefs are what help define effective coaching. The coaching beliefs that support a coach, which I'd like to focus on, are:

➡ I will maintain my commitment to support the individual.

➡ My coaching relationships are built upon truth, openness and trust.

➡ The coachee is responsible for the results they are creating.

➡ The coachee is capable of much better results than they are currently generating.

➡ I will maintain focus on what the coachee thinks and experiences.

➡ I know that coachees can generate perfect solutions.

➡ My coaching conversations are based on equality.

Once we've identified this common set of beliefs, they serve as principles we can operate from to achieve effectiveness over time. By reflecting on them and comparing them with our own behaviours and approach, we can often spot opportunities to improve. When sometimes our coaching isn't successful, they can help us to understand why. Perhaps a coachee seems to be happy to spend the whole coaching session complaining about his situation at work. In addition, the coachee refuses to consider potential solutions or what they might be doing to make things better. The coach tries in vain to help the coachee feel more positive about the situation and get into action to sort things out. Then, by reflecting on the following principles, the coach is reminded to coach from the assumption that the coachee is responsible for their circumstances and actions. It may be that the coach had become so frustrated with the whole situation that they forgot to focus on that simple principle. Sometimes issues within coaching can appear complex, when really a simple approach solves the mightiest of problems.

Some of the key principles occur as rules of behaviour, while others appear as perspectives of what the coach is there to do, or not do. Where a coach is consistently able to adopt these principles, this will improve their ability to coach effectively over time.

Maintain a commitment to support the individual

A good coach must want to coach the individual and remain committed to the coaching relationship. They must maintain a supportive attitude towards the coachee, or consider withdrawing from the assignment.

At the beginning of the coaching relationship, this appears fairly easy. The coach is probably thinking more about how to make the assignment successful than whether they do or do not want to help the coachee with their situation. As time moves on, the coach may experience factors that encourage them to withdraw their support. This withdrawal may or may not be something the coach is aware of. For example, simple fatigue with the coaching conversations or even the coachee themselves may creep in. Maybe the coaching process feels laboured, and is showing little sign of progress; the coach might start to withdraw their commitment, even without knowing it. For the coach, this may feel like a kind of resignation or boredom. It's important that coaches are self-managing in this instance. They must regularly evaluate where they are in their coaching relationships and identify any negative thoughts or beliefs about these relationships.

This reflection process can become a natural part of your coaching routine. For example, when I'm coaching, I like to have a couple of minutes' preparation before the coachee arrives. In that time, I'll read through my notes from previous sessions, reflect on what the individual's goals are, and remind myself how I'm contributing to that. It gets me into the mental mode of supporting the individual, regardless of how challenging the session might be.

Coaching from non-judgement

On a tougher note, the coach may decide that they do not actually like the person they are coaching very much! Remember, as humans, we have a natural tendency to judge others. We compare how someone else looks, thinks or acts with how *we* do. We might approve or disapprove of other people because of their hair, clothes, appearance, the words they use, their tone of voice, etc.

What if a coach disapproves of the person they are coaching? What if they hear of behaviour that they think is bad or wrong? A coach might hear of lying, cruelty and infidelity – any of which might encourage them to judge the individual as 'wrong' in some way.

Let's not debate whether any of those behaviours are 'wrong' or 'right'. As a coach, any disapproval impairs the ability to facilitate the process of a coaching conversation. In addition, the coach's disapproval usually communicates itself to the coachee – even if they don't voice it directly.

For example, imagine that a coach is working with an individual who reminds them very strongly of a domineering ex-partner. This coachee says something like 'You see, I have certain standards I will always live by' and the coach remembers that's exactly what their ex-partner used to say! Before long, the coach is comparing them to their ex-partner, and beginning to dislike them intensely.

The coach may begin to have internal thoughts or dialogue about what the coachee is saying, e.g. 'Ooh – that's just what they used to do' or 'You must be difficult to live with'. It's like trying to watch television with the radio on; your internal dialogue blocks your ability to listen fully.

Where we do not see someone objectively, with an open mind, we are less likely to begin to understand them. This lack of understanding has a direct impact on our ability to relate to the individual and how things are for them. At the same time, we've diminished the warmth and openness in the relationship, and so reduced our ability to influence the other person.

The other person is likely to sense the coach's disapproval of them, possibly from facial expression, tonality, gestures or simply the phrases the coach is using, e.g. 'So why did you do that?' As the coachee recognizes disapproval, they become more guarded in their responses.

Once a coach starts to see the coachee as 'flawed' in some way, they begin to adopt the role of 'fixer'. For example, making suggestions like 'Don't you think you should have apologized for that?' Again, the coachee is likely to sense disapproval, and perhaps feel defensive or detached.

Where a coach's ability to relate to and understand someone is key to their success, judgement becomes a real stumbling block. Instead the coach must work at simply observing the coachee objectively – without judgement. When a coach maintains a more neutral, open posture, they can gather much clearer information and so gain more relevant insights into the situation. A coach's own thoughts will be clearer, and they may even feel calmer, as they gradually begin to appreciate how it is for the person they're coaching. They aren't thinking things they can't voice, and generally their mind remains quieter during the conversation.

A coach's role is not to judge or disapprove of the way the coachee treats other people, or indeed how they live their life. A coach's role is simply to make clear links between the behaviours of the individual and the results they are getting. For example, the coachee might have aspirations of promotion at work and knows his lack of progress is strongly linked to the lack of support he is getting from his peer group. He discusses several confrontations with these colleagues and describes cruel things he's said, to 'get back at' or hurt people.

> **A coach's role is not to judge or disapprove of the way the coachee treats other people, or indeed how they live their life.**

It's a very simple link for the coach to make between the person's goals and his current behaviour. However, if the coach spends energy on convincing the coachee that his behaviour towards others is 'wrong' in some way, the individual may easily reject the suggestion. Far more straightforward and motivating for the individual is to highlight the fact that his behaviour simply doesn't work and has a direct impact on his goals. We then have the opportunity to discuss more positive behaviours that will benefit him and his colleagues.

What does non-judgement feel like for a coach?

Well, put simply, to be in non-judgement feels like nothing, because there's nothing going on! The coach is not having an internal dialogue along the lines of 'That's awful, cruel, dumb, etc.' The coach is not frowning with disapproval, shaking their head or making little 'tutting' noises. Instead, they are really listening and staying with the flow of the conversation.

Hopefully, judgement is replaced by a pervading sense of curiosity, towards what is being said and what the individual is experiencing. The coach's overriding sense of purpose is to seek to understand what's really happening, and what's relevant or important about that, given the goals of the coachee.

How do we let go of judgement?

Unless you've spent years gaining the enlightenment of a Buddhist master, I think you're going to have to accept a lifelong journey with this one. We all judge others, but the trick is to notice that you're doing that, and give it up whenever you catch yourself doing so.

The exercise in the Toolkit called 'Meditation for non-judgement' will help you practise.

Build the coaching relationship on truth, openness and trust

When you step into a coaching relationship, you seek to serve honestly the individual you are coaching. This is worth mentioning, as our integrity in this issue can be so easily corrupted.

One easy trap to fall into can occur when the person requesting and paying for your services isn't the person getting the coaching. This often happens in business, where a more senior individual has requested coaching for a colleague. I'll tell you about Scott as an example.

Coach's story   **A question of loyalty**

True story – names changed! Scott's manager, Gary, asked Carla (the coach) to give Scott a series of coaching sessions. Gary felt that Scott needed to deliver faster results and develop better relationships at work. Gary seemed pretty frustrated with Scott.

So Carla had a set of coaching objectives already decided for someone who may, or may not, want coaching. From the outset it was important to let Scott, the coachee, know exactly what had been his manager's thinking that led to Carla's involvement. Working with his manager, Carla discussed the specific areas of improvement that were the goals of the coaching activity and what the coaching would involve. They agreed that the coaching was a form of support that Scott could either accept or refuse at any point during the process.

Carla and Scott also spent time deciding how coaching might be an opportunity that Scott could benefit from and added his own objectives into the coaching. Carla explained what kind of updates she'd be giving his manager and assured Scott that the specific content of conversations would be disclosed to no one.

With Gary, the person paying her bill, Carla agreed that while she was happy to discuss general areas of discussion and progress, she would disclose nothing of the actual content of her conversations with Scott. She also agreed that if Gary wanted any more information, he'd ask Scott directly.

During coaching conversations, Scott welcomed the chance to discuss his situation. In short, Scott was questioning his desire to stay with the organization, and especially doubted his ability to build teams.

Carla's focus during those conversations had to be first to establish what was best for Scott, and then to work out how that related to his manager and the company he was working for. They worked through several different scenarios, including him leaving or applying internally for other positions.

If that sounds disloyal to Carla's client (Gary), let's acknowledge that this is the only principle we can effectively coach someone from. Had Carla tried to influence Scott to stay, or to take on more of the responsibilities that his manager wanted him to, she would have immediately corrupted the relationship between them.

There was also the issue of maintaining integrity between the sponsor, Gary, and Carla. From the outset, Carla made it clear how coaching ▶

As coach, it may sometimes be appropriate to ask your coachee to adopt a more powerful posture, by 'trying on' this principle of responsibility with you, i.e. acting as if it were true. Then examine a situation from this perspective, to discover new insights or learning:

COACH: If you were to accept some responsibility for what happened in the relationship, what might you see?

COACHEE: I'm not sure what you mean – why would I do that?

COACH: Well, it might help a little with getting more information that we can use.

COACHEE: OK. (pauses) Well, my partner was always saying that I wasn't really committed to things working out, that I didn't put enough into it.

COACH: OK – what else?

COACHEE: Well, my partner kept saying we should talk more, about how things were going, if there was anything we weren't happy about – you know the kind of stuff.

COACH: What was your response to that?

COACHEE: Well, at the time I said that was garbage, I just didn't agree with doing that.

COACH: Is there anything you'd add to that now?

COACHEE: Huh – yeah, I guess I should have stayed more aware of where my partner was at, at least that way I'd have known we'd got problems.

Now this might not be enough to save a relationship, but it may well create learning of a better quality than could be achieved by simply staying with a victim's perspective. From the dialogue above, you'll notice that the coachee sounds more powerful, more in control, later in the dialogue. They are discussing things within their own influence, namely whether they committed to the relationship or didn't, whether they talked to their partner or not.

Ultimately, when we're working with an individual to create change in their lives, this kind of fresh perspective may be just what's needed to cast new light on to a situation.

Try it yourself **Responsible or victim?**

If you want to coach someone from a principle of responsibility, then I recommend you be able to relate to that principle personally first. These questions can help you understand your own ability to take responsibility for yourself and your situation. Simply think about it for a while, then consider each question in turn:

Q Do you prefer complaining about problems rather than talking about solutions?

Q Do you frequently blame other people or things for your problems?

Q Are you able to make links to your own behaviours and the results you get? For example, 'I didn't put a ticket on my car so I got fined', or 'I'm now late because I didn't leave in time'.

Q In conversation, do you 'own' your own problems? For example, 'I need to do something about this'.

Q Do you complain that things 'aren't fair' or can you view situations more objectively?

If this is difficult for you to decide, maybe ask someone you trust for their opinion. Or next time you're discussing a problem or situation you want to change, notice how much you talk about that as a responsible, powerful person – or how much you simply moan and complain!

The coachee is capable of much better results than they are currently generating

A coach must believe that the individual they are working with is capable of being more, doing more and having more, especially in relationship to their stated goals. That might be anything from increased fitness to a lasting relationship, a better job, etc. If a coach secretly believes the coachee is unlikely to succeed in their objectives, feeling that they're simply not capable – then that simple belief is likely to undermine the coaching process.

For example, imagine as a coach you're working with someone who says they want to be able to speak confidently and powerfully to groups. After some initial discussions, you agree to work with them to achieve this goal.

As the coaching progresses, you hear them make some attempts at a speech and decide that the person is really awful, very nervous and you can't imagine the possibility of them ever giving a successful talk in public.

At this point, your ability to support the individual to achieve their goal becomes inherently flawed. You have a negative expectation of the outcome of the coaching and this is probably going to get in the way during conversations. You might already know that when parents or teachers have a positive expectation of children, the children achieve better results than where the reverse is true.

While it isn't an identical situation, I strongly believe that the same principle easily affects coaching, either of children or adults. As coach, if you say one thing and think another, somehow that communicates. Maybe through expression, tonality or gestures, your coachee will sense that you don't actually believe that they're capable of achieving their goals. Maybe you'll encourage them to settle for less, or learn to 'cope with' their 'weakness'.

As coach, if you say one thing and think another, somehow that communicates.

In a worst-case scenario, you may even undermine their confidence and make the achievement of their goals less likely. This must constitute the reverse of coaching!

Now, in some cases it may be quite appropriate for a coach to form this view. Coachees may set goals that you genuinely feel are unrealistic, or place too much pressure upon them. Please be careful, however, not to place your *own* limitations upon other people.

For example, imagine you're coaching someone who tells you they want to double their income within the next six months. Now while this kind of income increase rarely happens, it is actually very possible. It's up to you to decide whether you're willing to enter into a coaching agreement to support them to achieve this. To do so, you must believe that they are capable of creating the increase.

Do you say yes to the work, secretly believing the coachee isn't capable? Do you tell them you think it's not possible, but you're willing to coach them into a more likely goal and risk losing the work? This begins to surface the question of integrity, doesn't it? (By integrity, I simply mean being true to your word, i.e. telling your truth and doing what you say you'll do.)

I would suggest that where you're sure that something isn't possible for the person, you deal with it honestly. If you enter into a coaching relationship where you haven't told the truth about how you feel, then, again, the integrity of the relationship is corrupted.

As a coach, you would be constantly having second thoughts about what you had committed to and whether or not things were going to 'work out'. This is going to affect your ability to challenge and encourage the coachee in an honest manner.

For the coachee, having a coach who secretly feels that the coachee is going to fail is not the kind of support needed!

Testing questions   **Are you a support or saboteur?**

Think about an existing relationship where you coach or support the goals of someone else. The following questions will help you consider your levels of commitment to this person:

- **Q** How do you feel about the goals this person has described?
- **Q** How achievable do you believe this person's goals are?
- **Q** Do you believe this person will really benefit from the results they want to produce?
- **Q** How do you feel about the person you're coaching?

Focus on what the coachee thinks and experiences

The focus of coaching conversations should be on the coachee and not the coach. Does that sound obvious? It is possible for coaching conversations to be all about what the coach thinks, knows, does; as though the coach were an example to be followed.

When someone calls themselves 'a coach', it can set an expectation of what being a coach should mean. Maybe people imagine that a coach has sage-like wisdom, or limitless knowledge (a risky assumption!). For example, a coachee may think a coach must have seen their situation before and so knows what to do. They may imagine that the coach knows more about life, how to be happy, how to be successful or fulfilled. If, as a coach, you have experienced some great results with a few coaching conversations, it can be quite easy for success to go to your head. Maybe it's an idea you buy into yourself (another risky assumption ...).

Perhaps a coachee asks a coach, 'What would *you* do in this situation?' This is an unintentional trap, laid to catch the coach's ego. The coach's ego hears this and purrs – imagining that someone actually wants to know what they think, so that they can be more like them.

Remember that a collaborative coach is not there to tell people what they should do, or have them make choices based on their life and preferences. In collaborative coaching, you're working with someone, to help them get where they want to go.

The principal focus has to remain on the coachee's thoughts and objectives, as those are the reason the conversation is taking place. If, when coaching, I hear myself 'taking over' the conversation, introducing my beliefs and views or giving 'advice', I begin to feel uncomfortable, as I know I'm shifting the emphasis of the conversation.

As with all principles, sometimes you'll have reasons to work outside it. An example might be where the individual appears reluctant to share their experiences. Offering your own experiences or thoughts can create a greater sense of sharing and trust.

Try it yourself	But enough of me – let's talk about you!

Next time you're having a casual conversation with someone, begin to notice the change in focus of the discussion from them to you. In other words, are you talking about your experiences and thoughts, or theirs? If it's appropriate, keep the focus of the conversation completely on them for a while, e.g. what they've been doing, what they've been experiencing, what their thoughts and opinions are, etc. After the conversation, ask yourself:

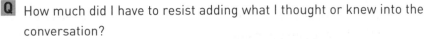 How comfortable am I when I'm not contributing my own thoughts and ideas?

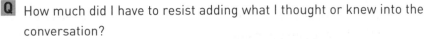 How much did I have to resist adding what I thought or knew into the conversation?

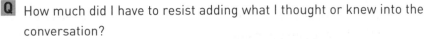 What effect did it have when I concentrated only on what they said or thought?

Coachees can generate perfect solutions

As humans we have an almost childlike wish to be the person who comes up with the best thought, the cleverest answer or the winning idea. It is like it was at school; where praise and reward come to those with the 'right' answer.

In collaborative coaching, the rules of your game are subtly different. To continue the classroom metaphor, you apply all your learning and experience to make sure that the person next to you comes up with the answer. That may or may not be the answer that you'd thought of. Clear ownership of the answer rests with the other person, who will normally go and use it on their own, to get what they want, together with the praise and reward.

As a coach, you win when someone else does. Your pleasure comes from being part of someone else's process, and helping them see different ways in which they can create the results they want. This becomes incredibly fulfilling for the coach and a huge motivation to continue coaching.

In practical terms, solutions or ideas spoken by the person being coached are often more reasonable, pragmatic and likely to be formed into action. That person will usually feel greater ownership of the idea and link that to a sense of responsibility for its success.

For example, I might be coaching a working mother having problems juggling her life between work and home. We may have explored lots of different aspects of the situation in order to understand the different values and factors involved.

45

As an observer, I might have the idea of changing her childcare centre, as this seems to be causing the problems. I might advise this, with the following potential consequences:

➡ It's a perfect idea for her and she seizes it immediately.

➡ She rejects the idea because she has a 'polarity response' to advice, i.e. automatically takes an opposing view.

➡ She rejects the idea because it doesn't feel right to her, or make practical sense to her.

➡ She initially accepts the idea, then disregards it later.

➡ She accepts the idea and switches to another care centre, but that makes things much worse and she then blames me.

➡ She accepts the idea and disregards her own instinct, which was to involve her mother in the situation.

A coach needs to resist the temptation to always have the answers. A good coach will often operate from the perspective that the best-quality solutions come from the coachee, not the coach. The coach might still influence those ideas and insights. The process of a coach's involvement guarantees this.

The coach's most common tools of influence are still questioning, listening, observation and reflection.

The coach's most common tools of influence are still questioning, listening, observation and reflection.

When we work with the rule consistently, however, we also develop an understanding of when to break it. I would recommend that a coach stay mostly out of advice and not 'tell' people what they 'should' do. Infrequently, I'll ask permission to offer a suggestion, e.g. 'Can I offer a thought?' and then, perhaps, 'How would switching your childcare centre affect the situation?'

By requesting permission, you're increasing the probability that the other person will accept your idea, whilst acknowledging the intrusion.

Once you've offered the suggestion, let it go. Don't become attached to their agreeing to it. They may or may not go with your idea, and that might be immediately, or some time afterwards.

Above all, remember to give up the idea of appearing 'smart' by having the 'right' answer. In the above situation, the best solution for the coachee may well have been her own idea to involve her mother, because of factors the coach wasn't aware of. Her mother might welcome the opportunity to spend more time with her grandchildren, be flexible when and where she looks after the children and do all this for free. Until now, the coachee's mother may not have offered her services as she respected her daughter's need for independence.

A collaborative coach needs to temper the basic human instinct to be 'right' about something. By giving up an attachment to finding a solution to a coachee's problem, we are actively encouraging them to find their own solution. Collaborative coaching encourages someone to be more powerful, more creative and more in action around situations, by helping them to find their own ways forward.

Try it yourself   Help someone else find the answer

For this exercise, you'll need to have a casual conversation with someone where they are discussing a problem or frustration. You can have this conversation by asking someone to do this, or you could wait for the next time this occurs naturally. It will be a conversation where the other person is not asking you to solve their problem; they're just talking, or complaining about it. For example, perhaps they're too busy, too tired all the time, fed up with their job, etc.

Rules of the game

During the conversation, you *must not* give them any advice or suggestions for a way forward. No matter how great your ideas or advice, just pretend for a while that you don't have an answer – and they do.

Step one – display the relevant facts

Ask them questions until you've (both) heard what you feel to be the 'key' or the relevant facts about the situation, e.g. 'What's causing this?' 'How supportive is your boss?' 'What actually is the real problem here?' If observations work better than questions, then use them, e.g. 'You seem to be spending a long time out of the office'.

Step two – discover their answer

When you feel you've got enough information for them to answer the following questions, use whichever seems appropriate:

 'What are you considering doing about this?'

 'What do you need to fix this/sort it all out?'

Q 'What could you do to improve the situation?'

Q 'What options do you have?'

Or any other question that requires them to think of their own solution to their situation.

Step three

(This step is optional.) If you are still 100 per cent convinced that you have a better answer, the right answer, and that they will benefit greatly from hearing it, then tell them. Perhaps use one of the following phrases to link to the previous part:

➡ 'Can I offer an idea?'

➡ 'As you were talking, I've thought of something that might help. What if ...'

➡ 'You know, I'm wondering if another answer might be to ...'

Sanity warning

This can be a difficult exercise! – especially if you're used to solving other people's problems for them. We can feel quite awkward or uncomfortable not 'fixing' things for people. So if the conversation isn't going well, for example:

➡ the discussion isn't flowing naturally;

➡ you can't think of the right questions or observations;

➡ they really (definitely) can't think of any ways forward;

give up, and have a go another day! Go back to having a normal, casual conversation, e.g. give your own views, experience, ideas, etc.

Alternatively, do step one on its own, then add step two when it feels right. Simply ask a few more questions than you would normally, before suggesting something. Before long, you'll find that feels more natural, as you feel less compelled to give your idea or advice. Then when that bit feels comfortable, simply ask them what their solution is, perhaps using some of the suggestions in step two.

The conversation is based on equality

As coach, you're working with someone else, to support them in achieving something that they want. Your relationship will feel more like a partnership of equals, rather than anything parental or advisory.

As you continue to work with someone, you strengthen the process of coaching. Together, you explore situations, causes, barriers and ways forward. The person you are coaching must feel they are receiving constant support, while remaining your equal. They must feel free to make requests or contribute to the discussion at all times.

Where coaches adopt the unfortunate posture of superiority, e.g. 'Trust me – I know about this', or 'Hey, I really think you should listen to me on this one', not only can they alienate the coachee, but they also run the risk of giving poor or irrelevant advice.

This imbalanced approach can also undermine the coachee's confidence, as they begin to feel subordinate in the relationship. Alternatively, they may dislike the inference that the coach is somehow 'superior' in matters relating to their own situation. Even where people are actually quite comfortable with a subordinate role, you diminish their ability to engage with their own problems, or seek their own solutions.

By acting from a sense of equality and collaboration, we promote an environment where the truth can be told, mistakes made and insights discovered.

Try it yourself   **Are we equal?**

For this exercise, you'll need to consider a relationship where you support, manage or coach someone else. The following questions can help you determine the levels of equality between you and this person:

 How much do you respect or admire this person?

 If you weren't managing or coaching this person, how comfortable would you feel asking this person for advice?

Q If this person really wanted to do something and you told them you didn't agree with that, what would they do?

➡ Go ahead and do it anyway.

➡ Ask you more about your views before making a decision.

➡ Go with your decision, as they will assume you 'know better'.

Chapter summary **Coaching principles or beliefs**

Coaches operate from principles of success, in much the same way as sports people or business people do. To repeat the key principles:

➡ Maintain your commitment to support the individual.

➡ Build your coaching relationships on truth, openness and trust.

➡ Remember that the coachee is responsible for the results they are generating.

➡ Know that the coachee is capable of much better results than they are currently generating.

➡ Maintain your focus on what the *coachee* thinks and experiences.

➡ Remember that coachees can generate perfect solutions.

➡ Make sure that your coaching conversations are based on equality.

4

Fundamental skills
of coaching

There are some basic skills, which can be learned and developed, that will distinguish a good coach from a 'not so good' coach. We all have some level of ability related to the skills required, e.g. we all have some ability to develop rapport. Other skills come less naturally, such as effective questioning, and may require learning and practice. I would recommend that anyone who wishes to enter a coaching profession take their own training very seriously. Untrained or sub-standard coaches can do more harm than good, creating an experience that's counterproductive for both the coach and the coachee.

Once skills are acquired, it's not like riding a bike – coaches do forget! These skills are more like muscles; they must be used regularly to keep them strong. This chapter focuses on the fundamental skills of coaching, as illustrated in Figure 4.1.

Can anyone coach?

In theory, anyone should be able to coach. In practice, however, some people are better suited to coaching than others; perhaps because of their natural character traits, attitudes and basic motivations. Some people find that coaching is a natural continuation of who they already are and what they already do. Others find coaching conversations complicated, laborious, frustrating or even pointless. Even if this is the case, any individual who is truly committed to developing the skills necessary to be a good coach will find that commitment will make it possible.

Only in a coaching type of conversation are you likely to be focusing on all these skills at once. Of course, many routine activities contain several of the following skills – the most obvious being basic conversation! However, for someone to use the full set of skills in all conversations would be tiring for the individual and rather strange for those they were talking to.

Skill one – building rapport or relationship

Rapport – the dance behind communication

The foundation for all coaching conversations is a feeling of warmth and trust felt between the coach and the coachee. Great coaches are fabulous to

Figure 4.1 Fundamental coaching skills

talk to and the coachee will experience them as warm, attentive and easy to relate to. This is due to the coach's ability to build rapport. Many people outside the coaching profession have this skill. You can probably think of someone you know who is able to put people at their ease and quickly build a feeling of familiarity or comfort when speaking to others.

Figure 4.2 Building rapport or relationship

The first time you do this, I'd recommend you tell the other person what you're doing. That way you can find out how it felt for them, how comfortable they felt, etc. When you think you've mastered the technique, use it whenever it seems appropriate for rapport.

Step one

Have a conversation with them, about something they are interested in, perhaps a hobby or particular area of study or learning. As the conversation progresses, gradually match their pace of speaking a little more closely. If they speak more slowly, gradually slow down your speech; if they are quiet, speak more quietly. Notice how your focus or attention has to change in order for you to do this. Do this as naturally as possible. Often slight adjustments work better than becoming an exact match of the other person.

Step two

Afterwards, consider the following questions:

Q What did you have to focus on to be able to do this?

Q What effect did your 'matching' seem to have (on you and on the other person)?

Q How did this affect the amount of rapport you felt?

If possible, ask the same questions of the person you were talking to. That way you'll get even more learning from the exercise.

Language/words used

We tend to notice the importance of words for rapport only when we get it wrong! For example, here is the initial part of a coaching conversation:

COACH: So, Jim, it's been nearly a month hasn't it? How have you been?

JIM: Well, OK I guess, I've kinda been feeling a little low though, a bit under the weather as they say.

COACH: Sorry to hear that – how long have you been depressed then?

JIM: Oh I'm not depressed! I just said a little low – how do you get from that I'm depressed?

As coach, you're now into a bit of a recovery situation, early on in your conversation – not a great start! This could have been avoided by repeating the same key words the coachee used.

As a more positive example, have you noticed how groups or communities of people often adopt the same words or phrases as each other? We notice this within certain professions or occupations especially. For example:

Phrase	Meaning
'Let's take that off-line'	'Let's discuss that outside this group we're in now'
'You're a star'	'You're great/thanks/well done'
'Break a leg'	'I hope it goes well for you'
'Same old same old'	'Nothing changes'
'Handball those bricks'	'Unload those bricks by hand'

Whether you're in construction, finance, the theatre or any other profession, you're likely to have your own words or phrases that help you feel related as a community. If you find yourself on the 'outside' of this kind of language, i.e. you don't understand it or can't use it, you might feel alienated when people use it.

Try it yourself   Who's playing word games?

Over the next few days, observe other people talking together in your work or social life (or simply go somewhere else and eavesdrop!). Listen to conversations, in particular the actual words and catch phrases that are being used. Judge for yourself the amount of rapport between people. Then consider:

Q What types of buzzwords or phrases are being used?

Q How much are these words being copied or repeated by individuals?

Q What effect is this copying having on the conversation?

Let's look at the previous coaching dialogue again – with the coach more careful this time to match the individual's words:

COACH: So, Jim, it's been nearly a month hasn't it? How have you been?

JIM: Well, OK I guess, I've kinda been feeling a little low though, a bit under the weather as they say.

COACH:	You've been feeling a little low?
JIM:	Yeah, you know, just odd days, it's almost like there's a little grey cloud over my head and it won't be shifted.
COACH:	This cloud – what's it about, what's in it?

You'll notice that the coach not only matches the words the coachee is using, but also the 'sense' of the images the coachee is building, e.g. by asking what's 'in' the cloud. As the coachee begins to feel understood, he begins to relax and explain what he's been feeling.

Coach's corner **Watch my feelings**

Where we want to acknowledge feelings

Sometimes, we need to acknowledge someone's feelings as a way of empathizing with them, or demonstrating an understanding of what they've said. Here, it usually works best to use the exact words or phrase they use. This is especially true when those feelings are negative. For example, if they say they're upset, say 'I appreciate that you're upset'. If they say they're worn out, use the words 'worn out' (not 'fatigued' or 'dog-tired').

Where we want to influence feelings

Sometimes, you might want to reduce the significance of someone's feelings in the conversation. Maybe you wish to make them feel a little better about what they felt, or help them calm down a little. If you have good rapport, use a diluted or reduced version of their word. For example, they say 'I'm scared stiff of making presentations' and you don't want to get 'stuck' in that feeling. So when you refer to these feelings, you might not use 'scared stiff' but instead use 'apprehensive' or 'uncomfortable', e.g. 'I guess you'd want to let go of some of those uncomfortable feelings wouldn't you?' You can then begin to use more positive imagery and feelings, e.g. 'What would it take for you to feel fantastic about giving a presentation?'

Beliefs and values

What we believe to be true about our world and ourselves can separate people, or bring them together. Religion is an obvious example of how beliefs can separate or unite people. On a simpler note, watch a passionate meat eater debate with a vegan about their eating habits and you'll see and hear how beliefs can divide.

Notice how a salesperson might find common ground with a potential client, to increase their ability to enrol that client. A good salesperson will often spend time learning about their client as a person, what they do, what they like, and what they don't like. By agreeing with the client on topics that they appear passionate about, e.g. the importance of a good education (or even the irrelevance of one), they build rapport based on implied like-mindedness. We tend to buy products and services from people we 'like' and we have a related tendency to like people who we believe are 'like' us. Building rapport is obviously a key behaviour for people in sales professions.

When to increase rapport

As well as knowing the ways we develop rapport, we should also know *when* to work at improving it. Where the coachee appears comfortable with the conversation, looks and sounds fairly relaxed, and is showing no signs of alienation or disassociation, my tendency is usually to forget about building rapport.

One point where a coach might work to build rapport comes during the initial stages of the coaching assignment. At this point, any individual they're working with may need to feel more comfortable with them before they can trust the coach and open up to the process of coaching.

The other obvious place where a coach must make sure they are building good rapport is at the start of each coaching conversation. No matter how warm or open the previous conversations have been, the time and distance between sessions create the need to reaffirm the coaching relationship.

Increasing rapport through simple matching

One well-known way of increasing rapport is known as matching. This means being literally the same in some way as the person you want to build rapport with. In a coaching environment, simple ways of building rapport would include matching: posture, voice quality, speed of speech, physical gestures, etc.

When you're coaching and decide that rapport isn't as good as it needs to be, first look for mismatches or differences between you and the other person. Perhaps do a quick check on physical posture, voice qualities, amounts of energy you're both displaying – what are you doing that's different? For example, if your gestures are more animated than the other person's, calm yourself down a little. If you're speaking much more quickly than they are, begin to decrease your pace. This needs to be done as a gradual process, so that the other person does not consciously notice it.

I'd suggest that you begin by subtly matching physical posture, as this has multiple benefits. First, it helps you to begin to focus more on the individual – to think more about what's happening with them and less about what's happening with you. Secondly, it often improves rapport quite naturally. Thirdly – and perhaps more oddly – once you begin to attune to the individual in this way, your concentration will increase or shift, so that at some level you might begin to notice other behaviours by the coachee. These might include subtle facial expressions, eye movements, changes in skin tone, etc. With this heightened concentration, you'll 'pick up' or 'read' other signals that previously you might have missed.

When is matching actually mismatching?

A word of caution on simple matching. If you 'overdo it', that is, match someone very obviously, or to an extreme level of detail, then instead of building rapport you will actually alienate them. There's nothing worse than having someone 'mirror' your every movement, behaviour and gesture. When you lift your hand – they lift their hand; when you cough – they cough. Sooner or later, you'll notice that you have what appears to be a very strange person behaving oddly in front of you! Instead of helping you feel more comfortable, you'll feel exactly the opposite.

Matching effectively is a subtle art. If you want to match someone who is leaning forward, first incline your body slightly towards them. If someone is continually smoothing their eyebrow, brush your hand across your own.

If they continually clasp or wring their hands, then occasionally bring yours together. This might sound strange, but it works!

The question of eye contact

Some people try to increase rapport with another person by looking directly into their eyes, for long periods of time. You might find that people in retail or sales professions are actually trained to do this when talking to customers. This is by no means guaranteed to improve the customer's sense of comfort with them, especially if the salesperson adds the trick of not blinking! Most people do not like to be 'stared' or 'gazed' at, and some may even find it threatening.

Again, when judging how much eye contact is appropriate with another person, we should work at matching them.

If the other person appears to give you lots of eye contact, then they'll be comfortable with you doing the same. If they look at you less frequently, then they are likely to respond to a similar level of eye contact. Simply notice and match the approximate proportions of time spent looking directly at the other person.

When to decrease rapport

There are times when it is entirely appropriate to decrease rapport or the levels of relationship that are occurring during the conversation. For example, when you want to close a conversation down, draw an end to the session and begin to summarize the key points and agree on actions.

There are also inappropriate as well as appropriate levels of rapport for the coaching relationship. Should too much familiarity, intimacy or warmth occur between the coach and the coachee, it is very easy for the relationship to become one of friendship, rather than a purposeful arrangement between two people.

There are also appropriate levels of rapport for the coaching relationship, and inappropriate levels.

I find it's less practical to coach my friends and impossible to coach my family, and this is one reason why! Other reasons relate to emotional attachment and personal agenda, which we'll cover later in the 'Barriers to coaching' chapter.

worthwhile. It is always possible to find some way in which you are related to another person, even if that's simply in your humanness.

In my own coaching, this often allows me to deepen the levels of rapport between the other person and myself. None of my internal thoughts or questions are communicated verbally to the person I'm coaching; I'm simply using the power of intention to focus my mind to where I want it to go. By the term 'power of intention', I refer to our innate ability to direct or concentrate our thoughts in order to create a specific outcome. In this instance I would use the intention of deepening rapport, coupled with a question, or thought, such as 'How can I increase my relatedness to him/her?' Gradually, as I leave the question suspended in my thoughts, I can begin to understand how. Maybe I'll suddenly realize that I'm staring too intently and this might be disconcerting; maybe I'm talking too much, or not enough.

Try it yourself   Use your intention

When we focus our minds on our intention, our thoughts and behaviours can often marshal themselves to show us the appropriate way forward. So go and have a conversation with someone you know quite well, but not very well. If you can choose someone who you'd like better rapport with, that might work even better.

During the conversation, have an intention to have great rapport with the other person. You want to develop that warmth and sense of connection that comes from having great rapport. You might use a word or phrase to remind yourself occasionally of this intention, for example: 'warmth and openness' or 'relationship'. During the conversation, simply remember the thought or phrase as much as seems appropriate. Remember that you also want to be able to have a conversation, so concentrate on the thought only as much as seems comfortable. If the thought begins to act as a distraction, then forget it – let it go.

After the conversation, ask yourself:

Q What was the rapport like within the conversation?

Q How did using your intention appear to affect your rapport?

Q How could you use your intention in the future?

Developing the coaching relationship over time

As a coach, once you've established rapport, you will then develop that relationship throughout your involvement with the coachee. The duration of your relationship might be just one coaching session, or it could last for many months or even years. In many coaching assignments an ongoing relationship is needed. So we need to consider the factors that will affect the sense of mutual warmth and value over a period of time. The skills of integrity and openness and trust add to the previous aspects of rapport, to give us a fuller appreciation of the importance of developing a coaching relationship over time.

Integrity

Integrity refers to the alignment between what we know to be true, right, wrong, good, bad and what we actually do. For example, if you know it's wrong to steal, then don't steal. If you believe it's wrong to lie, then don't lie. Integrity is a black and white, simple principle. For all that, integrity is not something that comes easily to many of us. For example, stealing logically covers all forms of theft, from taking someone's wallet to not putting a ticket on our car in the car park (which is technically theft from the owner of the car park). When we're pressured, short on time, or not feeling abundant, how easy is it to decide not to do what we say is 'right'? In the example of lying, are so-called 'white' lies still lies? Yes they are! So integrity calls upon us to be powerful in our own behaviours. To act consistently from a sense of personal integrity involves a lifetime of learning for most of us. Fortunately, in coaching the examples are probably simpler to debate and easier to adopt as personal standards.

Integrity causes us to be of our word. As a coach, what we say must match what we do. If you say you're going to call your coachee, then call them. If you say you're going to post them some information on Friday, then post it on Friday. This simple congruence of words and actions is very powerful within a coaching relationship. Your coachee is more likely to trust and respect you when you keep your commitments to them. This forms a contribution from you to the coachee, and over time your relationship will benefit. In addition, this can have a positive influence on a coachee's own behaviour. By setting high standards of personal behaviour you become an example to the coachee of what works and what doesn't. The consistency of your behaviour forms a further support to the coaching conversations.

As a coach, what we say must match what we do. Where a coach does not keep a commitment, they need to do whatever is appropriate to redress the situation. For example, if they didn't send information as promised, it's probably appropriate to apologize and offer to send on the information if it is still needed. If the coach didn't call, then the coach can acknowledge that, e.g. apologize and do whatever is needed to meet the needs of the call that didn't happen. If it helps the situation, then sometimes it's appropriate to explain why a commitment hasn't been kept. Maybe you're late because your car broke down. I'm cautious about over-explaining these reasons, as our explanations can easily become excuses. These excuses enable us to avoid responsibility for our actions. For example, we sometimes use the excuse of heavy traffic for being late. Actually, we're late because we just didn't leave the house early enough!

Here are the guidelines I have for myself:

→ Make commitments wisely – Can I keep this commitment? Is this a good/reasonable commitment to make?

→ Make commitments important: record them, make them a priority task.

→ Deal with the consequences of any commitments I haven't kept, e.g. apologize, make amends if possible (this one is good encouragement to keep them in the first place!).

So if you're doubtful about whether or not you can keep a commitment, don't make it! Or simply make an adapted version of the commitment, e.g. 'I'll post you the information on Friday if I get some free time, otherwise it will be either Monday or Tuesday of next week'. By building in an extension to the deadline, we increase our chances of meeting the commitment.

Try it yourself   **Are you keeping commitments?**

Use the following to reflect on your current tendency to keep commitments or promises. If you can't answer them, perhaps use them to monitor your behaviour over the next few days, or even weeks.

Q How readily do you make commitments or promises to do things, e.g. hear yourself saying 'I'll do that/send that by …' or 'I'll call you'? This includes doing things for yourself, e.g. 'I'm going to book that appointment this week'.

 How many of your promises or commitments do you actually keep exactly as voiced, e.g. by the deadline you gave?

 If you don't keep a commitment, what do you do, e.g. ignore the fact, use excuses to avoid responsibility or simply put it right?

When you have some answers to the above, consider the following question:

Which of the following could you use to get even better at dealing with your commitments?

→ Make commitments wisely – Can I keep this commitment? Is this a good/reasonable commitment to make?

→ Make commitments important: record them, make them a priority task.

→ Deal with the consequences of any commitments not kept, e.g. apologize, make amends if possible.

Openness and trust

A really successful coaching relationship will include a sense of openness and trust between the coach and the coachee. The coach can encourage this by being open with the coachee and being someone whom they can trust. The following are all ways that a coach can promote this trust and openness:

→ Share personal facts and details occasionally, e.g. mention your family circumstances, discuss personal plans, goals, etc.

→ Declare your own thoughts and feelings sometimes, e.g. about events outside coaching.

→ Speak your own truth consistently (see 'Strategizing in the conversation').

→ Be of your word (keep commitments made).

→ Keep any confidences between you and the coachee.

→ Support the coachee in conversation outside the coaching sessions, e.g. don't say anything about the coachee that you wouldn't want them to hear afterwards.

➡ Act in the coachee's best interests at all times, e.g. stay focused on their goals, make their success and fulfilment a priority during your conversations with them.

Section summary **Skill one – building rapport or relationship**

As a coaching skill, the ability to influence levels of rapport during conversations enables a coach to gain trust, engagement and influence during coaching conversations. Good rapport refers to the quality of relationship happening in the conversation, as the conversation is happening. It is directly affected by our thoughts or feelings being in some way the same or different from the other person. Where we are alike, we like, but where we are different, we feel detatchment or even dislike. Traditional techniques of simple physical matching might have a level of influence. However, other factors may be much more important. Our sense of shared values, common aims and intentions can be the underlying factors that create real relatedness within the conversation.

Over time, the positive development of a coaching relationship is affected by principles such as integrity, consistency, openness and trust. Our ability to act consistently from these principles influences the coaching relationship and the coachee's behaviour. The demands on the coach for high standards of personal behaviour require both commitment and self-discipline. The rewards of great coaching relationships and a clear conscience are worth the effort!

Skill two – different levels of listening

The art of listening is generally misunderstood and underrated as a skill – I firmly believe we should teach it in schools! The potential benefits of listening, for both the listener and the speaker, are not often acknowledged or valued. For example, good listeners obtain a better understanding of people and situations. Simple instances such as following travel directions, taking down telephone messages etc. are everyday occurrences that challenge our ability to listen. Someone who has a good understanding can respond to situations more effectively than someone who hasn't. In business, I notice good listeners make fewer mistakes, upset fewer people and generally operate using better quality information. A good listener also makes a contribution to the speaker they are focused on. The person speaking benefits by being encouraged to share their thoughts and ideas, and is viewed as someone who has valid opinions.

Imagine if we all raised the average quality of our listening for each other. We'd see greater mutual understanding, increase the generation of new ideas, experience fewer disputes and probably avoid a few small wars!

Much of the time, the consequences of poor listening aren't desperate, they're simply frustrating. Maybe we missed an appointment; maybe we didn't appreciate the full facts about something; or simply missed an opportunity.

Sometimes, the consequences of poor listening are more important. In coaching especially, poor listening by the coach can lead to an inability to understand a coachee and their situation. Where the coach is unable to develop this understanding, this becomes a real barrier to success.

The gift of listening

People who are great at listening can be found everywhere. Maybe you know someone you would call a 'good listener' or maybe you've had people

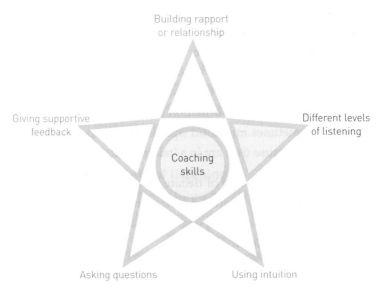

Figure 4.4 Different levels of listening

conversation, how we're feeling, etc. Some people talk much more than they listen, some people prefer to speak less and listen more, and some appear to have a pretty even balance of both.

Again, your objectives for the conversation will affect your listening. A police officer gathering facts at the scene of a road traffic accident is more likely to listen and internally process information before asking further questions or making observations. A person giving a stranger directions is more likely to be doing more of the talking and much less listening or processing of information.

Conversational listening is a natural activity for most people. It requires little effort, is present in most of our normal, daily conversations, and it can be tremendous fun and really quite energizing.

Coaching conversations are not the same as these day-to-day conversations, however, simply because of their purpose. Within coaching, we must develop a deeper form of listening.

Try it yourself   **Listen and learn**

Use your normal conversations today to consider the following:

Q How often do you pretend to listen to someone – and don't really listen?

Q How is your listening different, i.e. within different circumstances, or with different people?

Q What effect does the quality of your listening seem to have on other people or the conversation?

Active listening

One of the skills a coach must have is active listening. It has certain characteristics:

➡ The listener is using more effort to listen and process information than speaking themselves.

➡ The listener has the intention of staying focused on what the other person is saying, in order to understand fully what they are saying.

⇒ The listener is mentally registering and recording facts so they can potentially use them later (they might also take notes).

⇒ The listener continually confirms that they are still listening, by making appropriate sounds, gestures or expressions.

⇒ The listener will actively seek to understand what the person is telling them, by using clarifying questions, repeating or summarizing information back to the speaker and offering observations or conclusions.

A conversation where the coach listens attentively might sound like this:

SPEAKER: So the whole interview turned into a bit of a nightmare. I ended up wondering why the heck they'd invited me in the first place.

LISTENER: Really – why, what happened?

SPEAKER: Well, firstly, they kept me sat in reception for ages, so it was three o'clock in the afternoon before I got into the interview. My appointment was for two.

LISTENER: An hour late?

SPEAKER: Exactly, anyway, then I got in and I'm greeted by someone from Sales, and some bloke from the computer department – which was kind of strange. The least they could have done would have been to have someone in there relevant to the position they were hiring.

LISTENER: What was the position?

SPEAKER: Warehouse foreman – not the sort of job that you'd think those two would be interested in. They started asking me about what type of warehouse operations I'd run in the past, and how much I'd used computers! Apparently they were planning some fancy sort of system. Then the Sales guy starts getting interested in how the shops used to let us know what to order and what to deliver – they just kept going off at tangents.

LISTENER: Right – so what did you do in the interview?

SPEAKER:	Well, I just kept trying to bring them back to the important stuff like how important security is, fire prevention and how to stop staff stealing things.
LISTENER:	Hmm – so what's happened since?
SPEAKER:	Nothing, not a thing, no letter, no phone call – nothing!

You will notice from the dialogue that the listener is focusing very much on understanding what's happened. The listener is gathering facts, filling in gaps, working to get a fuller picture of events. The listener is not spending large amounts of energy giving their own thoughts and views, not telling stories of interviews that they've had and not offering advice and ideas. These behaviours would fit more into the scope of 'conversational listening' described earlier.

The listener is also following a fairly logical time sequence, i.e. asking about actions or events in the order they would have happened. For example, the question 'What's happened since?' comes at the end of the conversation not the beginning. This enables the speaker to recollect information in a way that feels more natural to them.

Deep listening

This last category of listening is unlike any other, in that it goes beyond what it is logically possible to achieve by listening to someone. I have heard people describe good coaches as 'almost telepathic' because of their ability to listen to and understand another person from insights into what they have said, or even understand what they have *not* said. Let me be clear – coaches are not telepathic. But there is a highly perceptive level of under-standing and insight that becomes possible when a coach is in a state of deep listening.

I have heard people describe good coaches as 'almost telepathic'.

When a coach is able to generate this quality of listening, they are able to experience the other person with a sense of who they are, as well as what they're saying. I can only describe this state of listening as a slightly altered mental state and would describe its characteristics as follows:

→ The mind of the listener is mostly quiet and calm.

→ The awareness of the listener is entirely focused on the other person.

→ The listener has little or no sense or awareness of themselves.

→ The listener is totally lucid and present to the person speaking.

→ This state can easily be broken or disturbed, e.g. by the speaker asking the listener a question, or seeking acknowledgement of some sort.

This state of listening feels almost elusive in nature, in that once you realize you have it and are in it the thought registers and it's gone again! This seemingly 'higher' state of listening has similar characteristics to meditation, in that the listener's mind is essentially quiet, with occasional thoughts or insights passing through.

Seeking to serve

What also seems present, however, is an intention towards the person you are listening to. In my experience, this intention is usually one of service – perhaps seeking to understand, seeking to help or provide support, something that contributes towards the individual and their learning.

For the listener, it almost feels as though you are experiencing 'being' the other person – although, of course, you are not. In terms of your ability to relate to the other person (what they are thinking and feeling about a situation) the quality of the information you are receiving is significant. For the person being listened to, as they are speaking they will undoubtedly feel understood and they also might experience a deeper sense of relatedness to the listener.

I should add at this point that to stay in continual deep listening for extended periods of time is neither desirable nor possible. It is not possible because the coach cannot only listen; they must also make observations, question and generally stay in the conversation. Plus, like meditation, it's a real challenge to maintain such a quiet state of mind. Long periods of deep listening are not desirable, because the coaching process demands that you are more than a passive observer. As a coach you engage in dialogue, in order to facilitate the other person's thinking. Your speaking, questioning, physical gestures or expressions are all essential to this process.

In addition, other forms of listening are sometimes more useful, for example when you need to gather the facts of a situation first, or help someone 'get something off their chest'. In such cases active listening works a lot better and more quickly.

Developing deep listening

I would recommend that anyone seriously committed to the field of coaching actively develop their own ability to listen in this way. Deep listening challenges us in a different way from a lot of other activities, possibly because working harder can actually work against us. The deep listening exercise in the Toolkit will help you develop your skill further.

Skill three – using intuition

Intuition – within coaching

Study any great coach and you will notice that they often seem to know in what direction to take a conversation, in order to gain information or insight that proves extremely relevant. The area they explore might appear unrelated and initially seem an odd thing to discuss. Subsequent conversation creates a real breakthrough in understanding or solutions for the coachee.

Figure 4.6 Using intuition

This is one of the great distinguishing characteristics of a coach, and one that makes the coaching role so valuable.

Sometimes a coach may spot what's missing from the conversation and become curious about something that's simply not being said. They may choose to ask a question, or make an observation that completely changes what's happening. From one simple remark or phrase, they may unlock an issue for someone or cast a whole new light on a situation. The way we explain this kind of behaviour is to call it intuition.

Intuition is actually an ability we all have, and one we can develop into a skill. For a coach, it becomes something they rely upon, to help shape and guide a coaching conversation. The following dialogue illustrates apparent intuition:

> **Intuition is actually an ability we all have, and one we can develop into a skill.**

COACH: So what is it about interviews that you don't like?

COACHEE: Well, everything, I mean, the whole situation doesn't suit me. I get in there and everything seems to start going wrong.

COACH: Perhaps say a little more about that ...

COACHEE: Well, it's probably the questions; I know what I want to say, it's just that my answers don't seem to flow in the right direction. I end up talking too much, about stuff that's irrelevant, sounding stupid. When I get out of there I realize I could have done so much better.

COACH: You know, I keep wondering – who might you be proving right here?

COACHEE: I don't understand what you mean.

COACH: Well, who might expect you to behave like this at interviews?

COACHEE: Aaah, that's easy, my Dad, I guess. He'd say I just couldn't cut it under pressure. 'Under a spotlight you'll blow a fuse' he used to say. My brother was always so much better at this sort of thing; I guess I kind of live in his shadow a little.

You will see from the dialogue that there are several different ways the coach could have approached the situation, many of which would seem more logical. What happened is that during the conversation the coach began to have thoughts and/or feelings that there was someone else involved in this issue. As well as someone else being involved, there was some sense of burden or resignation from the coachee. 'Who might you be proving right here?' is not a stock question for a coach. The question simply came to the coach as a thought and he went with that thought and asked the question.

Intuition – wisdom in action

Intuition is simply an access to our brain's potential to provide guidance and information free from the confines of our limited conscious mind. Through intuition, we are able to access vast stores of experience, knowledge and wisdom in a way that sometimes defies logic. Intuition is a way our brain has of communicating with our conscious mind and uses subtle means such as thoughts, feelings, sensations, imagery, sounds – or various combinations of those.

Intuition seems to be a function of both our brain and our body – think of how we talk about 'gut feelings', or 'having a feeling about something'. Intuition seems to potentially involve any part of our body, as it attempts to guide and direct our thoughts.

In the earlier example, the options for the next question were far too many for the coach to consider, assess and decide upon. Rational, practical thought would probably have explored techniques of great interview skills, preparing and rehearsing answers, investigating the interviewers beforehand, etc.

Even if the coach decided to analyse how the individual might be 'stopping' themselves from doing well during interviews, it would have taken a lot longer to arrive logically at the insight about the coachee's father. Instead the coach trusted a sense that someone was 'being proved right'. During coaching, this sometimes causes a coach to risk asking a dumb question, or receiving an uncomfortable response, e.g. 'I don't understand what you mean'. If the coach stays with his intuition, he'll continue until his curiosity is satisfied.

Communicating non-verbally

Intuition incorporates the brain's ability to understand communication from situations or people by going beyond the signals we normally respond to. Logically, we can respond to sight, sound, conversation, events, etc. I would also suggest that there are some forms of communication that happen where our conscious minds don't register them. It's a bit like dog whistles – we're simply not tuned into them. Our subconscious mind, however, is able to gather, assess and interpret different kinds of information from people and situations.

I believe that we can communicate quite well without language – after all, animals are able to do so. For example, after walking into a room where two people have obviously been arguing, we say things like 'You could cut the air with a knife' – but what do we mean by that? We probably mean that we have picked up enough signals or communication from within the room to 'guess' that an argument has just taken place. If we were to try to explain exactly what signals we got that caused us to decide this, we can't always give a detailed answer. Maybe the two people were sitting quietly, maybe they weren't actually looking at each other – does that explain the atmosphere in the room?

The human brain is known to be an underestimated resource. Research suggests that we currently use less than 10 per cent of our brain's true potential. In other words, our brain is a lot smarter than we are. While we struggle to compare more than three thoughts at a time, our brain's background processing is far superior.

I hear stories of doctors or emergency workers who need to – and can – assess a situation much more quickly and accurately than the conscious mind can. They often can't say exactly what led them to an almost instant certainty of what the person's problem was and what to do about it. Clearly, the brain is operating in a way we aren't aware of, in order to gain access to and compare information.

A practical tool

For me, there's nothing 'mystical' or 'spooky' about intuition; it's something that we all use, regularly and practically. We may use it to choose the perfect present for someone, avoid scheduling something in our diaries because we have a feeling something else might crop up, or know someone's not telling us the truth. Intuition simply builds on what you already know – knowledge you already have that is communicated to you via thoughts, feelings, images or sounds.

How do we develop intuition?

I hope to assist you in developing your use of your intuition. I'm also aware that your willingness to trust yourself and your inner wisdom is something you must journey with yourself. Improving access to and using intuition takes practice. It may help you to begin by acknowledging how you already use it. How many decisions or choices do you currently make with minimal rational thought? What happens with you before you do? Call it instinct, call it a gut feeling – you already have it. How do you know when you've left the house and forgotten something? How do you know when someone's telling the truth or not?

Because intuition speaks to us using fairly subtle signals (imagery, feelings, sensations, thoughts, sounds, etc.), we have to learn to become more receptive to this form of communication.

Once you have an awareness of the forms of 'language' your subconscious is using, practise tuning in. In order to tune in, you need to work at creating a state of mind, body, breathing etc. that enables you to hear, feel, or imagine the messages coming from your subconscious. However, if you are feeling nervous, angry, excited, or your mind is simply full of other thoughts, you are unlikely to be able to open up this channel for communication. Your strongest signals from intuition will come when you're feeling calm or relaxed.

Try it yourself   **Using your own intuition**

Choose your next meal according to what your intuition is telling you. If you're in a restaurant, read down the list of options and ask yourself 'What's the best choice I could make here?' Settle into the question peacefully, and make sure you're relaxed in order to hear, feel or see the response. If you're relaxed, your breathing will be slightly slower, comfortable and often you'll find yourself breathing from your stomach or mid-section.

This way of choosing food can actually be a good strategy for anyone wanting to eat more healthily or lose weight. Maintaining a relaxed state will give you access to your own wisdom. When your choice is based on this wisdom, you'll often find yourself choosing something that is a good choice for you and your body. Be warned, you may end up eating something unusual!

The subtle nature of intuition

Intuition is not infallible; it is simply another source of thought and ideas. Because it is a subtle channel of information, it is easily interrupted, or drowned out, by the thoughts already going on in our conscious minds. It's a little like tuning in a radio to a particular station. If you get two at the same time, the louder one is the one we tend to focus on.

Ask yourself what you want to eat tonight and your conscious mind might shout 'chocolate!' or 'pizza!' loudly and repeatedly, every time you repeat the question. When your mind becomes peaceful and quiet, however, you may get the sense of a certain type of food or combination of foods, maybe with a higher water or protein content – chicken salad!

The pitfall of intuition

In my experience, intuition also gets things wrong, or at least seems to. For example, I don't seem to be able to pick winning horses at a racecourse using intuition (yes, I have tried). Now I don't know if that's because my intuition is failing me, or I'm simply not accessing it properly, or maybe my attachment to winning money distorts my ability in that setting. What I do know is that a trip to the races usually costs me money! I would balance that by saying that I don't have any obvious knowledge or skill for picking horses. In other words, my subconscious mind has little information or experience with which to work.

What I am confident of is my own ability to use intuition within a coaching environment, because I do have both experience and developed skills in this area. I would suggest that the same is true for many individuals specializing within a particular field. For example, I bet a plumber can find a random fault in a heating system using his intuition faster than seems logical. Based on years of experience and technical skill, what looks like magic is simply wisdom in action.

An implied need to develop our own learning

If our intuition draws upon our latent wisdom and knowledge, then of course we benefit from increasing that knowledge. Continual learning and self-development will help a coach stay both effective and fresh. So, whether you learn by reading, attending courses or seminars, debating with others, seeking feedback, listening to tapes, keeping a diary, studying others, or a combination of all those – I encourage you to remain both focused and committed to increasing your own knowledge and skill.

Skill four – asking questions

If the coach and the coachee are to become travelling companions, then the coach's questions and listening are the quality of light by which they will travel.

Figure 4.7 Asking questions

Their answer is in your question

The ability to ask fabulous questions consistently is uncommon enough to seem like a rare talent. It's actually a skill that can be developed, with concentration and practice. In coaching, a beautifully timed, perfectly worded question can remove barriers, unlock hidden information and surface potentially life-changing insights. In other words, to be a great coach you need to be able to ask great questions.

> If the coach and the coachee are to become travelling companions, then the coach's questions and listening are the quality of light by which they will travel.

What does a great question look like or sound like? Well, it will have the following characteristics:

➡ It's simple.

➡ It has a purpose.

➡ It will be influencing without being controlling.

Keeping things simple

Simple questions often have the greatest impact, because they allow the coachee to use energy for forming their response, rather than trying to understand the wording of the question. In addition, they often get 'to the heart of the matter' more easily, simply because of their direct nature. We obviously need to balance 'direct' with a need to maintain rapport, and that is still possible. When asking questions, being clever just isn't clever.

Complex questions confuse people

Unfortunately for a coach, asking simple, straightforward questions isn't always automatic. Perhaps a coach hears the coachee say, 'Well, I need to earn more money you see – that's important'. The coach might decide that they want to understand the motivation behind that and so respond with the following:

Too complex a question: 'When you consider your motivations around this and what causes you to want to earn more money, what does this lead you to realize?'

This is not a great question. It's fairly long and too complicated. The listener is asked to compare, analyse and then 'realize' something. There's also an implied pressure to come up with a particular 'realization', as though the coach knows the answer, and the coachee needs to come up with it. As a result of the coachee getting the answer 'wrong' or, worse, not being able to produce an answer, the conversation may easily become uncomfortable or laboured.

Alternatively, the coach's question might be:

Too casual a question: 'So what's all this earning more money about then?'

Again, not a great question. Although it's brief, it's also too casual and lacks focus. The response to this question may be equally flippant, e.g. 'Dunno – that's just me I guess.' Additionally, there's a subtle tone that suggests the individual is 'wrong' to want to earn more money. The phrasing is similar to that used by parents discussing a problem with their children: 'So what's all this noise/crying/fuss about then?' Again, when we make a person 'wrong' in the conversation, we begin to lose rapport.

Another 'simple' option might be:

Questioning 'why': 'Why do you want to earn more money?'

Easy to understand, fairly easy to respond to, but it contains the word 'why', which has risks associated with it. When we ask someone 'why', it can easily be interpreted as a request for them to justify themselves. When a person feels that pressure, they can easily become defensive and begin to form a 'logical' case for their own actions, e.g. 'Well, I just do, why should I put up with the lousy wages this place is paying me?'

Questions can be like keys that open doors

The best question is one that the coachee is willing to answer because it's both simple to understand and inoffensive in its tone. In addition, if the question is right, it will surface the information you both need to increase progress within the conversation. Suitable questions might include:

➡ 'Can you perhaps say a little more about the importance to you of earning money?' This is a gentle, respectful question, maybe a little general, but it's likely to create progress.

➡ 'What is it about earning more money that's important to you?' This is more direct, and relies on you having good rapport, and a fairly gentle tone of voice.

➡ 'So money's important – can you tell me a bit more about that?' A little more casual, a little less direct and still might easily hit the mark. If it doesn't, you can be sure it's going to get you closer.

In coaching, simply worded questions encourage the smooth flow of a conversation, as the coachee is able to concentrate on their thoughts and respond naturally.

Questions with purpose

When we ask a question of someone, or even of ourselves, the question normally has purpose. For example, some questions gather information; some questions influence a person's thinking. In coaching, the questions that a coach uses often do both.

Table 4.1 illustrates examples of good coaching questions, along with their purpose.

Table 4.1 Good coaching questions

Purpose	Coaching examples
Gather general information.	'Can you tell me more about what happened with her?' 'Could you say more about that?' 'What else is there to say about that?'
Gather specific information.	'Specifically, what was it about her that you didn't like?' 'Can you tell me what she actually said?' 'What words did she use that upset you?'

▶

Help someone remember something more clearly.	'What can you remember about what happened?' 'What do you remember seeing/feeling/hearing?'
Shift someone's attention to the present moment, e.g. if they're becoming angry about something and you want them to relax a little.	'Okay, what else do you want to say about that to me right now?' 'So, what seems important about that right now?' 'Can you think of any other information that would be relevant about that for us here, now?'
Understand someone's values.	'What was it about her words that upset you?' 'What is important to you about that?' 'What would you have wanted her to say?'
Help someone appreciate another person's values.	'What was important to her in this situation?' 'What might be her reasons for acting like that?'
Get someone to link two thoughts, or situations, together.	'How does the location you described relate to what happened?' 'How does this situation affect how you are at work now?'
Help someone appreciate something from someone else's perspective.	'What do you think her experience was?' 'What might she be feeling at that point?' 'What might her intention have been?'
Help someone come to a conclusion	'What are your thoughts about that now?'

	'What is the conclusion you are drawing about that now?'
Influence someone to action.	'What could you do about that right now?'
Prepare someone to overcome barriers to taking action.	'What might stop you from doing that?' (Follow-up) 'So how will you overcome that?'
Influence someone to think about a situation positively.	'How have you benefited from this?' 'What will you get by sorting this whole matter out now?' 'What's the positive/up side of this?'
Influence someone to think about the effects of an action.	'What are the risks associated with your action?' 'How will this affect your other colleagues?' 'Who else is affected by this?'
Help someone gain learning from an event or circumstance.	'How has talking this through affected your views on the situation?' 'What learning have you taken from this?' 'How would you react if that kind of situation happened again?'

There are obviously lots of reasons to ask a question. For a coach, it's important to decide in what direction to take a conversation, and then construct the appropriate question that fulfils that intent.

Occasionally, a coach will ask a question without really knowing why they've asked it. Where the question is based on instinct and experience, this is appropriate. I would suggest, however, that this is the exception rather than the rule. To frequently ask random questions with no idea of their purpose would create a very strange conversation indeed!

Maintaining integrity of purpose

Questions may do many positive things in a conversation, such as create clarity, explore different perspectives, etc. Unfortunately they may also narrow options, imply judgement and leave the coachee feeling pressured or defensive.

It is important to make sure the purpose of a question is not corrupted by strong personal opinion. For example, a coach may hear a coachee describing his desire for a new job that involves more money and much more travel. The coach also knows that the coachee has recently said that his wife is expecting their first baby. Logically, it seems reasonable to look at the effect such a move may have on the person's family. The following questions may appear to do just that:

'Isn't that a bit unfair on your wife right now?'
'Won't that be difficult if your wife has just had a baby?'

Both questions, however, have an implied outcome and strong sense of judgement. The coach is expressing their own opinion by using words like 'difficult' and 'unfair'. The potential of exploring the effects of the job move is almost lost as the coachee is pressed to justify his statement.

With less of a sense of judgement, the following questions work better:

'How will this amount of travel affect things at home?'
'Who else is affected by you changing jobs?'

By keeping the questions open and more neutral the coachee can explore their own thoughts and awareness of the situation. This is an example of the non-directive approach outlined in Chapter 2, where the coach seeks to draw insights and learning from the coachee.

Influence versus control – leading the witness

Asking someone a question automatically influences the direction of their thoughts. For example, 'What was the best holiday you ever had?' causes you to think about holidays in the past. Although it subtly implies that you have had a great holiday at some point in your life, the question is fairly neutral, i.e. it doesn't tell you what you should think.

Within coaching, a collaborative (less directive) coach tries to maintain the balance between influence and control. Controlling questions can narrow down options, imply judgement, or create pressure on someone else to come up with the 'right' response. Perhaps when there's a time limit on a coach to reach a conclusion, these kinds of questions might be appropriate. Mostly, though, I'd discourage coaches from using controlling questions. They inhibit thought and self-expression, and the coach risks missing information, losing rapport, or both.

> Within coaching, a collaborative coach tries to maintain the balance between influence and control.

Table 4.2 illustrates controlling questions further.

Table 4.2 Controlling questions

Controlling question	Problem/issue
'And what did you feel about that – frustrated?'	Narrows down options of what the person may have felt, plus subtly assumes what they 'should' have felt, i.e. frustrated.
'What made you act in such a hostile manner towards her?'	Implies both criticism and a requirement for the other person to justify their actions.
'How is that going to put things right if Kathy's still so upset?'	Again, implies disagreement and requests justification.
'What could you do to completely resolve the situation for everyone affected?'	Places pressure on the individual to get the question 'right' while implying subtle blame.
'What is it about Kathy that you aren't able to deal with?'	Assumes that the other person isn't able to deal with Kathy, and that's a bad thing.

Making someone wrong

One other thing common to most controlling questions is that they make the other person wrong in some way for their actions. By making someone 'wrong' for something, we create difference or distance between us, e.g. 'Don't you think that was a little silly?'

When a coach frequently makes a coachee wrong, they risk damaging rapport and the ongoing relationship.

Table 4.3 gives more neutral alternatives.

The importance of voice

Any question is given further meaning by the quality of your voice when you ask it. Questions may be made clearer, colder, more supportive or more aggressive simply by the tone, warmth and speed of your voice.

Try it yourself   Use your voice

Using the question 'So what was important about that?' repeat it three different times, changing the quality of your voice each time, using the following characteristics:

➡ With a cruel sneer.

➡ With sarcasm (and end with a sigh!).

➡ With genuine curiosity, as though the answer is important to you.

You will notice that a great question can be completely wrecked by the wrong tonality. Also, use great tonality with a potentially risky or abrupt question and you're more likely to get a good response.

An appreciation of closed and open questions

Part of the flexibility a coach needs to develop can be found in the effective use of both closed and open questions. Closed questions can be answered with a yes or no and open questions can't:

➡ Closed questions (Y/N):

  – Did you enjoy that?

Table 4.3 Neutral questions

Coaching question	Benefit
'How did you feel about that?'	Open question enables the coachee to decide how they felt.
'What caused you to react like that?'	Helps the coachee disassociate in order to identify reasons for their behaviour.
'What was behind the way you acted towards her?'	As a follow-up to the above question, might uncover further information, e.g. values.
'What do you want to happen now?'	Helps someone disassociate from the past and associate with the future. Creates a focus on goals, a desired outcome, progress.
'What effect will doing that have upon Kathy do you think?'	Helps the coachee see the implications of their actions for others.
'What could you do to improve things now?'	Allows the coachee to consider options to improve things, plus imagining themselves doing them.
'What is it about Kathy's behaviour that's important to you?'	Distinguishes Kathy's behaviour from Kathy the person. Also, uses the word 'important' in a way that implies no judgement.

- Would you like this?
- Can you do that?
- Will that be here by Friday?
- Is that everything?
➡ Open questions:
- What did you enjoy about that?

- Who would like this?
- How can we get this done?
- When will it be delivered?
- What else is there?

Open questions encourage more information than closed. They also encourage participation and involvement in the conversation and allow us to explore someone else's thoughts and ideas. For this reason, a good coach will tend to use many more open questions than closed. During a typical coaching session I would expect the coachee to be doing at least 70 per cent of the talking. Using open questions is one way a coach can achieve this.

Nevertheless, closed questions may still be used to great effect, especially where we don't want a detailed response, e.g.:

Confirming information: 'Have I got that right?'
Moving the conversation along: 'Can we continue?'
Closing a conversation down: 'Have we finished?'

The exception is when people don't respond to closed questions with a yes or no – this is especially common with politicians!

Coach's corner

Q What if I can't think of my next question?

Sometimes a coach will go blank, get stuck and not know what to say next! This is normal, human and happens to all coaches at some time. Causes and potential options include:

The coach has lost concentration and has lost the thread of the conversation
Be honest, declare what's happened, and move on, e.g. 'I'm really sorry, I need you to repeat what you just said, I lost concentration just then.' Then make sure you refocus on the conversation and what the coachee is saying, in order to regain your involvement.

The coach is genuinely distracted by another thought, idea or insight

Be honest, declare what's happening, e.g. 'I'm sorry, but I keep thinking about what you said earlier about not liking things too easy, can we go back to that a little?' It might be that your intuition has made a connection that's worth exploring.

The conversation seems to be leading nowhere or seems 'stuck', e.g. maybe the energy has gone out of the conversation, or the conversation feels pointless

Be honest (again!). Say what you're feeling or thinking – after all, they might be thinking it too. For example, 'OK, I'm kind of stuck now because I don't know where our conversation is heading – is this still a useful discussion?' They might say 'Yes I'm actually getting a lot from this', so, if they think it's still useful, find out how, e.g. 'Help me understand a little more about that'. You'll then have a new focus for the conversation.

Alternatively, if they say 'I know what you mean, I'm stuck with it as well', you can then decide how it's best to continue, e.g. 'OK – do we leave that or do we want to know why we've got stuck with it?' or 'OK, what could we be talking about?'

The coach's mind has simply gone blank because they are nervous or new to coaching

This one is helped by a little advance preparation. Learn to relax yourself and refocus. Perhaps use your body to help you regain your sense of inner calm and confidence. Maybe sit back a little, pull your shoulders back and move your breathing down into your stomach (so that your tummy goes in and out as you breathe). Use a 'holding' phrase to enable you to refocus your thoughts, e.g. 'I'm pausing a little here, I just want to think about what you've just said' (then focus on to what they've just said). Remember that pauses are often useful for the coachee as well as the coach – silences can be powerful! Alternatively, do a brief recap, using your notes if you have them, e.g. 'Let's just recap a little, we've begun by saying that we wanted to …' Usually this is enough to reorientate you to the conversation, helping you decide what you want to explore or discuss.

Powerful questions

Powerful questions have many potential benefits, for example:

→ They refocus thought, e.g. from problem to solution.

→ They can help someone feel more powerful and constructive about a situation.

→ They tap into creativity and create options.

→ They can make a problem feel more like a challenge or an opportunity.

→ They create forward movement, i.e. out of the problem state and into solution or action.

Powerful questions are phrased in such a way as to encompass the problem and provoke an answer. The answer that they produce addresses the deeper problem, not just the surface issue. Table 4.4 demonstrates the journey between describing a situation as a problem and describing the same situation with a powerful question. The particular situation here is that the person is overworked and wants more support from their boss. They feel that their boss doesn't know much about their day-to-day situation and doesn't value the workload they are carrying.

When we ask a really powerful question in response to a situation, you can almost hear minds crunch into gear. It's as if the human brain can't resist the challenge of a really juicy question. For example, imagine you've been complaining relentlessly about needing a holiday but also needing the money to fix your car. You hate the car, you'd prefer something smaller, but it seems too much hassle to change it. Then someone asks you:

'How can you have *both* the car you want and the holiday you need?'

Hmm – gets you thinking, doesn't it?

Powerful questions are an invaluable tool within coaching and good coaches will ask them in a variety of situations. Perhaps the coachee is complaining repeatedly and not progressing towards a solution. Or maybe the coachee is blaming their situation on other people or things. Powerful questions often shift people's attention to a more powerful, responsible perspective. In addition, they

Powerful questions are an invaluable tool within coaching.

Table 4.4 Using powerful questions

Statement/question	Comment
'I'm really struggling with this job, and my boss doesn't support me – he doesn't even know what I do!'	This is a statement of complaint or problem; it focuses on what's wrong. It's not a question, and it produces no creative thoughts or ideas.
'Why can't my boss help me?'	This is a question, but it's not a powerful question. It's actually still a complaint. Also, if this question were answered, we'd get responses like 'Because he's not interested/ too busy, etc.'. Such responses are not going to progress this issue.
'How can I get my boss to know more about what I'm doing?'	This question covers only the superficial aspect of the problem and so evokes only a partial answer. Remember that the person also wants their boss to support them, not just be aware of what they do. Responses to this question might include 'Spend some time with him so that he understands what you do'. A powerful question will produce answers to the deeper problem.
'How can I make sure my boss understands more about what I'm doing, and encourage him to give me more support?'	This is a good, powerful question. The question digs below the surface, in order to bring up a complete solution. The likely response would create ideas that address all parts of the problem, i.e. make the boss aware, and get him to support more.

introduce the possibility of a solution in the mind of a coachee where previously none existed.

Table 4.5 shows some more examples of powerful questions.

Table 4.5 More powerful questions

Coachee's statement	Powerful question
'I've moved jobs, I've moved home and now I've got no friends and no social life – it makes the whole thing seem pointless somehow.'	'What could you be doing to feel more settled and meet some new friends?'
'I'm always worried about money, I'm worried about it regardless of how much I have. It's just always on my mind.'	'What's it going to take for you to feel more relaxed about money?'
'I want to go to night school but there's no one reliable to look after the kids, the situation's just impossible.'	'How can you get someone reliable to look after the kids while you go to night school?'

Often, people get bogged down by their complaints about how bad things are, or about how difficult their problems are, and never progress to sorting things out. In coaching, powerful questions can be a really effective way of moving someone forward from a problem, to a solution and action. This is a natural part of the coaching role and can be of great value to the person being coached.

Try it yourself   **Powerful questions**

The following will help you to experience powerful questions:

Step one – identify three problem statements

Write down three problems that you think you have. Choose things that are moderately important but not earth-shattering, e.g. 'I don't have enough time to exercise'. Leave enough space under each statement to write a few more sentences.

Step two – change problem statements into powerful questions

Under each problem, write down questions that provoke solutions to the issue, e.g. 'How can I create more time to exercise?' Remember, for a question to be powerful it must have the following attributes:

→ The question assumes that there is an answer to the problem.

→ The question provokes thought to begin to create answers or solutions.

→ The question digs below the surface, and thereby invites a more encompassing solution.

For further support, look back at the previous examples.

Step three – answer your own questions!

On a clean piece of paper, write your powerful questions down one side. Then, focusing on each question, produce ideas or solutions, e.g. 'Get up an hour earlier', 'Ask Jon to pick the kids up from school sometimes', 'Prepare more food for the freezer on weekends'.

Once you have some great solutions, simply decide which you're going to commit to!

What if your question doesn't create progress?

Sometimes, no matter how many great questions a coach might ask a coachee, the coachee is simply stuck and can't progress in the conversation. For example, a coach asks 'What else could you have done in that situation?' and the coachee simply can't think of an answer. The coach has asked the question because they want the coachee to understand their options, or perhaps produce some learning from a situation. The coach would prefer that the learning came from the coachee if possible. However, the coachee appears not to be able to think of anything as a response. In this instance, a coach has the following options:

→ Does the coachee need more time or silence in order to respond?

→ Is there another, similar question that might help them, e.g. 'What options did you have?' or 'What would Zorro do?' (OK, maybe not Zorro, but someone else, then.)

→ Is there something else bothering them that needs to be addressed before they can continue, e.g. 'Are you comfortable discussing this right now?'

Give an observation before an answer

If the above options still fail to create progress, the coach may be tempted to just give the coachee an answer, e.g. 'Well, you could have spoken to Bob about your plans first'. For reasons discussed previously, this may not be the best way to promote learning for the coachee, plus the coach might get the answer wrong. There is, however, a useful step towards giving an answer.

The coach has the option of first making an observation, as a way of encouraging the coachee's thinking process. Using the earlier example, the following observations may all be relevant:

➡ 'What you did was to prepare the report by yourself then introduce it at the meeting.'

➡ 'The report came as quite a surprise to everyone didn't it?'

➡ 'Well, you said that the report didn't get the response you wanted and I was wondering what else you might have done to make sure that it was well received?'

That last seems to work particularly well, as it combines an observation with a nice, gentle question.

So it's important to remember that just because a coachee can't answer a question quickly and easily, the coach still has options. A period of silence, asking another question or making an observation can all encourage further thoughts and ideas.

Section summary   **Skill four – asking questions**

The ability to ask great questions is one of the most important skills a coach develops. Great questions are simple to answer, give direction to the conversation and gently influence someone else's thinking. A simply worded question, delivered at the appropriate moment, can shift or shape someone's thinking dramatically.

Skill five – giving supportive feedback

Feedback as a way of learning

Figure 4.8 Giving supportive feedback

One of the great things about a coaching relationship is that it helps the coachee to experience a different view of themselves and their situation. One obvious way that they experience this view is through the eyes of the coach. The coach is able to give their own views of the coachee and so contribute to the coachee's picture of themselves and their experience. This might range from simple encouraging observations, to more challenging views of the coachee's attitudes or behaviours.

The ability of a coach to give their own views of a coachee constructively is important to the coaching experience. Effective feedback can accelerate a coachee's learning, inspire them, motivate them, help them feel valued and literally catapult them into action. So it's important that a coach learns to deliver feedback that is:

> **The ability of a coach to give their own views of a coachee constructively is important to the coaching experience.**

➡ Given with a positive intention.

➡ Based on fact or behaviour.

➡ Constructive and beneficial.

(We will examine these characteristics of feedback in more detail later in the chapter.)

What do we mean by feedback?

The term 'feedback' means literally to feed information back to someone. This information relates to the person receiving the feedback and provides data from which they can assess their performance or experiences. It can range from a general comment such as 'That was great/lousy' to more specific assessments of performance such as 'You've got your hand an inch too high'.

Many of us are familiar with the term 'feedback', maybe from situations at work, or learning situations, e.g. school or college. In recent years, the term has unfortunately become associated with criticism, due to how and when people choose to use it. The expression 'I'd like to give you some feedback' is sometimes used as an introduction to a fairly negative conversation. This is especially common in business, where praise and encouragement are rare and frustrations or disputes must be handled 'professionally'. By using the word 'feedback', individuals are able to give the illusion of professionalism to critical remarks.

It's a shame, because while critical remarks do constitute feedback (they're information), often the same message could be delivered in a much more supportive and probably effective manner. For example, the following statements all relate to the same situation:

> 'You keep upsetting people because you're so blunt with your remarks.'
> 'When you told Mark he'd no chance of getting the job, I thought he appeared upset.'
> 'When you told Mark he'd no chance of getting the job, how do you think he felt?'

All three comments have the same intention, i.e. to change the way in which the person speaks to others.

The first remark sounds like generalized, subjective criticism, and may easily upset the person hearing it. This remark is not a supportive way of giving someone feedback.

The second remark comments on specific behaviour in a more objective way and is less likely to offend the individual. The remark is fairly direct, although within a healthy coaching relationship this level of openness should be OK.

The third option uses a question to explore the impact upon the person, Mark. This is a much less direct attempt to influence someone's behaviour. This is not feedback, although it is a valid option to meet the objective of influencing the coachee's future behaviour.

Knowing when to give feedback

Within coaching, there are no hard and fast rules as to when to give feedback but there are guidelines. An opportunity for feedback may be prompted either by the coach or by the coachee. In either instance, the coach should offer feedback only in the genuine belief that it would benefit the coachee.

Potential benefits for the coachee when they receive feedback include:

➡ It has a positive impact on their learning.

➡ It offers useful information or perspectives.

➡ It encourages or motivates the coachee.

➡ It confirms or compares views and opinions.

➡ It prompts insights or ideas.

Sometimes, the coachee simply hasn't noticed something, is avoiding considering something or is simply stuck in their own thoughts. At these times, using feedback is often a good choice to make. By intervening with a piece of well-timed feedback, the coach can often clarify thoughts, offer alternative views and even unblock blockages.

Sometimes, coachees will look for reassurance and say things like 'I bet you think I'm mad, don't you?' or 'Do you think I'm being silly about this?' In this instance, the coachee is probably looking for some simple reassurance before continuing talking. In cases like this it's easier for the coach to make a quick comment like 'No, of course I don't. Carry on ...'

If a coachee asks for feedback and a coach is not willing to give it, the coachee can easily become uncomfortable. The situation might be important, e.g.

'I just don't seem to be making progress with this, why do you think that is?' If the coach refuses to comment, the coachee may view this as a withdrawal of some kind. The coachee might even become slightly paranoid, as they begin to suspect the coach has formed negative thoughts or judgements about them.

As a balance, there are some occasions where it would not be helpful to give feedback. For instance:

➡ Where it seems to be an excuse for the coachee to avoid taking responsibility, e.g. 'What do you think about all this?'

➡ If, giving feedback, the coach interrupts the flow of a conversation or the thought processes of the coachee.

➡ If giving feedback may lead to an inappropriate level of control by the coach, e.g. 'Let me tell you what I think about your situation'.

➡ Where the coach does not have enough information to give feedback effectively, e.g. 'Well, I could guess what might be happening is ...'

Imagine you are coaching someone who appears overly concerned with what other people think and it affects their ability to make decisions. Their first thought is to check what other people might say or feel about what they do before fully exploring what they themselves want. In the past, this has led to them missing out on opportunities, or suffering in silence instead of expressing their views and needs. A coaching dialogue on this might sound as follows:

COACH: So what will you do about the job offer?

COACHEE: Well, I'm not sure. I've been asking around, doing a bit of a survey. Trouble is, everyone seems to be saying different things. I mean, you know me, and what I'm good at – do you believe I'm capable of doing it?

COACH: Well, I can easily add my view, but what I'm really interested in is what you believe.

COACHEE: What I think? Well, I'm not sure I've thought about that!

It is appropriate for the coach to challenge the coachee's tendency to place too much importance on what other people think. In this way, they encourage the coachee to use a different decision-making strategy that relies more on what they themselves think and feel.

The decision when or whether to give feedback should be based on a balance of the potential benefits and risks of doing so. While the risks are rarely significant in isolated instances, over time, continual feedback can result in the coach taking too much authority within the coaching relationship.

The coach simply needs to balance the pros and cons of giving feedback and to act accordingly.

How to give feedback

As we mentioned earlier, feedback should be:

➡ Given with a positive intention.

➡ Based on fact and behaviour.

➡ Constructive and beneficial.

The person hearing feedback that is clumsily worded and badly delivered can experience it as criticism, e.g. 'You're being arrogant about this'. This can usually be avoided by the person giving feedback taking care about what they say and how they say it. Some people will be more receptive to hearing feedback than others and a coach must develop the ability to deliver a potentially difficult message in such a way as to maintain the motivation of the coachee.

Some people will be more receptive to hearing feedback than others.

Of course, not all feedback is related to difficult messages. Praise and acknowledgement of good performance or progress are equally as important as observations of someone's need to adopt change, or develop different behaviours. Where messages are positive in nature, the previous principles of intention, based on behaviour, fact, etc., still apply.

Whilst the following guidelines apply in a coaching relationship, they also work for anyone giving feedback outside a coaching situation.

This remark is too general, too vague for the person hearing it to do much with. They are left with the option of being someone who 'doesn't try so hard' – which may not be something they can do anything about.

In the same situation, the following feedback is more usable and likely to be more effective:

> 'I noticed that some of your answers to the questions were quite long and I suspect that caused some people to lose the sense of what you were saying.'

This is an observation of behaviour, plus a personal opinion of the effect of that behaviour. The person hearing it can disassociate from their behaviour enough to evaluate the situation more objectively. After all, most people know how to stop talking.

As a more positive example, if I notice that the coachee smiled a lot at the audience and that they responded by smiling back a lot, I can give the coachee that observation. In future, they can choose to repeat the behaviour, in the knowledge that it's likely to produce a good result.

The difference between objective and subjective feedback

It's useful to understand the difference between a statement that is objective and one that is subjective. Objective statements are based solely on fact, e.g. something that actually happened. Subjective statements contain the views and opinions of an individual person. For example:

Example 1: Objective   COACH: Before you said 'yes' to that question, you paused and smiled.

Example 2: Subjective   COACH: Before you said 'yes' to that question, you paused and smiled – for me, that's real progress.

The first statement comments only on behaviour, making it more objective. The fact that the coach chose to observe the behaviour at all suggests they think it is significant and that requires some judgement – but for the purposes of coaching, we'll consider it an objective statement. The coach simply makes the observation to enable the coachee to respond with their own thoughts. The coachee is likely to comment on what caused them to pause and smile.

The second statement obviously adds the coach's opinion that progress is being made. The coach intends the statement to be supportive and encouraging and the coachee is more likely to respond to the encouragement, e.g. with 'Thanks' or 'Great'.

While both statements are very similar in nature, notice that in their subtle difference they may create a very different result. However, I'd like to be really clear that neither form of feedback is right or wrong. What is important is that we appreciate the varying degrees to which we are being subjective or objective. The amount of fact and personal opinion within our statements affects the potential benefits, risks and results of feedback.

Subjective – the pros and cons
There are both benefits and risks attached to the coach giving subjective feedback.

Potential risks include being wrong and directing or controlling the coachee in an inappropriate manner. By using their own views and opinions, e.g. 'I think', the coach is introducing a form of guidance which might be directive.

This risk of over-influencing the coachee must be balanced with the potential benefits of providing support, acknowledgement and recognition. Once the coach has established both credibility and rapport with the coachee, their input is often welcome. Over a period of time, the coach gains valuable insight into the behaviours and tendencies of the coachee that might help them to progress towards their goals.

Again, it's a question of balance and a need to avoid extremes, i.e. too many personal views or no input at all. In practice, I tend to avoid giving personal views where possible as in general they get in the way of an individual's ability to find their own solutions.

Objective – the pros and cons
Objective statements reduce the coach's influence to a minimum and allow the coachee to respond only to facts. Of course, these 'facts' rely on the

ability of the coach to observe behaviour correctly, or else the whole process is flawed.

Objective, factual statements are more likely to be accepted by the coachee as 'true' than are statements heavily laden with the coach's opinion. With the former, there's less non-factual information to debate. For example, if I say 'You raised your eyebrows when I said that' as opposed to 'You don't believe me, do you?' the first observation is more easily accepted than the other.

The potential downside of the coach making only objective, factual statements is that the coachee may actually need the coach's personal input to progress. Some behaviour might benefit from the coach interpreting it, e.g. 'I sense that you're avoiding discussing your current partner' might work better than 'You've talked a lot about your previous marriage'.

The next examples illustrate the journey between objective and subjective feedback. The following coachee has a goal of being more influential in meetings.

Example 1   COACH: You said that you take notes throughout the meetings.

The above comment is fairly objective, although obviously there is some judgement implied by the fact that the coach has chosen to focus on the behaviour at all.

Example 2   COACH: You take notes a lot. That might be related.

The above comment is still fairly objective and has a hint of the coach's views.

Example 3   COACH: You take notes a lot. That's going to affect your influence.

That one was less objective, and contains more of the coach's views.

Example 4   COACH: You take too many notes. It's got to be causing you to lack personal impact.

This has a fairly hefty amount of personal opinion – subjective feedback – in it.

Example 5   COACH: Because you're taking notes all the time, it's causing you to lack presence. This is what's really affecting the situation.

Example 5 is an extremely subjective statement that suggests strong opinion on the part of the coach. It's also very risky, as the coach is making a statement based on their understanding of the situation, which is limited to their knowledge. Also, by suggesting that taking notes is the most important factor, Example 5 controls the direction of the conversation too much.

Remember, collaborative coaching is a less directive, less controlling style of conversation. That way, we place primary responsibility for the conversation and the situation with the coachee.

The coach needs to decide whether to give a simple objective observation as feedback, or subjective feedback containing more of their own opinion, as the following dialogue illustrates:

COACHEE: I don't know, maybe I'm worrying too much about the whole situation. What do you think about all this?

Now at this point, the coach has options:

➡ Decline to give input and simply continue seeking to understand the situation, e.g. 'Well, what I'm really interested in is how you feel about it – what do you think?'

➡ Offer a simple objective feedback, e.g. 'Hmm, well, we have been discussing this for most of the session'.

➡ Offer subjective feedback, such as 'Well, the discussion does seem to be a little out of proportion to the problem. It sounds to me like you're worrying unnecessarily'.

Again, there are no right or wrong options – only outcomes. It is important that the coach appreciates they have a choice of response and they should choose according to their desired result.

Try it yourself   **Who's being objective?**

This exercise is a bit of fun with a twist. You'll need your favourite newspaper or magazine and a piece of paper and a pen. Choose a fairly brief article you're interested in reading. Read the article once, so that you understand what's in it. Now, divide your paper into two columns, one headed 'objective' and the other 'subjective'. Using the columns, separate the objective facts in the article from the subjective or opinion-based statements. When you've finished, notice what and how much is in each column.

Q What does that say about your preferred reading material?

Feedback that is constructive and beneficial

If a piece of feedback is effective, then it will benefit the coachee in some way. The feedback may create deeper understanding, build an idea, encourage productive action or simply increase someone's sense of well-being.

Being constructive also relates to how the coachee experiences the feedback. One of the signs of a good coach is their ability to make a potentially difficult or awkward message easier for the coachee to hear and experience. In order to make this happen, the coach must maintain the emotional state of the coachee throughout the feedback conversation. To do this, a good coach will often:

→ Balance difficult messages with positive statements.

→ Take personal responsibility for the views he/she is giving, e.g. 'I notice' or 'I think'.

→ Use open questions to encourage the coachee to shift perspectives or explore other avenues of thought.

→ Use neutral or diminished emphasis of words and phrases to describe difficult situations or emotions, e.g. some discomfort, slight resistance, etc.

→ Communicate supportively using non-verbal signals, e.g. posture, facial expressions, tonality, eye contact, etc.

→ Link observations to goals, e.g. 'This may help you to approach your time management a little differently'.

For the coachee to judge the feedback as constructive, the conversation must be, in balance, positive to them. They must feel that the coach has their success and well-being at heart, and that it was a worthwhile conversation to have in support of their development. For this reason, the coach must be able to deliver messages and observations in a way that the coachee accepts. By effectively combining the above principles of style and delivery, the coachee is more likely to welcome the feedback as constructive.

Balance difficult messages with positive statements.

Clearly, there must be some benefit to the feedback conversation for the coachee. Where feedback is directly related to the coachee's goals, this is fairly straightforward. Where the feedback does not obviously relate to the coachee's goals, the coach should establish a relevant benefit when considering their intent for giving feedback.

Coach's corner — What if my feedback gets a negative response?

Sometimes, our feedback isn't received in the way we wanted it to be. Maybe the coachee responds in a way we feel is negative. Responses we hadn't hoped for might include the coachee being upset, angry, unpleasantly surprised, or maybe they simply reject the feedback given completely. Causes of negative responses to feedback can vary, from an unsupportive statement clumsily delivered to a simple misunderstanding of what's been said. Maybe as a coach we're not feeling great ourselves, maybe we're feeling pressured, stressed or just tired (these are not good times to give feedback by the way!). Or maybe we don't understand enough about the person or their situation to attempt offering feedback. There may be an external factor that affects their response. For example, we use a phrase or word that they are already very sensitive to like 'dominant' and this creates an overly defensive reaction. There are a number of principles that can support a coach if this should happen, namely:

Immediately after the coachee's response

Make sure that this is a genuinely negative response that you need to act upon

For example, what you decide is a 'stony silence' might simply be the time the coachee needs to consider what they've just heard. Perhaps re-play in your mind what's just happened and consider other possible causes of their response. Alternatively, if the coachee begins pro-testing, or becomes angry or upset, then listen to what they say before you decide what you need to do. If you know that your feedback has been clumsily delivered, then focus on making amends.

Take full responsibility for your unsupportive feedback

Acknowledge that your feedback hasn't worked out the way you intended. Apologize and accept that you have regret about causing their response, for example:

'I'm sorry, I've upset you and I didn't mean to.'
'I've upset you with what I've said, I'm sorry, that's my fault.'
'I'm now really regretting putting it like that, I'm sorry.'

If you're not sure what it was you said that caused the upset, then still acknowledge your responsibility, e.g. 'I think I've upset you with what I've just said – have I?'

If you find you're actually not responsible, then simply stay supportive of the coachee, e.g. by allowing them time to think, or listening to why they've reacted in the way they have.

Make amends, explain if possible/appropriate

Explain your intentions, but don't excuse yourself, stay responsible. For example: 'My intention was to be helpful but I haven't been have I?' or 'I wanted to give you another way of looking at the situation – I hoped that it might give you another way forward'.

After the session

While maintaining responsibility for causing the response, seek to understand what it was you did that caused it and learn from the experi-ence. Your options for learning include:

- When the coachee is in an appropriate state of mind, ask them to help you understand what you did that didn't work. Be careful to maintain a position of full responsibility and ask them to help you learn. Be prepared to explain your intentions, but avoid justifying yourself or making excuses.
- Review the situation with someone you trust to help you learn from the situation (while maintaining the confidentiality of the coachee).
- Read this chapter again and consider what principles or methods might have enabled you to give the feedback in such a way as to create a better response.

Coach's corner   **Summary**

If we're going to learn to give feedback we're going to make mistakes. So it's important to know the principles of giving good feedback and focus on them. Where we give feedback that is unsupportive, then we need to acknowledge that and make amends if possible. Then we need to learn from the experience. And please don't let a bad experience of giving feedback stop you from ever giving any more – the world needs you to be great at giving fabulous feedback!

An example of constructive feedback

Obviously the non-verbal element of giving constructive feedback cannot be demonstrated here. The other principles are, however, illustrated in the following dialogue:

COACH: I wanted to discuss a little more your desire for less tension at home, which is proving a little more difficult now you've got your parents staying for a few months.

COACHEE: A little difficult? – You can say that again!

COACH: I've noticed that when you're speaking about your mother mostly it's a complaint, for example, 'She's so moody' or 'She just loves being difficult'.

119

COACHEE: Right – yes, I suppose that's true.

COACH: The other thing that seems to relate to this is the way you portray your father in the situation.

COACHEE: How's that?

COACH: Well, you sound like you care for your father a lot. When you discuss him in relation to your mother, you say things like 'Poor guy, I don't know how he copes with her' and 'She must make his life a misery'.

COACHEE: Yeah, I guess I do feel pretty sorry for him.

Notice how the coach is gradually constructing a picture of the situation that the coachee finds it easy to accept. Observations so far are mainly objective, i.e. facts about behaviour.

In addition, the coach is careful not to use emotive or potentially sensational words that might cause the coachee to be uncomfortable or defensive. For example, instead of saying something like 'You don't want going home to be such a nightmare', the coach chooses to say 'You want less tension at home'. It's a subtle distinction and an important trick to use sometimes.

The same dialogue continues:

COACH: You know, I'm wondering if how you discuss the situation is affecting how you're responding to it, and perhaps how you're feeling about it.

COACHEE: OK – go on.

COACH: What effect could that be having on you do you think?

COACHEE: Well I guess I'm thinking about it more, I certainly seem to be discussing it with anyone who will listen. I guess I'm making the whole thing worse.

COACH: OK, so I hear you complaining about your mother yet discussing your father as someone to feel sorry for or sympathize with. How does this actually affect your behaviour at home with them?

COACHEE: Hmm, now I'm getting it. That's not a nice thought, actually. I'm seeing how I am around my parents at home and it does mirror what I say. I'm very different around my father than I am around my mother.

COACH: How's that?

COACHEE: Well, much more patient I guess.

COACH: And is there an opportunity here?

COACHEE: Yeah – I need to work out how I'm really featuring in all this – that's the opportunity to affect the whole thing, isn't it?

Notice from the dialogue how the coach carefully constructs an increased awareness of the situation in collaboration with the coachee. Open questions are used both to involve and to engage the coachee in the conversation. Gradually, the coachee builds a fresh perspective on the situation that enables them to create other options for a way forward.

Remember the importance of maintaining the coachee's emotional state. This includes not upsetting them unnecessarily or putting them on their guard. In general, an understatement is more likely to be accepted than an exaggeration. Within coaching I tend to use caution when describing situations. It's easier for a coachee to hear 'You have a situation that you want to change' than 'You've got a big problem here'.

To experience some feedback yourself, try the feedback exercise in the Toolkit.

Section summary   **Skill five – giving supportive feedback**

As a coach, your observations and experience can make a significant difference to the person you're coaching. By making observations on the coachee's situation, the coach provides an external point of reference that the coachee can use to compare with their own thoughts and ideas.

▶

flow. Maybe the coachee is discussing something really important to them, or maybe the coach feels that a significant issue or breakthrough is just surfacing.

As much as possible, a good coach works at managing the session time effectively. Surprisingly, this can be easier in short coaching sessions (20 minutes) than long ones (2 hours). In a short session, both parties are automatically focused on the time available. In longer sessions, it's easier to get lost in the conversation and allow time to disappear. One solution is to keep a clock or watch visible on the table, perhaps explaining at the beginning of the session the reason why it's there.

I find it's best to be open about checking the time during a session. At an appropriate moment, it's usually acceptable to say something like 'Let's just check how we're doing for time here'. That way, the coachee also becomes aware of the need to finish promptly.

Whatever the circumstances, the coach should do everything in their power to stay as resourceful as possible during the day. Simple things like drinking lots of water, taking regular breaks and eating the right foods help tremendously. I personally don't like to eat a large lunch when coaching as I find I get tired and can't concentrate so well afterwards.

Anything that creates a sense of tiredness in the coach, e.g. lack of sleep, alcohol, etc., is best avoided.

Behavioural barriers: 'what not to do'

Less obvious and possibly more harmful to the coaching process are behaviours that the coach might adopt during coaching conversations that obstruct the collaborative coaching process. For example, asking too many questions for the coachee to respond to or displaying impatience when the coachee becomes confused or unclear. Again, practicality and common sense are needed to consider which behaviours work in coaching and which don't.

The behaviours we're going to explore can be both subtle and damaging to a collaborative coaching conversation. As with most coaching principles, there are no rights and wrongs, only results or outcomes. For example, it's not wrong to ask too many questions, it's just unlikely to produce the results that the coach wants to produce.

The following three-step response will help you deal with these barriers when they arise; the more you practise this, the more 'instantly' you'll relax and refocus in a situation:

1 Awareness: You notice that you're doing or thinking something that's not working.
2 Acknowledgement: You acknowledge that – and give it up (let the thought go).
3 Refocus: You shift your attention to a more effective thought or behaviour.

I would also acknowledge that some of the following tendencies and behaviours might resonate with you more than others. For example, you may never try to control others in conversation or talk too much. I would still encourage you to reflect on these barriers, as the more self-awareness you have, the more choice you have.

Too much talking

It may sound obvious for a coach not to talk too much during a coaching conversation, but it's actually quite easily to slip into. Perhaps the coach is feeling particularly enthusiastic or energetic about a point they're making and 10 minutes later they are still talking. Alternatively, the coachee may seem reluctant to talk and so the coach fills the silence by chatting.

In a collaborative coaching conversation, the coachee should be doing at least 70 per cent of the talking, often more. The principles of collaborative coaching rest on the coachee being able to explore their own thoughts and experiences in a way that encourages insight and learning. This simply isn't possible if they have to constantly listen to the coach talking.

Instead, a good coach uses a gentle process that involves them listening, asking questions, making observations or offering feedback. Occasionally the coach may choose to illustrate a point they are making by telling a short story, drawing a simple diagram – whatever is appropriate. Overall, the balance of all the talking will still rest with the coachee.

Less is more

Periods of quiet are often preferable to the irrelevant ramblings of a coach who has been embarrassed by silence. For the coachee, silence is often a wonderful thing. By not having to speak or listen, they can take time to reflect on their internal thought processes. Some thoughts and feelings take time to form and further dialogue with the coach may distract or pressurize the coachee's internal process.

For the coachee, silence is often a wonderful thing.

A good coach will notice when the coachee appears to be reflecting on thoughts and ideas. Maybe the coach has just asked a question and the answer is not obvious, or maybe the coachee has just made an internal connection and wants to consider it a little. By allowing the room to fill with silence, the coach creates time and space for the coachee simply to think.

The following exercise will help you feel more comfortable about using silence.

Try it yourself   **Just be quiet ...**

Go and have a conversation with someone about something they are comfortable or familiar with. You might ask them about their weekend or something they're doing at work: anything that they can discuss easily. During the conversation, allow the conversation to fall silent if possible. For example, don't respond automatically when they pause in the conversation. Use one or two moments of silence as a way of deepening the conversation, or allowing them to speak again.

After the conversation, consider the following:

Q What effects did the silences have on the conversation?

Q During any silences, how did you feel?

Q What opportunity does silence provide in a conversation?

Q When does using silence not work?

Emotional states

Generally, a coach wants to be in a resourceful state of mind and body to be able to coach to the best of their ability. As well as physical conditions such as general fatigue, or even illness, the coach must be in a good emotional state to coach well.

Emotional states conducive to coaching include: feeling relaxed, feeling aware, feeling focused, objective, even slightly detached. Emotional states unsupportive of coaching would include: feeling stressed, frustrated, impatient, anxious or simply bored.

Good coaches learn over time how to manage their own feelings and emotions within a coaching session. Different factors may challenge the coach's ability to do this and the following could all knock a coach off balance:

➡ The coaching session is delayed by one hour and you're left to sit and wait.

➡ You arrive for the session to find the room you wanted is double-booked.

➡ People keep walking into the meeting room you're in without knocking.

➡ You're coaching all day in the same room, it's freezing, and the drinks machine is broken.

➡ The coachee begins the session by saying they want to quit the coaching as it's not right for them.

To name but a few! As much as humanly possible, a coach must maintain a way of being during sessions that enables effective coaching to happen. A coach's ability to listen, focus, ask the right questions and generally encourage progress depends on their emotional state. Whatever happens, they must respond resourcefully. For example, if the fire alarm goes off, leave the building in a relaxed manner and continue chatting if possible. If the room is double-booked, go and find another. If the coachee wants to quit, gently explore their reasons why (before jumping to conclusions).

I find that a combination of commitment and detachment really helps. For example, I can remind myself I'm committed to the success of the coaching but not attached as to how that might happen. Who knows? The fact that we have to break the session to walk out as part of a fire drill may be just the interruption we need to stimulate fresh conversation!

Sympathy as an emotional state

Within coaching, it's important that we understand the nature of both empathy and sympathy as they can create very different results.

Empathy means the ability to identify mentally with another person. In other words, if you feel sad, I can relate to that; if you are angry, I can appreciate how you feel. Empathy does not mean that I feel what you feel, only that I can relate to how you feel.

The word 'sympathy' means to share in an emotion or feeling with another person, so that two people experience similar emotional states at the same time. For example, if you feel sad, I am sad, and if you feel angry, so do I.

For example, a coachee is very angry or upset about something; maybe a work colleague has said something really cruel or unkind. Perhaps the coach sympathizes by also becoming angry and upset, 'Well that's awful, that makes me mad just to hear about it and I wasn't even there!' This is not a helpful view for the coach to take. The coach is becoming personally involved in the issue in a way that's not appropriate.

By sympathizing and becoming angry, the coach is also suggesting that they support the coachee's anger about the situation. If the coach becomes angry or upset as well, then rational thought is difficult. The coach has become subjective about what they are hearing, and no longer holds a balanced perspective on the situation.

In this instance, empathy would be a more effective way of responding to the coachee, e.g. 'You sound quite angry about that and I can appreciate why. Do you want to say more about what happened?' By acknowledging the coachee's anger while remaining fairly objective, the coach can continue to facilitate the conversation from a perspective of learning.

Additionally, a coach who continually sympathizes throughout coaching sessions is likely to become emotionally drained. Taking on the emotions of others is something that counsellors and therapists are trained to guard against or deal with because of the debilitating effects over time.

When empathy seems cold

There are times when empathy is not appropriate in relating to a coachee's emotion. Empathy is fine in response to more typical emotions of mild frustration, annoyance, disappointment, etc. The risk of merely empathizing with the coachee is that sometimes this can appear a little cold and unsupportive.

Sometimes, situations and events demand a more sympathetic response. For example, a coachee has just experienced a significant loss of some sort and is visibly upset by it. For a coach to say 'I can appreciate how that must feel' might be inappropriate. To begin to explore the situation objectively, or look for possible learning, may not be what is needed right then. Maybe the coachee simply wants to know that their sadness is normal and that the coach is genuinely caring in that moment. In this instance, sympathy often feels more caring to the individual, as the coach is demonstrating that they are willing to take on the experience of their sadness, e.g. 'Scott that's awful, I'm so sorry'. When the coach takes on the coachee's sadness, they obviously become more personally related to the coachee's situation.

This delicate balance rests on a combination of factors. The coach must consider what the coachee might want and what seems effective for the coaching at that point. The coach might also consider the potential impact on the ongoing coaching relationship. In addition, the coach needs to stay resourceful for the conversation and that isn't helped if they have sunk into a similar emotional state as the coachee.

Of course, sometimes this level of restraint just isn't possible. Some things strike such a chord with the coach that they will genuinely be unable to control their response. That's human, natural and a real part of the coaching relationship.

Seeking to control or dominate the conversation

Collaborative coaching is based on encouraging the coachee to explore their own thoughts or experiences in a way that promotes insight and learning.

Collaborative coaching is based on encouraging the coachee to explore their own thoughts or experiences in a way that promotes insight and learning.

If a coach controls the direction or content of a conversation in a way that inhibits its natural flow, then that's counterproductive.

It is important for the coach to maintain a balance between keeping the conversation focused and supporting its natural flow. The next dialogue illustrates too much control by the coach:

COACH: So tell me more about the situation with your father. I want to find out exactly what the problem is and also what's causing his behaviour. I'm going to make sure we get to the bottom of this now.

COACHEE: Well, what is it you want to know?

COACH: Tell me about the most recent argument you've had with him and how he made you feel.

As you can see from the dialogue, the coach is being both directive and authoritative during the conversation. In this case, the coachee adopts a compliant, almost submissive, posture, saying, 'Well, what is it you want to know?' This places the coach firmly in control of the direction and content of the conversation. The next thing they will discuss will be what the coach wants to discuss. There is much less space in the conversation for the natural flow of the conversation to emerge.

The next dialogue demonstrates a coach maintaining a focus, while enabling the flow of the conversation to emerge and develop:

COACH: So tell me a little more about the situation with your father.

COACHEE: Well, he's just being totally unsupportive of my efforts to get into college, he just keeps telling me to get out and get a job.

COACH: What else does he say?

COACHEE: He says I'm wasting my time; that I'm going to be disappointed and let down when I can't get the course that I want.

COACH: What might be his reasons for saying that?

COACHEE:	I guess because he thinks I might do what my brother did when he was rejected. My brother ended up doing nothing for a year, just sat round the house being miserable.

Clearly, the coach uses open questions to gently surface information from the coachee. If either party has the balance of control, it's probably the coachee. The coachee is causing the direction of the conversation to emerge based on the information they are offering.

Another subtle form of control is demonstrated in the following dialogue:

COACHEE:	So I've decided that I'm not taking the job – they can keep it.
COACH:	Before you met the manager, didn't you say you wanted the job?
COACHEE:	Well, yes – but things have changed now.
COACH:	And didn't you say you wanted a challenge?
COACHEE:	Yes, I still do.
COACHEE:	Well, if you wanted the job and you wanted a challenge, isn't this the perfect opportunity for you?

In this dialogue, the coach is using a series of tactically worded questions to close down the options of the coachee. The questions are closed questions (only 'yes' or 'no' responses are possible), leaving the coachee little room to explain themselves properly. The coach is adopting an inappropriate level of control over the conversation. As a result, the coachee's own thoughts and insights cannot be expressed fully and the full potential of the situation is unlikely to emerge.

This subtle form of control also places the coach in a superior position to the coachee. Rather like a cat toying with a mouse, the coach is adopting a position of intellectual superiority over the coachee.

A more collaborative version of the previous dialogue might be:

COACHEE:	So I've decided that I'm not taking the job – they can keep it.
COACH:	OK, can you tell me a little more about that?

COACHEE: Well, I don't seem to be what they're looking for I guess.

COACH: What are they looking for do you think?

COACHEE: Well, they seem to want someone energized and motivated, I've felt so low for so long in my current job I've forgotten what that's like.

As you can see, the conversation goes in a completely different direction once the coach adopts a more open style of questioning. So what might cause a coach to try to control the conversation? The following are all possible factors:

⟹ The coach thinks they've spotted a solution to a problem and wants to lead the coachee towards it.

⟹ The coach is frustrated at the amount of time it's taking to discuss a subject.

⟹ The coach thinks the coachee expects them to take control.

⟹ The coachee seems unwilling to discuss an area, and the coach really wants them to.

⟹ The coach has high energy or enthusiasm for the topic under discussion.

⟹ The coach knows a lot about the subject being discussed and wants to display this knowledge.

⟹ The coach has a naturally authoritative manner in conversation and is used to 'leading from the front', e.g. they have a very 'strong' personality, maybe they're a senior manager, etc.

Again, awareness is the key to choice. By noticing when we're controlling the content and direction of a conversation, we can reduce this influence immediately. Our efforts and energy need to go into listening and facilitating thoughts, rather than constructing the conversation. In doing so, we open up the potential for a natural flow of thoughts and ideas to emerge.

If you want to practise reducing control during a conversation, try the Toolkit exercises 'Help someone else find their answer' and 'Developing deep listening'.

Needing to be 'right'

We like being right and we don't enjoy being wrong. Some of us are better at finding out we're wrong than others. (Some of us are really lousy at being wrong!) In coaching, I would recommend that any coach give up an attachment to being right – it simply gets in the way of the conversation. An attachment to being right is closely linked to our need to look good in conversations. In order to let go of an attachment to being right, we must also give up an attachment to looking good.

For example, a coachee may be discussing setting up home with a new partner and complaining that they are having second thoughts. The coach may have a theory about why this is and become inadvertently attached to it:

COACH: Well, I think the reason you're having doubts is because you're anticipating everything that could go wrong. After all, it's a big step for you.

COACHEE: No, it's not that, I haven't actually thought about what could go wrong.

COACH: Yes, but a lot of these things happen subconsciously. I think you're experiencing transference – that means you're transferring the real problem in order to disguise it.

In this example, the coach has made several mistakes. Firstly, they've played a subtle form of 'fix-it', by seeking to come up with a reason for the coachee's misgivings. It might have been more effective to explore the situation more fully before making any observation.

Secondly, they've become attached to proving that their theory is right. Because of this attachment, they are influencing the conversation in a direction that is inappropriate. The conversation might easily develop into looking for things the coachee thinks might go wrong, or even why they haven't been thinking about what might go wrong.

Finally, the coach seems to have slipped into the behaviour of looking good. By using words like 'transference' the coach is displaying some knowledge of psychology. The effect on the coachee is likely to be one of confusion and/ or defensiveness.

If a coach makes a mistake or gets something wrong, they should deal with it in a mature, unattached way.

If a coach makes a mistake or gets something wrong, they should deal with it in a mature, unattached way. There's a simple three-step approach that I use:

1 Acknowledge I'm wrong, either to myself or the coachee (whatever is appropriate).
2 Put the mistake right if possible/appropriate.
3 Give up thoughts of being wrong – move on.

For example, to repeat the previous example in a more effective way:

COACH: Well, I think the reason you're having doubts is because you're anticipating everything that could go wrong. After all, it's a big step for you.

COACHEE: No, it's not that, I haven't actually thought about what could go wrong.

COACH: OK, that's probably me jumping to conclusions. Tell me more about what you've been thinking.

Very quickly and smoothly, the coach acknowledges the error and continues the coaching conversation. Both the coach and the coachee can carry on with the natural flow of the conversation uninterrupted.

Within coaching, it's OK to make mistakes and get things wrong. All coaches do. What's not OK is for a coach to spend time and effort justifying or disguising errors or mistakes. To do so may confuse, disrupt or impair the coaching process.

Playing 'fix-it'

When a coach plays 'fix-it' they assume that the coachee has a problem and it's up to them as coach to find the answer. The coach will focus their efforts on searching for a problem in what's being said and then trying to solve it. The drawbacks of this include:

→ The coach develops an inappropriate filter to listen only for problems.
→ The coach tries to come up with solutions without the input of the coachee.

➡ The coachee can end up feeling flawed or inadequate – something of a 'problem case'.

Watch the following dialogue for signs of the coach playing fix-it:

COACHEE: So really, I don't know why I've taken on organizing the party at all. It's typical of me to get stuck with something like this.

COACH: Well, why don't you cancel it?

COACHEE: Oh I couldn't do that, we'd lose money on caterers and flowers and things.

COACH: Can you get someone else to help you, then?

COACHEE: Not at this late stage, and besides, why should I ask? – They should be offering!

COACH: Could you move the date, then?

From the dialogue, the coach thinks that they have found the problem – namely that the coachee doesn't want to organize the party. Because the coach is playing 'fix-it', the coach is then reacting to incomplete information, guessing at possible solutions.

The coach needs to spend more time seeking to understand the situation and let the conversation develop naturally. The next example demonstrates a better approach:

COACHEE: So really, I don't know why I've taken on organizing the party at all. It's typical of me to get stuck with something like this.

COACH: OK, can you tell me a little more about that?

COACHEE: Well, I seem to be the one who ends up doing all the work. I wouldn't mind if anyone actually acknowledged me for it. A simple 'thanks' would do.

It is clear that the conversation has gone in a completely different direction, as the coach gently explores the situation. The 'problem' (if there is one) may turn out to be entirely different from initial impressions. Maybe the coachee simply wants to be acknowledged for their efforts, or for efforts they've made in the past.

By ignoring any temptation to find a problem and solve it, the coach helps both understanding and resolution emerge more naturally.

If you want to stop playing 'fix-it', take another look at the Toolkit exercises 'Help someone else find their answer' and 'Developing deep listening'.

Assuming your experience is relevant

This trap is an easy one to fall into. When a coach does a lot of coaching, sometimes what the coachee is saying sounds just like something other coachees have discussed in the past – a sort of flawed version of déjà vu. Because the coach thinks the conversation or the situation is the same, they also expect other aspects of it to be the same as well. This might cause the coach to assume other facts around the situation to be the same, and the same solution or way forward to be of benefit.

For example, a coachee is describing problems with their boss at work. The coachee says that their boss interferes too much in their work and this is causing them frustration and annoyance. The coach is listening to the coachee and an internal voice says, 'Aha, this sounds familiar, this is just like that other situation – it's all about lack of understanding of the boss's intentions'.

From this thought, the coach can easily begin to jump to conclusions, e.g. that they totally understand the situation, or they know what will work as a way forward.

When coaching I'm mindful that what worked yesterday won't necessarily work today. Whatever totally brilliant insight, question or idea we had in a previous session, it could easily be irrelevant or inappropriate in the next one.

Staying focused

The other pitfall of assuming relevant knowledge or experience relates to the coach's focus or attention. Once again, if the coach diverts their thoughts to recalling past coaching conversations, they might easily spend time drifting off thinking about previous events and lose focus on the present. In this way, the quality of the coach's attention and listening is impaired. This in turn affects their ability to appreciate fully what the coachee is telling them and so coach effectively.

Looking for the 'perfect solution'

Sometimes in coaching we experience a magical 'Aha!' moment between the coach and the coachee. A fabulous idea or insight presents itself and the perfect way forward for the coachee appears. Problems dissolve, blockages are cleared and the sun comes out. For a coach, this feels great. They know that by the process of their conversation they have really made a difference to the coachee. The 'buzz' of the whole experience can be quite uplifting for the coach and also mildly addictive.

The issue arises when the coach attempts to repeat it in subsequent coaching sessions. The coach assumes that there's a wonderful solution to every coachee's situation and attempts to find one in each session. In this way, the coach is guaranteed obvious results in the form of amazing breakthroughs and ideas. Also, the coach will regularly experience the 'high' of that wonderful moment when the magical solution or insight is found.

In reality, these moments are fairly rare in coaching and usually occur when a coach least expects them. Certainly trying to produce them rarely works. Personal coaching is usually an ongoing process, where insights and learning can emerge as much between coaching sessions as they do in them. For a coach to try always to produce fast or amazing results can distort their view of the conversation.

> **Personal coaching is usually an ongoing process, where insights and learning can emerge as much between coaching sessions as they do in them.**

Ultimately, the coachee determines the value and effectiveness of coaching. Some coachees don't need amazing insights or breakthroughs. They simply need support with their learning and development processes.

Perfection is in the eye of the beholder

Sometimes the perfect solution for the coachee doesn't look perfect to the coach. For example, a coachee is describing how his studies at night school are interfering with his social life. The course that he's taken falls on the same night as his bowling club's match nights.

During the process of the coaching conversation, the coachee realizes that if he leaves the evening class 30 minutes early, he can still make the bowling evening. At this point, the coachee seems pleased he's found what feels like a workable compromise. The coach doesn't think that this sounds like a perfect solution. After all, the nursing qualification the coachee is taking is really important to his life goals.

At this point, the coach has three options:

1 Accept the coachee's choice of a way forward.
2 Explore the potential risks and benefits of this option further.
3 Encourage the coachee to think of something else.

If the coach is still looking for the 'perfect' solution, they will pursue option 3 and continue looking for another idea. This may cause the coachee to feel uncomfortable as what feels to him to be a great idea is being disregarded.

If the coach genuinely feels that this is a flawed idea but simply accepts it anyway (option 1) then they risk sharing the burden of the ultimate consequences. Maybe the coachee's coursework will suffer and he won't get the qualification that was so important to him.

Bad ideas usually expose themselves very quickly when they are explored more fully. Likewise, apparently flawed ideas expose themselves as perfect by the same process of exploration. The following dialogue illustrates this principle, as the coach takes option 2 and explores the potential risks and benefits of the idea.

COACH: How will leaving the class early affect your studies?

COACHEE: Oh, not at all. The last half-hour is always a reading time. I can do that on the bus ride home.

COACH: And what will your tutor say if you request to leave early?

COACHEE: Well, if I'm doing the reading I don't think she'll mind. She's very easy-going as long as we keep up with our homework, which I always do.

So ultimately, the coachee's idea appears workable. It may still not seem perfect to the coach, certainly not enough to produce lightning bolts or cries of 'Eureka!' However, if the coach persists in pursuing a perfect solution, it may become a frustrating and pointless process for both parties. They may easily end up back where they started, with the coachee's first idea being the only practical way forward.

Trying to look good in the conversation

As humans, we have a need to look good in the eyes of other people and ourselves. In coaching, this can get in the way of an effective conversation. It gets in the way because it diverts the coach's attention from staying fully present in the conversation. When the coach is not fully present, the following can be true:

→ The coach's mind can be focused too much on themselves and not enough on the coachee.

→ The coach is not as truthful, open and honest as they could be.

→ Because the coach is not as open and honest, they are less powerful in the conversation.

By 'looking good', I refer to our almost subconscious tendency to maintain an appearance that we feel is in some way positive. When a coach devotes effort or energy to looking good in the conversation, it detracts from the quality of their attention and the effectiveness of their coaching. A coach may do or say things in order to impress, rather than for the actual benefit of the coaching conversation.

This probably relates to the ego, our sense of self or self-consciousness, and some instinctive reluctance ever to seem vulnerable to others. Whatever causes it, it helps to try to recognize it in yourself and your behaviour – although it's not always easy!

Within coaching, there are various pressures upon the coach to 'look good'. Where a coach is delivering the service of coaching, it follows that the coachee may have certain expectations of them. For example, the coach should appear to:

→ Be professional, businesslike.

→ Say clever or smart things.

⇒ Be very experienced/knowledgeable.

⇒ Have all the answers.

⇒ Have a real impact.

⇒ Know just what to say within the conversation.

⇒ Have a happy, fulfilling life, free of problems or conflict.

Wanting to look good isn't a 'bad' thing; it's a way we've learned to cope with some of the risks and pressures of life. We might assume that the alternative to 'looking good' is 'looking bad' – and that feels wrong to us. Actually, the alternative to using behaviours intended to make us 'look good' is simply to be our natural selves.

For example, a coachee is saying how they'd really like to exercise more but they just don't feel like it. The coach just happens to have studied various theories of human motivation. So the coach spends the next 15 minutes describing Maslow's hierarchy of needs and drawing diagrams on paper as proof of this knowledge. The coach forgets the original point which led to the discussion of this theory, as they are enjoying demonstrating how much they know. In the meantime, the coachee has become bored with the conversation and doesn't see how it relates to why he can't be bothered to go to the gym.

The coach has fallen into the trap of wanting to appear knowledgeable to the coachee. This may be in order to gain more credibility, or simply because they enjoy appearing knowledgeable. Unfortunately, the coach effectively diverted the conversation from something important and relevant, namely the coachee's lack of motivation. Instead they focused the conversation to something less relevant, i.e. a lengthy, theoretical explanation of Maslow's theory. If we'd interrupted the coach part-way through his explanation and asked him, 'Why are you saying this stuff now?' a really truthful answer would be, 'Because I think it's impressive/sounds good ...'

Staying present in the conversation

Any time we increase our awareness of ourselves, our appearance, how we're sounding, etc., we decrease our awareness of the other person. We become 'not present' to the person and to what's happening in the conversation. As a result, our quality of listening diminishes and our ability to notice non-verbal signals from the coachee is impaired. Literally, we become less conscious.

Staying present to what's happening requires commitment and concentration. Our reward within coaching conversations is better understanding and a sense of relatedness.

Try it yourself   **Are you present?**

In conversation, we focus quite a lot on our own thoughts, what's being said, what we're thinking of saying, etc. This exercise demands that we let those thoughts go, as we focus solely on what's really happening. This can be a real challenge and also incredibly rewarding!

Step one – on your own

Becoming present requires us to refocus our attention into the here and now. Do it now. Lift your head up from reading this and focus on wherever you are – your surroundings. What can you see and what can you hear? Let your mind go quiet, as you become acutely aware of what's actually going on.

Step two – with someone else

Go and have a conversation with someone and practise being 'present' while you're talking to them. Really focus your attention on them and what they're saying. The more you get present with them, the more your mind will go quiet as you begin to notice them properly. Any time your mind drifts off, wanders, starts thinking of something else, simply bring it back to what's happening there and then. When you speak, get really present to what you're saying, experience your own words and the impact they have.

Step three – focus on learning

After the conversation, ask yourself the following questions:

Q What was different about the conversation when you remained present?

Q What did you have to do to become present?

Q If you remained present more in your conversations, what impact would that have?

Confusion can be powerful

Another form of the 'looking good' trap arises from the gentle expectation from the coachee that the coach has all the answers and will always know the perfect thing to say. Sometimes, the most authentic and powerful thing a coach can do is to acknowledge that they are as confused by a situation as the coachee. At least then they can work through the facts and issues together. For the coach to pretend they understand, or take a wild guess at what might be an answer, may take the conversation in a wholly inappropriate direction. One valid option is to give a brief summary instead. As well as displaying the facts for your coachee, you'll give space for reflection and thought. Summarizing the conversation isn't something you'd want to do every few minutes as it can have the reverse effect of slowing things down. But a well-timed 'OK, let's look at where we've got to …' can be the pause that creates progress.

Strategizing in the conversation

Another barrier to effective coaching is a subtle form of control known as strategizing. Strategizing is what happens when the coach starts saying or doing things in order to create a certain outcome. For example, a coach may say something in order to provoke a reaction or deliberately take an opposing view. The coach might reason that they had good intentions for playing these mental tactics with the coachee. Whatever the coach's reasons for doing it – they were still strategizing.

There are many ways a coach might strategize in a coaching conversation, and they all have one thing in common: when a coach is strategizing, they are saying what they are saying 'in order to get a certain result' and they prefer this motive to remain concealed from the coachee.

That might be to get the coachee to do or say a certain thing, in order to get them to see something a certain way, feel a certain way, etc. There's a subtle note of covert manipulation to strategizing that enables us to distinguish it from anything else.

For example, maybe a coach is thinking, 'This conversation just isn't working, and I don't know why'. The coach might feel uncomfortable about voicing that and so decides to take another route to explore the issue. So the coach says, 'Let's look at our original goals here'. This may or may not address the underlying issue, i.e. that the coach doesn't think the conversation is 'working'.

If the coach were being more truthful, they would say, 'I'm not sure that this conversation is working – can we explore that a little?' This is likely to open up a conversation that exposes what's happening. If the conversation isn't working for the coach, it probably isn't for the coachee either. By approaching the subject openly and directly, the coach can explore what's really happening. Maybe the coachee wants to talk about something completely different, and has been preoccupied with that from the beginning of the session. If the coach hides what they are thinking and asks, 'Let's look at our original goals here', the coachee's preoccupation is unlikely to surface. By strategizing, the coach has avoided tackling the issue directly.

Being authentic – speaking our truth

The opposite of strategizing is being authentic. When we are authentic, we speak our truth, we say what's there and this is not corrupted or changed in any way. For example, if we're worried about driving on the motorway we declare, 'I'm worried about driving on the motorway'. We do not say, 'Let's go the country route, it's prettier'. In coaching, this level of honesty is needed to create openness and trust within the coaching relationship. It's also a more powerful way to communicate.

If the coach is busy strategizing, they are not fully present with the coachee and are not being authentic in their views. The mental effort of translating one thought into different words diverts energy from being with the coachee and developing the conversation naturally. It's almost as if the coach is having two conversations: one with themselves and another with the coachee.

> If the coach is busy strategizing, they are not fully present with the coachee and are not being authentic in their views.

Example of strategizing

COACHEE: Well, I just don't agree with the feedback forms from my colleagues, how can they say I withhold information? I think we should disregard those comments as malicious rubbish.

COACH THINKS:	*[I've heard you say 'Information is power in this place' repeatedly and also that you don't tell anyone anything that they don't need to know.]*
COACH SAYS:	[In order to avoid giving more difficult feedback] What might have caused these comments, do you think?
COACHEE:	No idea. Some people just don't like to see others getting on, I guess.

The coach is effectively hiding what they are thinking. This may be to protect the coachee from a potentially hurtful thought, or even avoid a confrontation. Unfortunately, this may not create much learning for the coachee. One of the core coaching skills is the ability to give challenging messages in a constructive way, as supportive feedback. This skill enables the coach to say what needs to be said, in order to progress the coachee's awareness.

Example of being authentic

COACHEE:	Well, I just don't agree with the feedback forms from my colleagues, how can they say I withhold information? I think we should disregard those comments as malicious rubbish.
COACH THINKS:	*[I've heard you say 'Information is power in this place' repeatedly and also that you don't tell anyone anything that they don't need to know.]*
COACH SAYS:	That's quite a tough message, isn't it? Although I can see some potential links to something you said in our last session – can I remind you of those?
COACHEE:	Sure – I'd love to know what's going on here!
COACH SAYS:	When we were discussing the management team meetings, you said you reported the minimum of your department's plans as 'Information is power in this place'. And when we talked more about that you said you saw no reason to tell anyone anything that they didn't need to know. I'm just wondering if we aren't seeing some of the effects of that here.

COACHEE: Yes, but everyone does that, don't they?

COACH SAYS: I don't know. And right now what's important to me is you, and what works for you. Right now it seems like this approach to reporting information might not be working for you.

COACHEE: Well, maybe I need to think about that – it's silly isn't it? You think you're playing by the rules and it turns out you're not!

Giving up strategizing

The way to avoid strategizing begins with catching ourselves doing it. We need to develop an internal alarm bell for this behaviour. When coaching, if I notice I'm saying something in order to produce a result that I've predicted, mine goes off! For example, I might decide I know 'the answer' to the situation. Then all I have to do is get the coachee to see this answer.

The trouble is, as soon as I start doing this I begin strategizing. Using the previous example, maybe I think that it's a good idea to talk to a certain person about the coachee's concerns. I then start to ask a series of questions to lead them to that conclusion. Now, I may or may not be right with my idea. The point is that strategizing with it can lead me into trouble. It is actually far more honest, and usually effective, simply to declare my own thoughts at that point, e.g. 'I keep thinking about the option of speaking to Deborah about your concerns. What do you think?'

Another place to practise giving up strategizing is in normal everyday conversation. Wherever we have an agenda for a conversation, or think we know how it's going to go, we tend to strategize. Have a go, especially in conversations with people you're a little wary of, and observe how we make 'moves' in conversation, rather like intellectual chess!

A simple example: your partner wants to go out for dinner tonight and you're too tired. You don't want to say so, because you think that sounds lame. So instead you start asking questions to change your partner's mind, e.g. 'Won't it be difficult to get a booking?', 'Aren't we supposed to be saving money?' or 'Who's going to drive and not drink?'

Once you have noticed yourself doing it, you can give it up. You might choose to declare your hidden thought or feeling, or simply let it go. Maybe a good night out is just what you need to refresh your spirits!

Try it yourself   **Where are you strategizing?**

The following exercise is intended to help you develop your own awareness of when you might be strategizing. In addition, it will also help you speak your own thoughts more authentically.

You will be using a conversation with someone to notice the difference between what you think, and what you actually say. Pick a conversation with someone you're not very close to: perhaps you're less relaxed in their company, or just never became really familiar with them. A work colleague might work well – a partner or best friend might not.

Step one – develop awareness

During the conversation, develop an awareness of that moment just before you say something. Maybe the other person has just said something to you and you're going to respond to their statement or question. At that moment, you might first have a thought, maybe an opinion – do you respond with that thought? How much difference is there between what you're thinking and what you're actually saying?

Step two – practise authentic responses (optional)

Where you notice a difference between your true (authentic) thought or view and the response you might normally give, instead give a response that more accurately reflects your views. This will feel like you are speaking your own truth, rather than what you think might sound 'right' or appropriate. It's probably easier to begin with something minor, like a true response to the question 'How are you?' or 'How did you like that film?' So say what you really think, rather than what you think might be expected.

Step three – focus on learning

After the conversation, consider the following:

Q How much did your speech match your real thoughts and views?

Q What causes the difference in what you thought from what you said?

Q How does speaking your real thoughts and views feel?

Q What would happen if you matched your thoughts to your speech more often?

Q When might this not work very well?

Exercise summary **Where are you strategizing?**

This exercise is simply to draw our attention to times we might be strategizing, and that's not always easy is it? When you're feeling more comfortable, you might choose other conversations to speak your truth more powerfully on more significant matters. For example, what you think about a difficult situation or perhaps a decision that's being made.

Focusing on what not to do

So now that we've discussed several things a coach needs 'not' to do during coaching sessions, I've created another. There's an obvious risk in focusing on 'what not to do' during a coaching conversation. For example, if I tell you *not to think about* a blue rabbit wearing sunglasses, what do you think about? (Surely not a blue rabbit wearing sunglasses?!)

So a coach needs to not think about what they are not supposed to be doing ... Confused? That's exactly the point.

If a coach's head is full of thoughts like 'Don't control the conversation', 'Don't treat them like they're a problem', 'Don't take on their feelings too much', obviously that's not going to work. The coach's head is then full of their own internal conversation rather than listening to the coachee. In addition, by focusing on what not to do, they may easily end up doing it. Did you ever have an awkward conversation where you knew you shouldn't use a word and yet that was the only word that would come? For example, 'Just don't say failure' – and the word failure is the only word you can think of?

Within coaching the three-step process of awareness, acknowledgement and substitution can help to refocus thought.

The power of substitution

One way for a coach to let go of a thought is to replace it with another thought in order to refocus their mind. For example, if a coach notices herself playing fix-it, she might remind herself, 'Just let the solutions emerge'. Alternatively, if the coach notices that they are talking too much in the conversation, they might silently say, 'Listen and focus back on them'. It's like realizing that a lamp you have is shining on the wrong side of a room. You simply move the light. By moving the light you illuminate a better area, while returning the other side to darkness.

Chapter summary **Barriers to coaching**

Much of the skill of coaching lies in what a good coach doesn't do, as well as what they do. Some behaviour is counterproductive to the coaching process and simply gets in the way of a great conversation. Some of these are simple behaviours, like talking too much, while others relate to the coach's belief, e.g. a need to be right, or to find the 'perfect solution'.

Once we become aware of these behavioural barriers, we are able to let them go. This follows a three-step process:

1 Awareness: You notice that you're doing or thinking something that's not working.
2 Acknowledgement: You acknowledge that – and give it up (let the thought go).
3 Refocus: You shift your attention to a more effective thought or behaviour.

The way to avoid these barriers to good coaching is an ability to develop an intuitive sense of when we're doing them. As I've mentioned before, this begins with awareness. This includes awareness of the pitfalls, which might begin by you reading this. Then develop this awareness by consciously noticing your own tendencies to adopt these behaviours. First, create a focus for just one of them, e.g. playing 'fix-it' in your next conversation with someone who appears to have a problem. Make it a game to catch yourself doing it, then decide to give up doing it.

Over time, you won't have to wonder if you're doing it, as your subconscious will let you know. Intuitively, you may get a feeling or thought that you're not comfortable with the conversation. If you attend to that thought, you'll probably notice what it is that you're doing. At that point, simply acknowledge the realization, give up doing whatever you're doing and move on, letting the thought go.

chapter

6

Coaching conversations: the coaching path

This chapter offers a supporting structure, or guide, for a typical coaching conversation. By 'typical', I refer to most formal coaching conversations, as well as many casual or unplanned conversations. The 'coaching path' is intended to help any coach navigate through a conversation. It is not intended to provide a definitive formula, or to inhibit your natural creativity and flexibility. Please use what follows to support and encourage your coaching, rather than be restricted by it.

Figure 6.1 illustrates the basic path that a typical coaching conversation might follow. Although there are five stages illustrated, you'll see that the first and last are very basic in terms of the skills you'll need to use (and you're already familiar with greeting people and ending conversations effectively). Stages 2, 3 and 4 are what actually distinguish this as a coaching conversation, rather than any other type of conversation. At each stage there are both principles and example dialogue to guide you along.

The coaching path: guiding principles

To continue the idea of a path, imagine the different stages as places to dwell or rest a while. Activities along the path may be returned to and also combined. For example, you may initially agree on what topic the coachee wants to work on and then need to revise that when you surface a more important issue or topic. Occasionally, you'll find yourself 'looping back through', e.g. going back into enquiry as you find that something towards the end of a discussion is incomplete.

Activities, not 'tasks'

The coaching path is a series of activities that blend together, rather than a list of tasks to 'get done'. Please remember that if you approach the phases as tasks, you're more likely to focus on completing tasks and so develop a 'mechanical' feel to the conversation. You may also feel more determined to 'get to the end' and could miss subtle cues from the coachee that you need to backtrack, or simply stay where you are a while longer.

> The coaching path is a series of activities that blend together.

For example, you're at the stage of 'surfacing understanding' – although your coachee

Figure 6.1 The basic path of a coaching conversation

tells you the cause of their frustration at work is the long hours, you may still not truly understand what's going on. But if you think your role is simply to 'collect' an answer to the question, then you may move on to the next phase, 'agreeing ways forward'. The coachee may then come up with ways forward, which include refusing to work overtime, or even quitting the job completely. However, if we'd stayed in enquiry a while longer, we might actually have surfaced the person's underlying reluctance to ask for help in an area of the job they are finding particularly difficult. If we had released our agenda of 'making progress' and relaxed into the activity of enquiry more, then we'd have noticed that actually the coachee had more to say about the topic. Our focus would be on the coachee and hearing what they are really saying, rather than getting through the stages. So, on hearing about the issue with long hours, we might have picked up a note of discord, or something not quite 'ringing true'.

A worked example   **Coaching Phil**

We're going to use a scenario to demonstrate how the coaching path unfolds during a discussion. Phil is our coachee and you might imagine yourself as the coach. For the purposes of this example, let's acknowledge that it's a distilled version of a conversation. This means that we've reduced the dialogue to leave the key principles exposed. Normal conversation when written down would not make for great reading! In

▶

155

real life, I would expect much less 'coherence'. For example, from the coachee, we'd hear more 'stalls', half-sentences and repeated information, or even nonsense. From the coach I'd expect more 'umms' and 'aaahs', plus more questions that didn't add much value, a few blind alleys, etc.

In this scenario, the coach will be using principles, behaviours and skills outlined elsewhere in this book. In particular, the skills described in Chapter 4: Fundamental skills of coaching, will provide support for your reading. So, let's use the scenario to travel along the coaching path.

Stage one – establish conversation

This first stage is about the coach building the basics of a conversation, e.g. saying hello, having the other person feel comfortable, welcoming them into the conversation and creating a good balance between warmth and formality. You'll see we're at the start of the path in Figure 6.1.

Our objectives at this stage include:

- Greet your coachee in an appropriate manner.
- Establish warmth and rapport.
- Deal with any housekeeping, e.g. duration of session, how long the room is booked for, any potential interruptions, etc.
- Create an appropriate sense of occasion, i.e. 'We're beginning a coaching session now'.
- Create a sense of leadership in the conversation, e.g. 'You're in safe hands'.
- Identify a future point for the conversation to end.

Let's assume familiarity

The following dialogue shows how a coach might build the foundation for a session in an ongoing relationship. We're assuming the coaching has been happening for a while and the coach and coachee are comfortable with each other. Where this is the very first session of an assignment, this stage

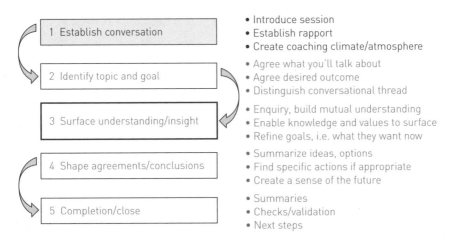

Figure 6.2 Establish conversation

requires more preparation. For further information on a first session, see Chapter 7: Coaching assignment: structure and process, and also 'Summary of a first session' in the Toolkit.

In this example, I hope to illustrate the balance between warmth and professionalism from the coach:

COACH:	Hi Phil, how's it going? [shakes hands] You're early I think! Have you been waiting long?
PHIL:	Aaah you know me, I'm keen to get on ... [laughs] Sorry, do you need time to prepare or something?
COACH:	Nope, I'm all set, I've been reading through my notes on the train, just let me grab those and we'll get started – can I get you a drink or something?
PHIL:	Actually I've ordered some coffee to be brought in; it should be here any minute I think.
PHIL:	Lovely. Now let's see where we are. [pauses] We've scheduled around two hours for this – is that still possible?
PHIL:	Yep, I'm fine until four o'clock.
COACH:	Great. Let me just check my phone is off. Yes. Perhaps we can begin with a brief recap from last time, and then we can focus

> on what you want to get from this session – how does that sound?
>
> PHIL: Sounds good.
>
> COACH: OK, so this is session three out of six, and we last met on the 21st March didn't we? Let's look at what came up in that conversation.
>
> PHIL: Well, you'll be pleased to hear I did actually talk to Mike and Jayne after last time; those were good conversations actually.
>
> COACHEE: Really? – That's great; I look forward to hearing what happened. OK, last time we covered three main areas really didn't we ... [coach begins to run through simple headlines from the previous session, plus any actions agreed]

That's obviously a fairly fast set-up to demonstrate the principles. Some sessions need more set-up than others, e.g. maybe the coachee needs to query something, or introduce a new piece of information. I've omitted the update from the previous session to maintain our flow.

Facilitation, navigation

Notice how the coach is willing to lead the process of the discussion, by keeping time, performing the recap, and focusing the coachee, Phil, on his goals for the session. This 'light touch' is probably all that's needed to enable Phil to simply relax into the conversation, knowing that the coach will navigate. When the coach is navigating the process of the session, then the coachee only needs to focus on the content. I must stress that 'navigating' is different from *controlling* the direction of the conversation. It's a little like helping someone to go clothes shopping. Occasionally you may need to remind them that the purpose of the trip was actually to buy trousers not shoes, or help them find what they want. Then all they need to do is try on clothes, while you offer the appropriate challenges and feedback!

Stage two – identify topic and goal

This activity agrees a place to begin and a desired destination. It's a gentle orientation to where both the coach and the coachee want to work during the session, rather than a rigorous, detailed assessment. We're balancing clarity and a sense of direction, while maintaining pace with the coachee. Our progress from the previous stage is illustrated in Figure 6.3.

Our objectives at this stage include:

⇒ To help the coachee to become clearer as to what they actually want.

⇒ To encourage the coachee to 'own' the direction and content of the conversation.

⇒ To help the coachee to 'expect' a potential solution, e.g. realize that there can be a solution.

⇒ To have the coachee feel comfortable that the coach is facilitating the conversation in a professional, structured way.

⇒ To give the coach a clearer sense of what he/she needs to navigate towards.

Right now our role is to surface a desirable goal for the conversation, without putting pressure on the coachee to 'know everything'. For example, the coachee is more likely to arrive with a general idea of what they want to talk about, i.e. a topic. Maybe they'll also have an idea of what they want to get from the session, i.e. results. The coach needs to help refine these a little at this stage, to distil one or more 'threads' for the conversation. With gentle questioning, some clarity can be gained at this point, while more might arise later. Again, a light touch is often best. For example:

Figure 6.3 Identify topic and goal

COACH: Alright, so what is it you'd like to get from this session?

PHIL: Well, I'd like to talk a bit more about my impact in meetings. Since our last discussion I've noticed that I am actually a bit unpredictable, I want to look at that a bit.

COACH: OK, so ... thinking about your impact in meetings, what would you actually like to get from this session?

PHIL: I guess I'm just looking for ways to be a bit more consistent. I do want to understand what goes on with me, but really I want some ideas as to how to come across as a bit more confident ... a bit more of the time.

COACH: OK, right, I've got that [takes short note]. What else would you like to work on?

Get clarity, rather than detail

For me, the dialogue above gives enough clarity to continue, without the coach getting 'pulled' into the next stage ('understanding') too early. You may disagree and I encourage you to decide for yourself when you're happy to continue. I think that without the coach asking 'What would you actually like to get from this session?' the initial objective is too vague. The response to the question, i.e. 'I want to understand ... I want some ideas ...' creates the clarity we need at this stage.

Vague leads to drifting

I would discourage any coach from hearing a vague statement from the coachee and then continuing without getting more specific. You are the best judge of what's vague. Vague is indicated by the sense that you 'sort-of' know what they mean – but not exactly. For example, the following are vague answers to the coach's question, 'What would you like to get from this session?'

➡ 'I thought we'd work on my confidence a bit.'

➡ 'I need to look at me and what I do in presentations.'

➡ 'I want to look at how I'm coming across in top-team meetings, I'm just not making progress.'

Hopefully, you'll notice the potential for misunderstanding. The coachee is using vague terms that could mean something different from what the coach assumes. In the first statement, their need to work on their confidence may refer to a specific event in the future they want to prepare for, or a past incident they are upset about. The coachee could be referring to a range of topics, from speaking to large groups to a recent argument they've had. Or actually they may not mean confidence at all! Most of us would feel the need to dig deeper at this point.

Continuing with a vague topic and goal risks misunderstanding and mistakes then being made by the coach. If the coach takes too long to realize what the conversation is really about, the coachee may feel confused and slightly 'adrift' in the conversation. However, if the coach continues without clear direction, the conversation may literally go round in circles. The best option is to gain sufficient clarity at this early stage from the coachee. That requires asking the coachee what their objectives for the session are and probing further if that's appropriate. In the following dialogue, the coach encourages the coachee to relax and explain further, without suggesting they've been misunderstood:

COACH: Alright, so what is it you'd like to get from this session?

PHIL: I thought we'd work on my confidence a bit.

COACH: [gently] Can you say a little more about that?

PHIL: Well, it's to do with presenting in meetings ... sometimes everything's fine, but in the exec. sessions I just don't seem to be able to function.

The coach makes a gentle request ('Can you say a little more?') and that helps the coachee open up. With little additional prompting, the coachee will normally continue talking around the topic and offer further insight into what they want to talk about. If they don't and we still need more specific information, the coach may continue to question to gain further clarity:

COACH: Alright. So what's your goal, for when you're presenting in exec. sessions?

PHIL: I guess I just want to be able to perform better. You know ... like I'm professional, like I know what I'm talking about. I want to create a good impression. Instead of what I did last week – which was mess up.

By now the coach should be getting much clearer about what is in the coachee's mind. Once the coachee has offered a little more information and explained their need further, I'd normally summarize what I think our start-point for the conversation is, before continuing to the next stage, e.g.

COACH: OK Phil, let me just check: you'd like to be able to present professionally in the senior exec. meetings and create a really good impression; for example, that you really know what you're talking about. In this session you'd like to know a little more about why in other meetings you can present well and also why that's not always true in the exec. sessions. You'd like to be more consistent. How does that sound?

PHIL: Yes, that's it.

With our initial questions, we're simply identifying broad topics and goals, e.g. confidence, senior meetings, good impression, understanding, etc. Normally you'll refine what Phil actually wants more during the next stage in a natural way.

Of course, there may be other goals for the session, so you'll want to check by saying something like, 'What else would you like to cover?' 'Is there anything else you'd like to cover?' etc. You may end up with a list of things to work through. Simply note those down and agree a suitable order to work through them, e.g. 'Right, where seems the best place to start?' For the purposes of this scenario, we're only using one topic – Phil's confidence in meetings.

Remember the person within the process

It's important to balance the need to get a detailed objective with a consideration for the feelings of the coachee. When a coachee arrives ready to tell a big story about a recent incident and the coach wants to spend a long time identifying detailed goals, we are mismatching the coachee in a way that might be counterproductive. Perhaps the coachee wants to tell a story and do so quickly, while the coach seems to want them to think of detailed objectives and slow things down. The coachee may feel that too much time spent 'preparing to have a conversation' is pedantic. We need to balance both positions. In these circumstances you could let the coachee talk a little, release any tension or emotion for a while, before referring them back with a statement such as:

'So you've talked a little about your frustration with your presentation to the top team last week and the disappointing feedback since. That's obviously important and something we need to focus on. I wondered if I might just confirm before we continue … what is it that you'd like to get from *this* conversation?'

Again, it's down to your own judgement. As coach, you need to have enough sense of direction to navigate confidently, without getting stuck in detail.

When you decide you need a more specific goal upfront

Of course, there are exceptions to every rule. Sometimes you'll decide you need a specific goal much sooner. For example, if the individual does not really know what they mean themselves by the term 'confidence'. Maybe they're confused and feeling a bit emotional about something that hasn't gone well. Or maybe they don't seem to have any real goal. You may then decide to be a little more rigorous at this initial stage, for example:

➡ 'Tell me a little more about confidence, what does that mean to you?'

➡ 'What specifically is it about confidence that you'd like to work on?'

➡ 'So Phil, by the end of this session, what would you like to have achieved?'

The goal for the session is not the same as the goal for the situation

It is worth noting that the coachee may have a goal for the session which is slightly different from their goal for the situation they are focusing on. For example, during the session, Phil's goal is to come up with some *ideas* to help him perform better in meetings. That is what the coach needs to help him produce. But his goal for this session will relate to other goals he has, like gaining the respect of the senior team, gaining promotion, or just feeling more comfortable when presenting. As coach it is likely you will begin with one (the session goal) and then surface his other goals later. For example, as you work through the next stage of 'understanding' his issue, you are likely to ask questions which surface goals relating to his topic of performance in meetings, such as, 'How do you want to feel while you're giving presentations?' or 'What kind of impact do you want to have?' It's often inappropriate to try to gain that goal now, as the coachee is unlikely to have the clarity of thought yet. That will come later, as we truly understand what's happening, and what Phil thinks or feels about what's happening.

Strangely, in some situations you may hear a goal that seems really definite, but you suspect it needs thinking through, e.g. 'Operating at this senior level just isn't right for me, I'm just messing things up. I need a job that's more in line with my strengths. So I've given myself three weeks: I want to find something by the end of this month.' In the next stage, you may find further enquiry into that goal renders it less relevant. The coachee may find that actually it's a hasty decision based on an uncomfortable experience. For now, you need to capture it and perhaps check if the individual has other goals for the session. (For a way of helping someone work through this kind of thought, see 'Building a clear goal' in the Toolkit on p. 289.)

When you feel you've got enough mutual clarity and agreement to continue, simply go to the next stage.

Stage three – surface understanding and insight

This stage begins the real process of enquiry, in order to surface real understanding and insight for the coachee. As the coach, you will also become clearer about the situation, although the primary goal is to support the awareness of the coachee. I'll whisper that, sometimes, this stage is where the magic of coaching reveals itself. As we gently surface someone's thoughts, feelings and realizations, we may uncover a perfect idea that moved unnoticed in the swirl of other thoughts surrounding it.

Especially relevant to this stage is the listening exercise in the Toolkit on p. 284, which helps you practise your style and approach. Please avoid fixing, advising or jumping to quick conclusions. Instead seek to understand, look for 'gaps' or contradictions, and gently probe into what seems to be happening.

So, we're at a key place on our path, as illustrated in Figure 6.4. Our objectives at this stage include:

➡ To enquire into the situation(s) that relate to the coachee's goals or issues.

➡ To paint a 'fuller picture' of the situation(s) above.

➡ To increase the self-awareness of the coachee, in relation to the topics under discussion.

➡ To deepen understanding for the coachee, leading to clearer thought.

➡ To help the coachee begin to form ideas or decisions based on clear thinking.

Revisit the facts

There's a subtle trap to fall into at the beginning of this stage, which is to hear a familiar situation and imagine we understand it. Let's continue the thread from the previous examples. So far, you know that Phil wants to improve his confidence when he's presenting, particularly in meetings with senior people present. He's had a bad meeting last week and really wants to improve his performance at the next one. But actually, we still don't know much about what's really going on. After all, Phil is a unique person with his own experiences,

Figure 6.4 Surface understanding/insight

beliefs and values. So let's begin by assuming there's still lots for us to learn about Phil. And lots of opportunity for Phil to get clearer about himself.

Build an understanding

Start by asking for some simple, factual information about the situation (whatever the situation might be). Allow yourself to be curious, give yourself permission not to know everything, and ask questions that build a clearer picture of what's going on. Remember, while you're laying out the facts for you, the coach, to understand, you'll be helping the coachee become clearer about both the situation and how they feel about it. For example:

COACH: So, can you tell me a little more about what happens in meetings?

PHIL: I guess it varies a lot. Sometimes everything's fine. I come across completely naturally. But then sometimes I just don't seem to be able to find my voice, it's like I can't even express a simple thought or piece of information. I come out wanting to kick myself. It's horrible actually.

COACH: OK, so what actually happens?

PHIL: Well, it's like last week. I'm presenting our progress to the top team and it should have gone well. I'd got some good figures after all. But somehow my whole presentation was a complete mess. Then when it came to the questions, I couldn't even remember basic data. My boss had to jump in and help out. Later he told me what I already knew really, that I didn't do myself justice at all.

COACH: Alright, so you also said that sometimes you come across completely naturally, and everything is fine – can you tell me more about those situations?

Notice how the coach is gathering basic information, without going really deeply into anything, then shifting the balance from one unpleasant situation to a better, more pleasant situation. It's a little like emptying someone's pockets on to a table. We're just getting items on to the table at this point, not studying any of them in great detail. If something troubling comes to light, simply observe it and move on. Let's continue:

PHIL: An easy example would be my client meetings. I presented a similar update to those guys yesterday and it's fair to say we really shone. I mean, by the end of it the client sounded delighted with how it was all going.

COACH So, can you tell me what was different from the session last week, with the top team?

PHIL: Well, with the top team the whole thing seemed more pressured somehow. I mean, it shouldn't have been; I knew the results were good. But I guess I'd worked myself up a bit before going in. When those guys start drilling me with questions, they can really chew people up.

COACH: And how was that different from the session with the client?

PHIL: [pauses] I think really that's about what we are there to do. My focus is different. At this stage it's to make the client feel comfortable we're doing a good job, and we are. Also, I'm there to support some of my team. I want them to have a good experience that gives them confidence.

Hopefully, as you're reading this you'll be developing your own questions about what you see is happening. Your natural powers of observation will have you comparing facts, seeing differences or even illogical statements you want to explore further. Avoid jumping to conclusions, don't try to fix anything, stay in enquiry mode. For example:

COACH: What else was different?

PHIL: [pauses] Well, I guess because I'd had the run-through the previous week, I felt more prepared. I mean, I know it didn't go well the first time, but at least it all felt familiar.

COACH: Familiar?

PHIL: Yeah, you know, the running order of the slides, the questions I was likely to get. I felt more prepared.

Although it may not be true when you first begin coaching, over time you need to develop a style that's natural for you.

Let's imagine the coach has let Phil 'rest' in silence for a while before continuing:

COACH: Might it be helpful if I just summarize where I think we've got to?

PHIL: Sure. Although I think it's already dawning on me.

COACH: OK. So, as we started you talked about confidence; although when we looked at that really you mainly focused on this recent topic of the top team meeting.

PHIL: Right.

COACH: Can I just check; have we narrowed this down too much by focusing on just these two meetings?

PHIL: [pauses] Well, no, not really, I mean there are other occasions, but I'm beginning to suspect that it's all wrapped up in the same stuff. This is a good example.

COACH: OK. So, you're describing the two sessions quite differently, although the broad content of the presentation is the same – you're presenting good results that relate to the performance of your team.

PHIL: Yup.

COACH: In one session, the top team, your focus is more about you, your performance, and the fact things may go badly.

PHIL: [laughs] Yeah.

COACH: And in the other, your focus is much more about your team, supporting them – plus you expect a great outcome.

COACH: Yes, I do – I just imagine the whole thing differently. [pauses] In fact, the thing in the top team is all about me, but with the client I'm much more about everyone else, you know, looking after my team, helping the client feel comfortable and confident – what I think I'm there to do is rather different.

COACH: You also mentioned that you felt more 'prepared' in the client session, partly because you'd had the experience of the first one.

COACH: I did. Partly that's because I knew it was unlikely to go like the first one, but more importantly I'd just had a run-through.

A summary for you and me

Let's take a quick look at where we are with progress in this stage of 'surface understanding and insight':

➡ We've focused on what Phil seems to want to talk about.

➡ We've laid out some facts of the situation, e.g. two meetings, different start points, different outcomes.

➡ We've dug a little deeper to create clarity, e.g. how are the two meetings different? How does he prepare differently for them?

➡ Oh, and remember, we've shortened the investigation for the purposes of this written example.

So, we've reached a point where Phil appears ready to make his own links, come to his own conclusions and decide on his own realizations. Again, as coach our role is to support him with this, not do the work for him. Rather than 'drill' him down into what we think he should be 'deciding', instead you can ask a question that's general enough to encompass wherever his thoughts might be, but one that also encourages his conclusions to surface:

COACH: So, what thoughts are you having now?

PHIL: Well, I think a lot of it is in the way I set things up. I mean, both practically and also in my head. I just imagine the two things as completely different experiences.

COACH: And how does that affect what actually happens?

PHIL: It means that what I'm doing in the session is different. Like in the top team session, my whole game plan is about not screwing up. But when I'm in front of a client with my team I'm on a roll, I feel so sure of myself.

COACH: So, how can you feel that sure of yourself in the other meetings, the top team meetings?

PHIL: I think there's a fair amount of things I can do. Some of it's in practical preparation and some of it's to do with mental preparation. Some of it's simply about staying relaxed, making that more important.

COACH: Alright, so how would it be if we work through some of those things you can do and get them out on paper?

Phil now seems ready to list some of his ideas and options. Let me just acknowledge the question that helped him reach that point: 'How can you feel that sure of yourself in the top team meetings?' This is what I would call a 'powerful question', which is a question that encompasses the problem, while assuming a solution. For more explanation, please look at the section called 'Questions with purpose' within Chapter 4: Fundamental skills of coaching, on p. 91.

Develop a sense of possibility

What's also occurred is that Phil seems to have moved from a perception of 'no possibility' to 'possibility'. By the phrase 'no possibility' I mean not being able to imagine that a better way might be available or possible. For example, when Phil first began talking he was focused on what had gone wrong and also his feelings about the situation: 'I just don't seem to be able to find my voice' and then, 'It's horrible actually'. At an extreme, he may even have imagined that it was 'impossible' for him to perform well in a top team meeting.

Phil may have been feeling so frustrated about the poor outcome of the 'bad' meeting that he was a little 'stuck'. For example, maybe in his mind he was replaying what went badly, focusing on the negative feedback, dreading the next meeting, etc. By gentle questioning, comparisons and observations, the coach helped Phil regain the sense of possibility that he could actually perform well in that kind of meeting and enjoy doing so. It's a subtle form of magic, but magic nonetheless.

Regain a feeling of influence

Phil also moved fairly rapidly to a sense of influence over his situation, e.g. 'I think there's a fair amount I can do'. At the beginning of the session he made comments like 'I want to understand what goes on with me', and then, 'Somehow my whole presentation was a complete mess'. He seemed to have lost a feeling of influence over what happened during the meetings. We might wonder if he was operating from more of a 'victim' posture in regard to the issue. By this we mean he thought something was 'happening to him' rather than he himself was the cause of his own experience. For further discussion of this key principle, see 'Coaching principles and beliefs' on p. 37.

While acknowledging that our enquiry with Phil has been brief, let's leave the stage of 'surfacing understanding and insight' and continue.

Stage four – shape agreements and conclusions

Ideally, this will feel like a natural progression from the previous activity. Here we are shaping the previous elements of the conversation into conclusions, or raised awareness, or maybe actions to encourage further progress. Figure 6.5 shows where we are on our path and our objectives at this stage include:

⇒ To acknowledge what insights or conclusions the coachee has gained.

⇒ To refine and/or summarize ideas and options.

⇒ To surface any additional conclusions, ideas or options.

⇒ To agree specific actions if appropriate.

⇒ To create a sense of the future, e.g. help the coachee find the motivation to act.

Pulling the conversation together

The key to this stage is actually the previous stage. Where the coach has effectively surfaced the relevant information, feelings, contradictions, comparisons, etc., this stage is normally straightforward. The previous discussion has helped the coachee clarify what's actually happening, what they think about what's happening and also what they might want to do about it. Our

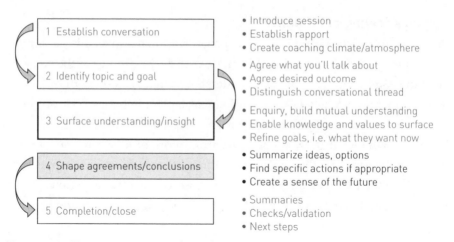

Figure 6.5 Shape agreements/conclusions

role now is to help refine their thoughts so that they can maintain progress after the session.

Using the scenario with Phil, let's continue:

COACH: So, you've mentioned that there's some practical preparation and mental preparation for the top team meetings that would help. Can you tell me more about those things?

PHIL: I think I need to involve my team more: either by having them present or by simply rehearsing with them in advance. As a minimum, I need to rehearse with them in advance.

COACH: And what effect would rehearsing have?

PHIL: It would mean that I felt prepared, that's a big one. But also I think I'd remind myself that the whole team are involved, that I'm presenting 'our' results, not 'my' results. More 'we' and less 'I' – I think that's quite important to me.

COACH: OK, great, and how feasible is it that they can be present?

PHIL: It's certainly possible. Maybe not all of them, but it's up to me who I invite in. I think actually it might reflect well on the whole team. Certainly my boss would be supportive.

COACH: Great. OK, so what about when they can't be there, how else can you prepare?

Refine ideas

The coach is obviously drawing Phil's ideas out, testing them for practicality and creating more clarity about what Phil is deciding to do. In addition, the coach is also creating a sense of the future. By asking the question 'What effect would rehearsing have?' we are testing the validity of the idea: after all, it might not be the full solution. We're also encouraging Phil to imagine doing something practical to create a benefit. Hopefully, Phil's optimism is increased as he becomes motivated to make the effort of rehearsing. Notice also how the coach challenges a potentially 'imperfect' solution, e.g. 'What about when they can't be there?' Of course, Phil may say that simply rehearsing is enough. But let's not assume he will. Maybe there's something else. After all, he's hinted earlier that there's 'lots' he can do.

Let's continue:

COACH: Great. OK, so what about when they can't be there; how else can you prepare?

PHIL: You know, a lot of it is mental. It's the way I'm drawing it in my head. I think I need to set myself up for success, rather than anything else.

COACH: How might you do that?

PHIL: It's simple things, like focusing on a positive outcome, reminding myself what I'm there to do. Making sure I stay relaxed.

COACH: OK, I guess I'm wondering how you'll do that practically, you know, what will you be doing?

PHIL: Well, the rehearsal will definitely help, help me relax. But actually just the realization that I let myself imagine the worst, predict failure – I just need to stop myself doing that, see it more like I see the client session.

COACH: OK, so instead of predicting the worst, how do you want to see the session?

175

PHIL: You know, like I'm on a home run, on a roll, like it's already gone well.

COACH: Great, I get that, 'like it's already gone well ...' You've said that a couple of times. And you know, you do seem a bit brighter about this whole thing now.

PHIL: Yeah, I feel brighter. That's silly isn't it?

COACH: [laughs] Well, not so silly if it helps you do well. OK, let's just check what we've got.

Agreements and actions

Often it is appropriate for a coachee to agree to actions following a coaching session. Certainly in the above scenario it seems relevant that Phil take action. I'll acknowledge that this is not always true. For example, imagine that during the conversation Phil had realized that he wasn't actually happy in his current job. Obviously that would be an entirely different (and longer) conversation than the one we've portrayed. But if Phil had reached that conclusion, is it wise to move straight to action? Maybe look for another job, tell his boss, etc. Probably not. Maybe the most Phil should commit to doing is 'go and reflect on the situation further', before meeting his coach again. That doesn't sound perfect either, but I'm sure you get the point. Some progress is made through direct, positive action – but not always.

Summarize and agree

When the coach feels that they have mutual clarity about what the coachee has decided and also what they are going to do, it's time to summarize and agree on the next steps. As mentioned previously, a summary may actually release further thoughts for consideration, so please be ready for that.

Let's resume:

COACH: You've said you want to prepare in two ways, both practically and mentally.

PHIL: Right.

COACH: Practically, you want to rehearse with your team, get them involved earlier, and maybe even take some of the team in with you?

PHIL: Yes, probably just one person, that would be fine.

COACH: OK, are there any other ways you might practically prepare?

PHIL: [pauses] Well, I do keep thinking about my boss, Mike. I keep thinking I should involve him more.

COACH: That's interesting, how might you involve Mike?

PHIL: Well, I think I need to show him the presentation in advance, get his thoughts and ideas. Maybe not all the presentation, but some of the slides that I think will provoke questions.

COACH: How will Mike respond when you approach him?

PHIL: Fine, I think. He won't want too much detail but he's brilliant at anticipating what those guys will do.

COACH: OK, I've got that one. Let me just check, are there any other practical ways you want to prepare?

PHIL: [pauses] No, I don't think so, I'm happy with that ...

Precision in language

Some of you may be noticing a slight repetition in the conversation. In written dialogue it's probably more noticeable than in real life. You'll see that the coach seems to be covering the same topic more than once, or simply using Phil's own words and phrases. This is all normal, and actually part of an effective conversation. The coach is using repetition to confirm the coachee's thoughts and also as a way of navigating through the conversation.

Using someone else's precise language and phrases can be fundamental to building rapport and also clear meaning. For example, when the coach says 'You've said you want to prepare in two ways, both practically and mentally', it serves as a reminder, a clarifier and a prompt to focus on doing that.

Phil doesn't need to wonder what the coach is referring to, he can simply relate to the point. The coach might have said, 'OK, so there were two significant ways you wanted to get ready in advance', but Phil might hesitate, thinking 'Did I?' or 'What were those then?' The phrase doesn't have the same impact on Phil, since it's not Phil's phrase. It's a simple yet effective option to use the coachee's terminology where possible, to keep things clear between you both.

Avoid embedding negative emotions

Of course, there's an exception that proves the rule. Where a coachee is using words to describe extreme negative emotion, I would normally avoid repeating those back. For example, 'I was absolutely terrified/distraught/raging angry', etc. When we repeat those words back exactly, they may actually emphasize something that you don't want emphasizing, e.g. 'OK, you say you're absolutely terrified when you present to your top team'. That doesn't feel good does it? It simply accentuates the feeling. When I hear a really negative emotional phrase, I would normally dilute or amend it slightly, e.g. 'OK, you mentioned you're less comfortable presenting to this group'. Our aim is to reduce its impact, or create distance from the emotion of it. This might often be something you do instinctively, perhaps as a sensitive gesture.

Let's continue with the scenario:

COACH: Alright, so in your mental preparation, you want to imagine the top team session in a similar way to how you imagine the client sessions. You mentioned 'on a roll' and 'like it's already gone well'.

PHIL: Yes, absolutely.

COACH: You also said you wanted more of a sense of 'we' in the conversation than 'I'.

PHIL: Yes. I want to remember that actually I'm there to represent my whole team, not just my own efforts.

COACH: OK, great. So are there any more ways you might mentally prepare?

PHIL: [pauses] Well, I'm not sure. To be honest, it's all mental preparation really, even the rehearsals and asking Mike for advice. It's all to help me be in the right frame of mind on the day.

COACH: I can really see that. I guess I'm just wondering if there's anything else you feel you want to do?

PHIL: [pauses] No, I'm happy. I think the realization of what's been happening, plus the actions we've got ... it's enough.

COACH: Great. And when do you next have a chance to put this preparation into practice?

PHIL: Oh, very soon; we've got another review three weeks from today. I probably need to start getting that ready from Monday.

COACH: Sounds perfect timing.

PHIL: [laughs] You could say.

So, a little more refinement, confirmation and encouragement. Hopefully you'll get the sense that the coach has gained sufficient agreement to suggest that Phil is both engaged and enthusiastic about taking on the challenge of the next top team meeting.

Drilling for detailed actions

I must acknowledge that some coaches would want to press for more detail on actions, e.g. 'What exactly will you do by when?' Occasionally that's appropriate and you as coach are the best judge. In the above example, I'm assuming Phil is a mature person, running a successful team and he's capable of keeping his commitment. I think it would be a little patronizing to insist on a detailed list of tasks and timescales. I'm guessing he is capable of what he's decided to do. I also know that some of the benefit of the session has been in his realizations and they will continue after the session. Plus, the situation is important to him and for him to avoid building on his fresh perspectives seems unlikely. Now it may be that in the next session he reports little action or progress. Since all the indicators are against that happening it's a risk I'm willing to take. Remember, we operate from a principle that the coachee is responsible for the results they create. Phil is in the driving seat and must continue to steer his own course.

Here's a balanced way of ending this segment:

COACH: Alright, I've got the following, let's see if you agree:

1 Arrange to rehearse with your team. You want to get their input but also involve them more; make it about them as well.
2 Speak to Mike in preparation; gain his input, advice and ideas, especially in regard to how the group might respond.
3 Invite someone from your team into the next presentation, if that still seems appropriate.

PHIL: Yes, what I'll probably do is ask Mike what he thinks about that first.

COACH: Great, obviously there's a shift in ways you want to think about it: the mental preparation. Do you want to note anything down about that?

PHIL: No, it's not necessary, I might talk it through with my wife maybe, but it's fine, I've really got that one I think.

COACH: Right. How might it be if I just pop those on an e-mail to you, for our records?

PHIL: That works for me.

Notice the coach has agreed to note the actions and send those to Phil. Not everyone will agree with this. Some coaches feel that the coachee should take all their own notes, record all their own actions and the coach should abstain from any responsibility. I feel that's unhelpful and impractical at this point. After all, the coach is there to serve the coachee. After a coaching conversation the coachee is normally fairly tired at this point and their ability to retain and record information is reduced. The coach will have been taking a few notes during the session. It's a simple matter for the coach to draft a quick e-mail soon after the session as a record of agreements. As well as a courteous professional gesture, it has the following benefits:

➡ It creates an accurate mutual record of what's been agreed.

➡ It can be used as a start-point in the next session.

➡ In the e-mail you might also check if they're still happy after the session, maintain rapport, etc.

Nearly there, we're now ready for the last stage.

Stage five – completion/close

This final step is about drawing the conversation to a professional close. As in the first stage, you will already have experience as to how to complete a conversation.

Figure 6.6 indicates where we are on the coaching path. Our objectives at this stage include:

➡ To summarize, indicating that the session is complete, e.g. no outstanding items.

➡ To help the coachee feel that the session is being handled in a professional, confident manner.

➡ To maintain mutual clarity, e.g. what happens after the session.

➡ To emphasize a sense of progress made during the session.

➡ To leave the coachee feeling comfortable to continue items discussed following the session, e.g. without direct involvement from the coach.

➡ To close the session in a natural way.

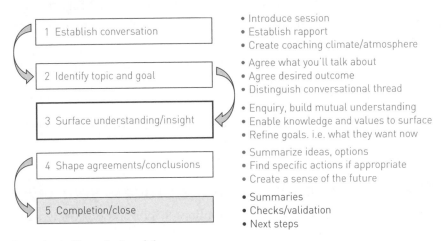

Figure 6.6 Completion/close

As you'd expect, there's no 'right' or 'wrong' way to close a session. Your own personal style will dictate your manner. Here's an example using the previous (abridged) scenario:

COACH: OK, we're nearly there I think, in terms of this session. Let me just check your original objectives. We had just one, which was this confidence topic we've just covered. Was there anything else you wanted to talk through?

PHIL: Nope, I'm happy with where we've got to.

COACH: Great, has that been useful?

PHIL: It has actually; it's given me a few things to think about.

COACH: Good. So, the next session, shall I book that as usual through your office?

PHIL: Yes, I'm away from the end of next week, but only for 10 days.

COACH: Work or pleasure?

PHIL: Bit of both I hope – over to Singapore but with a quick stop-over in Hong Kong. Anyway, thanks for today. [shakes hands] As usual, very interesting.

COACH: You're welcome, I've enjoyed it too. OK Phil, have a good few weeks and I'll see you in about a month or so. I'll confirm those actions by e-mail this evening. As usual, if anything else crops up, do get in touch.

PHIL: Lovely, thanks.

So you see, all fairly natural and probably something you can imagine yourself doing.

The coaching path: make the process your own

Over time you'll develop your own routines, habits and process to suit the way you work. For example:

➡ You might always begin sessions by revisiting the overall assignment objectives from your first session.

➡ Sometimes you might decide to call a tea/coffee break halfway through the session, to allow the coachee to 'rest' a little.

➡ You may choose to send a few notes from the conversation, plus a list of agreed actions.

It's important that you feel that you 'own' the structure of your coaching conversations.

As a rule, I'd encourage consistency and personal discipline. Consistency enables the coachee to trust in your professionalism and also be comfortable that they know what to expect. Personal discipline promotes high standards of behaviour from yourself and your coachee. For example, if you say you'll call before the next session, make sure you call. If you offer to e-mail some notes, make sure you send them. As previously described, the integrity and professionalism you demonstrate are vital to the ongoing relationship. Wherever possible, keep your word, or make amends if, for some reason, that doesn't happen. I'm sure you'll find a way of working that creates a sense of balance you can maintain.

Chapter summary **Coaching conversations: the coaching path**

Most formal coaching conversations will follow a similar path, with a common flow of activities. Those stages are:

➡ Establish conversation – build rapport, sense of occasion, etc.

➡ Identify topic and goal – for the session.

➡ Surface understanding and insight – regarding the topic and situation.

➡ Shape agreements or conclusions – arising from the 'fresh' understanding.

➡ Completion and close – checks, validations, end session.

The above stages are activities, rather than 'tasks'. At all times, the coachee needs to feel that they are 'in safe hands'. When the coach is aware of the core stages and activities that underpin the conversation they can navigate the coachee through to conclusion. Like all journeys along paths, sometimes we need to backtrack or retrace our steps. For example, we may need to revisit a goal, or check understanding. It is important that any coach develops his or her own authentic style of coaching. The coaching path above is designed to encourage this personal style, while supporting an effective coaching conversation.

chapter

7

Coaching assignment: structure and process

In the previous chapter we looked at the structure of a single coaching session. This chapter offers a structure of an overall assignment, i.e. a series of coaching sessions. For example, six sessions over a period of seven months, which are a complete coaching experience for the coachee.

Building a good supporting structure or process is key to the overall success of a coaching assignment. Several factors that alter the effectiveness of coaching are independent of what actually happens in each session. These factors include: length of sessions, duration between sessions, keeping appropriate notes and records, etc.

Logically, the initial coaching sessions will be distinct from, say, the final sessions, as the objectives for those sessions are different. At the beginning of a coaching assignment we're placing more emphasis on seeking to understand the coachee and their goals. By the final sessions we're consolidating our learning and finding ways to continue learning. We need to appreciate the overall coaching cycle we are working within and maintain a view of this 'bigger picture' when needed.

Understandably, coachees like to know they are receiving a quality service from a coach with professional standards that they can rely on. Agreeing a foundation for coaching that is mutually understood helps with this perception of the coach's services. A coach might be great during sessions, but if they are managing the overall situation badly then the coachee is going to be disappointed. For example, if the coach can't remember what was discussed in the previous session, or recall basic facts about the individual's goals, this can easily cause frustration for the coachee.

By introducing a certain amount of structure to an assignment, a coach can achieve some basic standards, for example:

➡ *The coachee understands key information relating to the coaching*: it is important that the coachee knows as much information as they need to feel comfortable and enthusiastic about the coaching relationship they're entering into. This might include a basic knowledge of what coaching is, or simply how often sessions are going to be and how long they'll last.

➡ *The coach demonstrates a commitment to the coachee's success or learning*: the coachee needs to know that the coach is working hard for them, focusing on their progress and taking their development very seriously. The coachee may judge various things as signs of commitment, e.g. the coach's enthusiasm and energy during sessions, or simply the fact that the coach turns up on time and appears prepared.

➡ *The coach develops an approach tailored to the coachee*: the coachee needs to feel that the coach is approaching them as an individual and adapting their approach accordingly. This would include requesting the coachee's views as to what is working for them and what isn't, i.e. requesting feedback, reviewing progress on goals, etc.

➡ *The coach is a professional and can be relied upon*: a coach will often encourage high standards of professionalism or integrity from the coachee, e.g. keeping promises or commitments made. To make that more acceptable, the coach must lead by example. The coach needs to demonstrate that they are a person of integrity. This can be illustrated in simple ways, such as keeping appointments, delivering information or documents promised, etc.

So, it is important that a coach considers these factors before beginning a new assignment and decides how much process and rigour is needed to support that assignment. For example, if you have agreed to supply six general coaching sessions over a seven-month period, it makes sense to agree an outline schedule of sessions upfront. You will probably want to plan your approach over the course of sessions, e.g. What performance measures are possible? What might be appropriate points at which to give or receive feedback?

Alternatively, if a coachee wants only two sessions around a specific area or situation, then spending time agreeing lots of principles of approach and guidelines may confuse the coachee, or get in the way of the coaching conversations. You must then consider what is the minimum structure needed for the sessions, to create a balance and focus for each session.

Four stages of a coaching assignment

The following four key activities or stages might effectively support a series of coaching sessions. These stages are shown in Figure 7.1. Some of these stages will often happen naturally, while others require you to make them happen. I find that most assignments are more effective when I work with these stages as a foundation.

While a series of coaching sessions never develops according to a perfect formula, I find that working within a flexible framework still feels useful. Additionally, it is easier for me to demonstrate to a client that they are buying a quality service that has some robust thinking and principles as a foundation. It's natural that people want to balance investment with real results, or the probability of results. The stages or activities that follow can support that conversation, by demonstrating a clear focus on achieving the coachee's outcomes.

A set of four developing activities

Once begun, the four activities are like plates that must be kept spinning. For example, throughout the assignment the coach will always be developing understanding and maintaining direction, constantly reviewing progress in some way, etc. Much of this happens naturally, with little additional effort from the coach.

The following begins to build a picture of the various activities and stages of a coaching assignment. Let's assume that a typical coaching assignment is between three and ten sessions long.

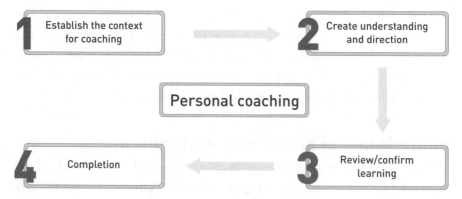

Figure 7.1 Four stages of a coaching assignment

Stage one – establish the context for coaching

First, we must build a supporting context within which to coach. By context, I mean anything surrounding the actual coaching conversations that might help or hinder those conversations. This might be anything from physical aspects, such as the room, lighting, etc. to non-physical aspects, such as the coachee's understanding of what's happening, their enthusiasm, etc. This is essential because we are forming expectations, ground rules and awareness that we will use throughout the coaching relationship. Upon these principles, we can build a foundation for subsequent coaching conversations.

Conversely, too much explanation to the coachee can be counterproductive to the coaching experience. Part of what happens in coaching can only be described as magical and too much discussion of these aspects in advance can simply spoil the surprise. If the coach explains the possibility of amazing insights, wonderful events or mind-blowing breakthroughs, then the secret is spoilt, isn't it? Worse, the coach might over-promise on results that aren't delivered – which benefits no one.

Let's look in more detail at some factors that can contribute to building a great context within which to coach.

Make sure the physical environment supports coaching

We must make sure the room is quiet enough, private enough, and suited to coaching conversations. Are the chairs comfortable enough? Is there a table if we want one? Do we have other facilities available to us to enable some flexibility within the session? For example, flip charts, white boards, drinking water, paper, pens, etc. all help spontaneity during the coaching session. Maybe an idea is easier to understand when it's drawn as a picture; maybe the coachee is being distracted because they're thirsty. Both parties need to feel positive about working in the surroundings. If all we've got is a room and two chairs we can easily create the impression of an interrogation room rather than a place to relax and talk freely.

Both parties need to feel positive about working in the surroundings.

Ideally, a room to be used for coaching sessions should be comfortable and not too cosy

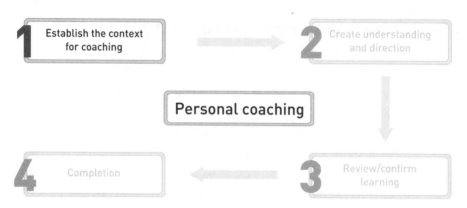

Figure 7.2 Establish the context for coaching

– it's important that people can both relax *and* stay alert. Ideally, the size of the room should create a subtle sense of warmth or intimacy. If the room is huge, the coach and coachee may feel 'lost' in the space or end up sitting too far away from each other. Alternatively, if the room is too small, the space might feel awkward and the coach and coachee may have to sit unnaturally close to each other.

Make sure the mechanics of coaching are mutually agreed

Here, we make sure that both the coach and the coachee have agreed the basic facts of the coaching sessions, for example:

➡ Schedule/dates of coaching sessions.

➡ Duration of coaching sessions.

➡ Location of coaching sessions.

➡ Who else might be involved in the coaching, e.g. their manager, colleagues, etc.

➡ Key milestones or stages, e.g. 'After three sessions, let's review progress with Geoff'.

If an intended schedule is available before the sessions start, then share this with the coachee in advance of the coaching session. That way, the coachee can put all the sessions into their diary immediately. As well as the obvious practical benefit of securing dates, the coachee is also encouraged to begin thinking more about the coaching and what the sessions might bring. Even by committing dates to their diary, the coachee becomes more engaged in the future process, as they imagine the journey ahead. Plus, the coachee is likely to work better between sessions if they understand when the next one is.

Where possible, this information might be recorded/photocopied so that both the coach and the coachee have the same information. Misunderstandings at this point may easily lead to either person showing up late or not at all for sessions. That's a risk we want to avoid.

Coach's corner

Q I'm not a full-time coach, I'm a busy manager who wants to coach my team, how do I make the time?

This is a common situation: a manager is trying to run a busy operation plus make time to coach colleagues and team members. If this sounds familiar, please consider the following questions:

➡ What are the benefits you will get from coaching others, both personally and professionally?

➡ What are reasonable (and still challenging) goals to set for your coaching?

➡ What other situations give you an opportunity to develop coaching skills, e.g. questioning, helping others find their own solutions, supportive feedback, etc.?

➡ How flexible can your colleagues be, e.g. sessions at short notice?

➡ How can you create more time to coach? (Make a list!)

I would encourage any manager to think flexibly to create more opportunities to coach. Many everyday conversations have the potential for some coaching type of input (many of the exercises in this book are based on this simple principle). Rewards over time include colleagues who are more effective, make better decisions and solve their own problems. So if you are a busy manager who wants more time and less pressure – get coaching!

Is the coachee aware of what to expect?

Here, we make sure that the coachee appreciates what coaching is, how it generally works and what they might expect during the coaching sessions. For example, they need to understand that coaching is not training and that this kind of learning happens in a different way to training. They need to know that you'll be encouraging them to gain insights, ideas and perspectives on situations that will enable them to act differently and get different results. They need to know that you will encourage them to focus consistently on their desired goals or outcomes, as a way of maintaining an effective course of action.

I will sometimes give coachees a written overview of what coaching is, broadly how it works, and what I'll be expecting of them. This is best before the first session, to enable the coachee to read and digest the information. This works well where the coaching engagement is going to be fairly brief, e.g. one to three sessions. Additionally, some people welcome reading material as a way of preparing for a coaching relationship.

The following identifies the key elements of a coaching overview:

Checklist **Coaching overview – key points**

What does it do?

⇒ Gives someone an initial understanding of coaching: what it is, possible benefits, etc.

⇒ Encourages a coachee to begin thinking about any goals or objectives they might have.

When might I use it?

⇒ During initial discussions about the potential of coaching.

⇒ In advance of the first coaching session.

⇒ When beginning a new coaching relationship, to give a new coachee some background information or reading.

What does it cover?

⇒ A brief description of what coaching is.

⇒ How coaching works, e.g. compared with other forms of learning or training.

⇒ What situations might be suited to coaching and what are the typical benefits.

⇒ What the coachee can expect from their coach, e.g. behaviours.

⇒ What the coach will expect from the coachee.

⇒ Questions that begin to engage the reader, e.g. How might coaching benefit you? What goals or objectives are you focused on? What would you like to change, do more of, etc.?

The key is to find a balance of background information and discussion that is going to engage the individual. Using both documents and discussion up front often helps, enabling the coachee to orient to, and benefit from, the experience.

For an example of a 'Coaching Overview' see the Toolkit, or download a PDF from www.starrconsulting.co.uk.

Taking notes

If you expect the coachee to take their own notes, then they need to know that they're responsible for that. They also need to know that you'll be taking your own notes and intend to review them before each session. This demonstrates both commitment and professionalism from the coach. In addition, it's a practical way of ensuring continuity between each session.

I sometimes type my own notes up afterwards and offer to send a copy to my coachee, as an additional support. This can be a valuable discipline for both the coachee and myself. I can reflect on the session as I'm typing it up, which helps me consider the discussion, my approach and other perspectives on the situation. For the coachee, they get to read someone else's view of what happened, perhaps remembering a thought or idea as they read. I also make sure that I record any agreements made, so they can be reviewed during the next session.

I would also balance any advice to take notes with another that says don't take too many! Some coaches take too many notes, perhaps because they are anxious not to miss anything. Unfortunately, when a coach is writing notes their ability to observe or listen to the coachee is usually impaired. I tend to write brief 'memory-joggers' and then add other points from memory when I type the notes up afterwards. Alternatively, if the coachee stops speaking to write some of the conversation down, I might use that moment to record a point.

Another option is to record the session for the coachee. They can listen to this later, and review their session. This can also be a useful way of continuing learning, even after the assignment has ended. Of course, the coachee needs to be absolutely comfortable with this technique.

The coach and the coachee need to find a good, practical way of recording key information from sessions. In order to maintain both continuity and learning, it's important that both have an accurate picture of broadly what happened and what actions were agreed on. For an idea of how you might do this, see the 'Summary of a first session' in the coaching Toolkit.

Engage the coachee in coaching

When we begin to build the context for coaching, we are also beginning the process of engagement. By engagement, we simply mean that the individual is interested, involved and actively part of what's going on. If an individual isn't engaged in the experience of being coached, then they are much less likely to enjoy and benefit from it. When a coachee is really engaged, they are completely committed to getting the most from the experience. I would say that the more engaged an individual is, the more coachable they become. When someone is coachable, they are more receptive to finding new ideas and fresh perspectives – they are eager to learn.

> I would say that the more engaged an individual is, the more coachable they become.

For the coach, the difference between coaching someone who's engaged in the coaching versus someone who's not engaged or 'bought-in' can mean the difference between fabulous results and no results. Consequently, a coach must carefully consider factors that might affect the coachee's openness to being coached, both before beginning to coach them and during the initial stages of an assignment. The following checklist helps us focus on this a little more.

Checklist	Signs that the coachee is engaged in the coaching

→ The coachee's levels of enthusiasm for the conversation: energy, ideas, questioning, etc.

→ How active the coachee is between sessions: completing actions, reading background material to the coaching, even over-performing on agreements or commitments made.

→ Level of openness in discussion, positive comments or questions, willingness to consider fresh approaches or ideas.

I would also acknowledge that if any or all the above are missing, then that doesn't automatically mean that the individual is not engaged! This is tricky, but nevertheless true. Some people learn and respond differently and some people become more engaged over time. For the coach, patience, commitment and flexibility will sustain you towards success.

The coach must view each coachee as an individual. Some people are unlikely to respond positively to coaching in the first few sessions. They may by nature be initially cautious in their response to anything new. This might display itself as reluctance to discuss certain situations, hesitation when changing behaviours or even a challenging attitude towards the coach. The coach must balance a commitment to create progress with sensitivity towards the coachee's way of learning.

We can now look in more detail at those factors that might affect an individual's sense of engagement.

Does the coachee want the coaching?

If someone has requested, and paid for, coaching, we can usually assume that they want the coaching. This becomes less straightforward when coaching in business, as the coachee may not have asked for it and not be paying for it. Indeed, in that situation the coachee may resent being coached. Where a different person or department has enlisted the coach's services, it's important to spend time making sure the individual is happy being coached and aware of the opportunity that being coached presents to them.

Where an individual has been requested by their manager to attend some coaching sessions, they might easily be sceptical and/or mistrustful of what this means for them. They might imagine coaching is happening because of a problem with their behaviour that they aren't aware of. Or they may wonder if the coaching sessions are actually some kind of 'vetting' activity, e.g. for redundancy or promotion. They may be concerned that whatever they say during coaching is reported back to their manager or colleagues.

When the coachee has not requested the coaching, I'll usually encourage the requesting manager to spend time explaining the arrangement and the reasons for it. I normally request that the manager brief the coachee personally, in advance of my first session. While I can tell the coachee why I think they are having coaching, they really want to hear this from the manager. If it's possible, I would encourage any coach to sit in on the session between the manager and the coachee. That way they can help the conversation to be effective, by asking questions or clarifying comments. In addition, the coach also gets to see the manager and the coachee together, which may provide useful insights into that relationship.

What does the coachee expect to happen?

If what begins to happen in the coaching is not what the coachee was expecting, this can cause them discomfort. For example, do they know what sort of approach the coach is going to use in the coaching? If they're expecting magical answers or knowledge to be given to them by the coach, this can lead to silent frustration and disillusionment during sessions. This might easily disappear over time, as they become aware of the benefits of a less-directive approach. More preferable is that they are open to this approach from the very beginning of the sessions.

Negative expectations may arise when the individual has a poor view of coaching, based on previous experiences. For example, maybe they work within an environment where people are regularly critical of each other and call this 'coaching' or 'feedback'. A colleague may have been disparaging of them and told them to view it as 'coaching'. Not surprisingly, someone with this type of experience might not welcome an offer of further coaching.

Managing these expectations can be helped both by the coaching overview document in the Toolkit and by the coach discussing expectations at the initial coaching sessions.

Does the individual really want change?

This is a similar point to whether they want the coaching, but subtly different. Some people say they want coaching, involve themselves in a coaching relationship, attend sessions, join in conversations – and don't actually want anything to change. Perhaps we have problems that we don't want to solve, simply because, by solving them, we see that we could end up with what seems like a bigger problem.

For example, I might say I hate my job with its lack of responsibility and low salary. I might spend a long time describing why it's so awful and what kind of job I'd really like to be doing. Between coaching sessions, however, I might do nothing. Each coaching visit, my coach listens to my complaints and wonders why I'm not acting from the insights and decisions I appear to be experiencing.

The answer possibly lies in the fact that I never completely wanted the change. You see, to go and get a better, more responsible, higher-paid job might confront my ability to actually do the job. Maybe the thought of that scares me. Alternatively, I've been discussing a subject that's easy for me to explore and non-confrontational in nature. I may have other issues that are more challenging, but I'm simply not up for talking about them.

This is another opportunity for the coach to use their advanced skills of supportive feedback. Here, the coach needs to be open and honest about what they think is happening, i.e. a reluctance to embrace change. This enables them to explore what might be causing the apparent block and appreciate the coachee's views on what's happening. Together, the coach and coachee must find ways to create progress. It might mean that the coachee needs to consider what they really want more fully, or perhaps how they're stopping themselves from having it.

Try it yourself — **Does someone want change?**

What is this?	⇒	A way to help you to evaluate a coachee's appetite for change.
What does it do?	⇒	Causes you to reflect on how receptive the coachee is to learning and change.
When might I use it?	⇒	In the early stages of a coaching assignment.
	⇒	At any point during a coaching assignment when you consider that a reluctance to change may be a reason for little or no progress.

Consider the following questions:

Q During sessions, to what extent does the coachee demonstrate enthusiasm for new thoughts, e.g. seeking other ways of doing things, 'What could I do to change that?', 'What would I need to do?'

Q During sessions, does the coachee prefer to discuss problems rather than solutions?

Q Between sessions, how 'in action' is the coachee, e.g. do they complete agreements, use new behaviours, continue to learn, read, do their own research, etc.?

Section summary — **Does someone want change?**

There are many reasons for a coachee not to appear engaged in the coaching, and not really wanting to change is just one. Later in this chapter we look at another, more structured approach to this situation.

Begin to focus on desired outcomes

When building context, we also begin to explore what the coachee wants to get from the series of coaching sessions. I would hope to start this enquiry before the first session takes place. Using the coaching overview document, the coach can suggest that the coachee consider what their goals might be and what situations or issues currently relate to those goals.

By helping the coachee to begin thinking in this way, the coach helps the coachee to enter the initial session with a sense of preparation. Perhaps they've thought a little more about what areas of their life or work they want to work on, or simply have some questions based on the information they've been given.

Also, by encouraging the coachee to imagine the future series of coaching sessions – what might happen, etc. – the coach is also initiating the learning process. This is sometimes called 'future pacing'. When we 'future pace' someone's thoughts we are beginning to engage them in their future, helping them imagine what's going to happen before it actually does. For example, if I want to future pace your goal of losing weight and becoming much more healthy, I'm going to encourage you to imagine what having that goal will be like. That would include how you would look, how you would feel, how your experiences of life would be different – a really rich appreciation of what losing weight and being healthy would be like.

Future pacing is a valuable technique in any change process, as it has the effect of drawing someone's mind towards having a goal. This has both a practical and motivational result. By really thinking through what the goal of health and weight loss would be like, we begin to identify any practical issues with that. Maybe I don't actually want to lose as much weight as I thought and by imagining myself this much lighter I can see that clearly. Also, when I imagine myself looking slimmer and fitter I can become quite inspired by how that might feel and look – and that's going to motivate me towards my goal even more.

The same principles apply when an individual begins to imagine what benefits they might experience from being coached. Harnessing the power of the coachee's imagination begins to create a strong 'pulling' effect towards a desirable future.

Stage two – create understanding and direction

The second stage of a coaching assignment places a stronger emphasis on what the coachee wants to achieve within the coaching while identifying where they are right now. Once understanding and a sense of direction have been established, these can be developed throughout all sessions.

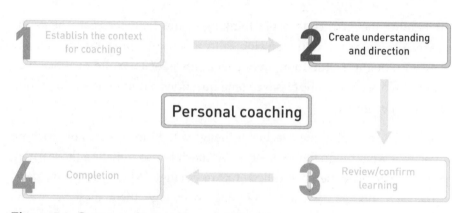

Figure 7.3 Create understanding and direction

Getting to know the coachee

Initially, the coach needs to form an appropriate level of understanding of the coachee as a person, their current circumstances, issues, etc. This information gathering will ideally begin before the coach and coachee sit down to a coaching session. Before I begin any new coaching conversation, I like to know:

→ The coachee's full name and age.

→ What they do for a job/occupation.

→ A little professional history, e.g. what did they do before they did this?

→ Where they live and where they work (and the type of journey between).

→ Family circumstances; partner's name; number, names and age of children, etc.

→ What general areas they would like to work with, e.g. confidence, productivity, health or finances.

→ Whatever else they want to tell me that seems appropriate to this general fact-building part of the conversation (be ready for anything at this point please ...).

Some of this is personal and asking for such information on a form or over the telephone is inappropriate. I tend to gather the most basic details before the session, i.e. name, occupation and perhaps areas they want to work on. Then at the beginning of the first session, I ask for the other information:

family, where they live/work, etc. People are sometimes surprised that I'm interested in knowing their partner's name, where they live, or even how long they've been married. However, most people happily accept that all these factors have a potential influence on the work we are embarking upon.

For example, perhaps in the second session we are discussing a recent job offer. I would want to understand the impact this might have on the coachee's home or family life and, at that point, it's better for me to be able to ask 'And what does Rachel think about this?' than 'Can I ask, are you married?'

Both for the flow of conversation and for the sense of a relationship between the coach and coachee, it pays to have some basic knowledge of a coachee's life and circumstances upon which to build.

Getting to know what the coachee wants

From the first session, we need to begin agreeing what areas of their life the coachee wants to change or improve on and what specific goals they might have in those areas. This begins the ongoing process of keeping a focus on those goals or desired outcomes. These stated goals and aims form the basis for each coaching conversation. The goals may change, or be refined, but a coach must always keep the coachee's goals as the background for the sessions.

Without this constant focus, coaching conversations can develop into cosy chats, with no real purpose or sense of direction. The coach and the coachee may update themselves on what's been happening with the coachee, what was interesting about that, enjoyable or frustrating, etc. The point is, with no underlying goal or sense of direction, this is just a cosy chat. Not that there's anything wrong with cosy chats, I love them – they're just not coaching!

Maintaining direction within each session

The need to establish purpose and direction is also important within each session. At the beginning of each session, a good coach will normally want to set a target for the coachee, e.g. 'What do you want to achieve in today's session?' By agreeing on expectations, the coach can review progress against that target if the discussion is drifting, e.g. 'We said we wanted to find ways of creating more time for your children today – are you happy that we continue with this discussion of promotion at work?'

The coach needs to find ways to maintain progress and stay flexible as to the natural flow of the coaching discussions. Sometimes, the coaching conversation that occurs seems unrelated to any of the coachee's goals, but a good coach may choose to continue. This is when experience and intuition tell the coach that the conversation that's happening is valuable and worthwhile. In these cases, such conversations can prove incredibly relevant to the coachee's overall progress and are easily worth the digression.

The coach needs to find ways to maintain progress and stay flexible as to the natural flow of the coaching discussions.

Using the previous example – by discussing the promotion at work, the coachee may realize that the price she's paying for career success is often her relationship with her children. She may decide that she needs to find ways of balancing these different aspects of fulfilment and happiness.

Developing goals

So when a coach begins working with someone, it makes sense to develop a true understanding of what the individual really wants to work on. For example, if the coachee wants to get a better job or career, both the coach and the coachee need to understand:

➡ What specifically does 'better job' mean? Is that defined by an increase in salary, benefits, responsibility, working conditions, job content, working location, job title, training, etc.? The possibilities for how a person might decide a job is better than the one they have right now are endless.

➡ What circumstances currently relate to that goal, e.g. money problems, frustrations with current employer, contractual obligations, notice period, etc.?

➡ What are the coachee's reasons (motivators) for wanting the goal, e.g. financial security/freedom, lifestyle, personal profile, respect, etc.?

➡ What might stop, or form a barrier to, the coachee achieving this goal, e.g. fear of change/risk, academic qualifications/work experience, peer pressure, etc.?

Often, just discussing what a coachee actually wants and defining that with real clarity can be of tremendous benefit. By creating a richer appreciation of the motivators, circumstances and issues that are involved in a person's goals, we can often create an immediate shift in their perception. It is not uncommon for a coachee to have a complete change of heart about what they want, when they gain this richer understanding.

Coach's story	Understanding what we really want	

Eddie, our coachee, wanted to find ways to support his son's education. Eddie was frustrated at his son's lack of progress at school in some subjects (in particular, maths) and wanted to look at options, e.g. private tuition or changing schools. Carla, our coach, decided to explore the situation a little more. For example, not just what Eddie was saying he wanted to provide for his son, i.e. a good education, but also what might be causing his frustration.

During gentle enquiry, Carla discovered that Eddie didn't actually mind that his son was no good at maths. After all, his son was excelling in other areas that came more naturally to him. What frustrated Eddie was that his son seemed so relaxed about the situation (instead of being worried or stressed about it). His explained that his son loved English, history and sports, and saw maths as something to be 'tolerated'. This contrasted with Eddie's values from his own childhood, where his strict father had taken education very seriously and taught Eddie to worry a lot about any areas where he might be 'failing'.

During the conversation, Eddies saw that he didn't want to teach his son to worry, or become stressed about things, such as his lack of natural ability for maths. Eddie decided that teaching his son to live an enjoyable and productive life, one that fulfils him, was a lot more important. Strangely, Eddie began to see his son as someone he can learn from. He found that he actually admired the way his son could find real pleasure

▶

at being good at something. Conversely, his son could also accept things he's not good at and view them in a relaxed way.

This was quite a shift in perception for Eddie, who tended to disregard all his own successes, and worry instead about the areas in his life where he thought he might be 'failing'.

By exploring Eddie's goals further, Carla was able to reach this conclusion fairly quickly. In addition, Eddie now had a new goal that would benefit him, i.e. learning a new, relaxed way of being from his son.

For any coaching assignment, goals are essential to success. It follows then that the goal should be defined and understood in a way that enables both the coach and the coachee to create forward movement and progress. For support on goal setting, check out 'Building a clear goal' in the Toolkit.

Using personality profiling or 360° feedback

Developing an understanding of the individual can be greatly enhanced by the use of personality profiling and/or 360° feedback. Both methods normally consist of a series of structured questions used to assess the characteristics of an individual. In personality profiling the coachee completes a questionnaire themselves. The characteristics assessed will depend on what kind of test is used, e.g. communication styles, thinking patterns, etc. In 360° feedback, we question a coachee's colleagues, to indicate strengths, character traits and development opportunities. Sometimes the coachee may complete the same set of questions, to allow us to compare their perception of themselves with that of their colleagues.

Personality profiling

Personality tests examine our individual character traits from an independent/objective view. Normally, we fill in a form and our responses are analysed to give us some results. The results might point to what we like, what we don't like, what kind of jobs we'd be really good at, how we typically approach problems, etc. There are many different types of test – too many to list here. Some popular examples are Myers–Briggs, the Insights

'Colours' profile, and Belbin, all of which can be used to understand teams, as well as individuals.

Some tests focus on certain qualities, or competencies, e.g. leadership, whilst others are much more general, e.g. are we creative, are we a 'people person', etc. Personality tests are useful as they can help a coachee discuss themselves and their typical behaviours in a much less emotional or attached manner. No one can be right or wrong in a personality test, as there are no good or bad personality types. In addition, it can help the coach learn to relate to the coachee in a way that the coachee will naturally respond to. For example, if the coach knows that a coachee likes to learn by reading, they can offer book recommendations.

360° feedback

360° feedback is subtly different, as people who know the coachee, plus the coachee themselves, give their opinions, or fill in questionnaires. For example, in business the coachee's colleagues, manager and subordinates might all contribute their views on a coachee. The feedback might be gathered in person, e.g. the coach interviews people using a structured questionnaire, or individuals may simply input to a web-based form. Again, the questions involved might be general or specific, e.g. 'How much do they motivate others?' or 'How well do they handle pressure?'

Gathering 360° feedback via personal interviews

I often interview someone's colleagues, as they provide a rich insight into the impact they are having on the workplace. Early in an assignment, I'll agree which four or five individuals it would be useful for me to speak to. Normally I'll agree the best individuals with both the coachee and the coachee's manager. I want to get a good cross-section of people, who can provide differing viewpoints. For example, as well as close colleagues that the coachee knows and trusts, I might also interview someone with whom the coachee has some discomfort or conflict. I'll also interview the coachee's manager, as they are both a stakeholder and influencer in the coachee's success. These interviews can be conducted either in person or by telephone and normally take around 30 minutes. All comments given will be attributed, i.e. the coachee will hear both what was said and *who* said it (obviously it's important to make that clear to everyone). During feedback interviews, I use the following questions, and they serve me well:

→ What is this person (my coachee) good at?

→ What do you value most about them?

→ What do they need to get better at?

→ What do they need to do to be successful in their current situation or role?

→ Do you have any other messages for this person?

Delivering 360° feedback to the coachee

After the interview, I'll type up the session and approve it for release with the person who made the comments. People might want to reshape their comments, making them clearer, or more constructive. Once the individual is happy for me to use their feedback, I can share the same document with the coachee. For an example of this document, visit the Toolkit.

I'll normally do this face to face, and try to deliver all feedback at the same time. This helps illustrate any strong themes or messages, as well as a broad selection of opinions. After telling the coachee a little about what to expect, I'll read out directly from the document and then leave all documents with the coachee. I'll add any balancing statements I think will help, e.g. 'I notice that everyone I spoke to all seemed keen that you lead more from the front this year ...' While I don't want to tell the coachee how to respond, I do feel I can help them distil key messages, or keep messages in perspective.

It may surprise you that in many years of using this approach, no coachee has ever responded less than gratefully to receiving this type of feedback. One of the keys to that is to encourage statements in a balanced, constructive manner and discourage any harsh or insulting language. I rarely hear insulting language and if I did, I would ask for a more helpful version of the statement. For example, if someone tells me, 'Jayne's team is making a fool out of her, instead of her managing them it's the other way round', I may say, 'OK, that sounds a tough message, what's appropriate for me to record here?' The person will normally give me something more constructive like, 'She needs to lead from the front more and find a way to keep the stronger characters following policy'. The coach needs to help people give feedback that is clear, objective and balanced. You are a natural 'filter' in the process and your job is to encourage openness, clarity and constructive comment.

When delivering feedback to the coachee, it's important to remind them that all comments are reflecting a perception that has been created. People's comments are not 'true', they are simply that person's perception of the coachee. For example, in the feedback a colleague may have described my coachee as 'disorganized'. That does not necessarily mean that the coachee is disorganized (although they may admit to that!), but it does mean that they have created the *perception* of being disorganized with the person giving the feedback. The coachee is more likely to accept responsibility for having created the impression of chaos than the fact that they are truly 'disorganized'.

When a coachee gets 360° feedback, it can be both informative and provoking. Rarely do they see a view of themselves through the eyes of others. The coachee may be surprised by how other people experience them. So getting this feedback can lead to breakthroughs in a coachee's understanding. For example, a coachee is frustrated with her lack of acknowledgement or promotion at work. When her 360° feedback is returned, she gains information that helps her understand why. Her manager and colleagues view her as happy, contented and unambitious. In addition, she is viewed as someone who prefers a small group of colleagues and does not actively seek new friends or contacts. By receiving this feedback, the coachee can decide for themselves what the important messages are and what they want to do about those. Their goals for the coaching assignment can be refined or changed, e.g. 'I need to promote myself and my goals more. I also need to develop relationships with a much broader group of people.'

Clearly, the use of personality tests and 360° feedback requires the coach to be skilled at giving feedback. The information these tests produce should be experienced by the coachee as valuable, insightful and stimulating. This requires the coach to devote time and energy to delivering the results in a supportive, sensitive manner. For further information, please refer to the supportive feedback section in Chapter 4: Fundamental skills.

Ongoing development of direction and goals

Once an initial direction and understanding are established, they must be developed throughout the coaching assignment. Understanding is one of the keys to the coachee's development, and coaching discussions are a constant process of enquiry, insight and conclusion. It's an ongoing journey of discovery and learning, for both the coachee and the coach. Success is reached by staying committed to the destination and flexible as to the journey. This is why the skills of careful listening and questioning are so important to a good coach.

Success is reached by staying committed to the destination and flexible as to the journey.

Stage three – review/confirm learning

Regular reviews help maintain progress during a coaching assignment. A good coach is interested in both the effectiveness of the coaching sessions and whether or not the coachee is making good progress in reaching their goals. During a review activity, we might explore any or all of the following:

⇒ Are the coaching sessions working well, e.g. are they productive, worthwhile, etc.?

⇒ What impact are the sessions having on the coachee?

⇒ What progress has been made on the coachee's goals?

⇒ Is the coach's style and approach working for the coachee?

⇒ Are there any issues that need to be resolved, e.g. what's not working?

⇒ How could the sessions be improved?

The above questions are relevant for both the coach and the coachee to answer. Mostly it is the coachee who places a value upon the coaching, as they are the focal point of the conversations and the person who should be benefiting from them. However, the coach will also have views on all of the above, as well as other coaching experience to draw upon. In addition, the coach may have their own goals during the assignment, such as improving their listening or rapport skills. It makes sense, therefore, that both the coach and the coachee have an opportunity to give their views.

Checklist   Ways to review progress of the coaching

→ Give the coachee a questionnaire to complete between sessions.

→ Use a questionnaire to conduct a structured review session with the coachee.

→ Schedule an unstructured discussion with the coachee to explore the progress of the coaching.

→ Conduct regular, smaller, reviews with the coachee, e.g. at the end of each session.

→ Ask for informal feedback from the coachee on an ad hoc basis, e.g. when it seems appropriate.

→ Arrange for a third party, e.g. another coach, to facilitate a discussion between the coach and the coachee.

→ Complete a feedback questionnaire on your own experience (as coach).

→ Supervision: arrange a coaching session with another coach to review progress (very useful where you are having some difficulty or issues with the assignment).

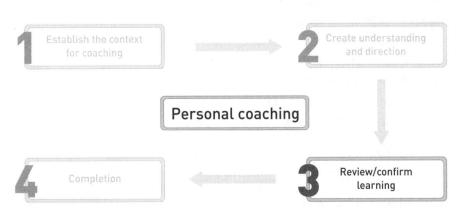

Figure 7.4 Review/confirm learning

Deciding when and how to review

A coach needs to strike a balance between how much time is spent reviewing the coaching, and how much time is spent actually coaching. Too many reviews can easily impair the flow of coaching conversations, causing an unnatural focus on the conversations themselves. Alternatively, if a coach disregards the review process, they risk missing an issue or an opportunity to improve the effectiveness of the sessions for the coachee. Imagine that you and I were doing a 1,000-piece jigsaw puzzle together. Occasionally, we might step back to review our progress and check everything was going OK. However, if we stopped to discuss every little piece going into place we'd slow our progress considerably!

There are no strict guidelines, although I like to schedule at least a couple of formal checks into any coaching assignment more than five sessions long. This might consist of one check around the mid-point of the coaching initiative and one a few weeks after the coaching has finished. The prompt of giving feedback three to four weeks after the coaching has finished gives the coachee an opportunity to give a reflective view, based on their experiences after the coaching has ended. In addition, the activity of giving feedback reminds them of the insights and learning they have gained and perhaps encourages them to apply those lessons a little more rigorously.

As well as this, I like to include some informal reviews in the sessions. These will normally consist of a few open questions, to explore how things are with the coachee. Maybe at the beginning or the end of the sessions, I might ask things like, 'Was that conversation useful?', 'Is the coaching what you expected?', 'How are we doing, do you think?' Obviously that's not going to produce good quality feedback but it can give a coach some clues as to an underlying problem. If a coachee answers such a question with an emphatic 'Yes – absolutely', then the coach can assume that there are no major problems. If a coachee pauses, and perhaps with less energy responds 'Yeah – I guess so', then further exploration is probably needed.

Occasionally, I'll also do my own reviews of progress, by re-reading all the notes I've kept on the coachee from the beginning of the sessions.

Table 7.1 shows a typical schedule of reviews over a ten-session coaching assignment.

Table 7.1 Schedule of reviews over a ten-session coaching assignment

	Nature of review	**Comment**
Session one	Informal check at end of session, e.g. 'Was that what you expected?'	Helps match the coachee's expectations to reality.
Session two	Informal check at beginning of session, e.g. 'How were you after the last session?' At end of session, quick informal check, e.g. 'Was that a useful discussion to have?'	
Session three	Informal check at end of session, plus coach reviews all notes before next session.	
Session four	Informal checks at start of session, based on coach's view having re-read the notes, e.g. 'Let's have a look at how we've doing so far. I want to do a quick recap using the session notes.'	
Session five	Informal check at end of session, e.g. 'Was that useful?' plus a request that the coachee completes a feedback questionnaire before the next session.	Need to engage the coachee in the value of giving open feedback.
Session six	Acknowledge results of feedback and discuss any matters arising, e.g. need	▶

	Nature of review	Comment
	to alter session times, focus more on work issues, etc.	
Session seven	Informally review what progress is being made on the coachee's goals. Agree what further progress the coachee wants to make before the final session.	This discussion is normally at the beginning of the session.
Session eight	Acknowledge focus of session, i.e. the coachee's goals. Confirm that any review points from structured feedback (session six) are now working, e.g. new session times, etc.	
Session nine	Informal checks at end of session, e.g. 'Are we still on track to meet our targets by the next session?' Tell the coachee you'll be reviewing progress more formally next time.	
Session ten	More formal review of progress on goals, record in notes. Give final feedback form for completion after session.	Final feedback form is useful a few weeks after completion, e.g. three to six weeks.

Other options for reviews include a telephone call between sessions, or maybe an e-mail to check how things are.

If the above appears to create a lot of reviewing, remember, the coachee will really only notice the more formal stages consisting of the two questionnaires. For the coach, much of the above can happen almost subconsciously, e.g. as I'm filing someone's notes, I'll sometimes re-read the others that are there. This will often provoke me to think about what's happening with that coachee generally and I may choose to do something different in the next session because of that.

Confirming learning

By reviewing the progress and results of coaching, we are able to affirm learning with the coachee. By this affirmation, we are simply linking what the coachee is learning with the benefits they are experiencing as a result – benefits such as better relationships with others, increased personal productivity, increased health and well-being, etc. By forming a clear link between the coaching and the results of coaching, we achieve several aims, namely:

➡ *The coachee realizes the benefit of their commitment to coaching*: the coachee now sees an obvious return on the effort they have put into coaching so far, e.g. trust, openness, completing actions etc.

➡ *The coachee is encouraged to develop new behaviours further*: by seeing how much they have benefited from taking on actions or new behaviours, the coachee is motivated to continue, in order to generate more positive results.

➡ *The business gains an appreciation of the potential of coaching*: where the coaching has been sponsored by an organization, e.g. a training department or senior manager, they can most likely link the results of coaching to a business benefit. Perhaps the individual has a marked improvement in productivity or personal effectiveness – these are both results that directly benefit the organization.

Linking results to coaching

Sometimes you might need to make a clearer link to the benefits your coaching has achieved, e.g. to evidence a commercial benefit to your work. There are lots of ways to do this, for example:

➡ Give the coachee a structured questionnaire, asking them to identify what they are doing differently now and the benefits of that.

➡ Have a structured conversation with the coachee, to explore what differences they are noticing.

➡ Speak to colleagues or friends; ask for feedback on the individual. To maintain trust, the coach must be really open with the coachee about doing this, i.e. ask permission to do this and share information with the coachee.

➡ Observe the individual in their workplace or indeed anywhere that seems appropriate to view results, e.g. if they wanted to be better at public speaking, go and watch them do that.

➡ Repeat 360° feedback later with the same group of friends or colleagues and look at changes in the results from the first exercise.

Obviously, the coach needs to appreciate the individual coachee's situation, before deciding how to make these links from coaching to results. It may be that an informal discussion is all that's needed. Alternatively, if from the outset the coach and coachee have agreed on some very specific behavioural changes as goals, then observing (or shadowing) them may be a good idea.

Checklist Linking coaching to results

The following is a checklist of questions you might use with a coachee to understand the impact of coaching conversations. They are very simple, and you'll probably want to add your own:

➡ What benefits do you see from the coaching?

➡ What effects are the coaching conversations having on your work/home/relationships etc.? (choose whichever is appropriate).

➡ If you hadn't had the coaching, what would be different now?

➡ If you continue with these new behaviours and routines, how is the future different? e.g. what impact will this have at work/home etc.?

➡ What have you got from the coaching conversations?

What if there aren't any results?

Where the individual is experiencing no results and neither are friends or colleagues, then recognizing this is important. If the coach neglects to iden- tify that the coaching is having no effect, then they have no opportunity to improve the situation. Plus, where the coach works within a business environment and their sponsor is not the coachee, the sponsor must be happy they are investing time and money wisely.

Sometimes, the coaching doesn't produce the results that we hoped it would. By identifying that the coaching seems to be having no effect on the individual, the coach is then able to explore that with the coachee. Together, the coach and coachee can look at what's happening and why, and decide what to do about that.

> **Sometimes, the coaching doesn't produce the results that we hoped it would.**

What if the results are not good?

Sometimes, an individual having coaching may find that things get worse before they can get better. This is a natural part of the learning cycle and both the coach and the coachee should be prepared for it as a possibility. For example, a coachee is used to getting results at work by using demanding, controlling behaviours. They are used to getting quick results, but find over time that colleagues either refuse to help, or simply avoid working with them. The coachee recognizes this and wants to learn other ways of making requests of people, while maintaining a good relationship with them.

Now, at first, the coachee simply stops barking orders at people, as they are now aware of the impact this has been having on their colleagues. As a consequence, important tasks aren't delegated and the coachee is overloaded with work. As coaching continues, the coachee realizes this and practises new ways of making requests of their colleagues.

The coachee returns to the work environment to try out these new behaviours. It seems it may take a little time for them to find the right balance between making an open request of someone and maintaining rapport at the same time. Until they learn the best way to do this, they may experience a combination of positive results and lousy results (or results that are somewhere in between).

Stage four – completion

This is logically the final stage of coaching, as its purpose is to bring the coaching assignment to a conclusion. No matter how amazing the benefits from the coaching have been or how enjoyable and stimulating the coaching relationship is, each coaching assignment should have an end to it. Just as there's something very exciting about embarking upon the beginning of a coaching initiative, there can also be something wonderfully liberating about ending one.

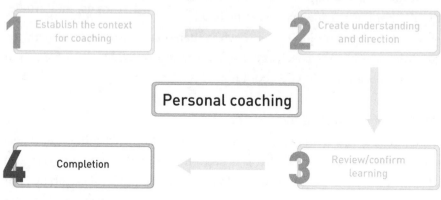

Figure 7.5 Completion

So while an assignment with a coach might easily be extended, I would recommend that it not become a permanent arrangement. A coach acts as a catalyst, bringing fresh perspectives, different ideas and a constant focus to the goals of the coachee. If a coach had regular sessions with the same personal coach for a long period of time, e.g. years, I would expect the value of that coaching to diminish over time. Maybe the relationship becomes too familiar and so less challenging. Or perhaps the coachee becomes 'immune' to the ideas and conversation of the coach. It's also possible that the coach becomes so used to the typical behaviours and language of the coachee that they almost stop noticing or questioning them.

In addition, the coachee must assume ultimate responsibility for themselves and their circumstances. With the same coach as a constant companion, some of this sense of independence may be lost.

I would also acknowledge that an individual may choose to return to a coaching relationship for periods where they need a clearer focus or more support over a period of time. I would recommend that individuals consider using different coaches, who have strengths in different areas. I know of coaches who work exclusively in one area, such as time management or relationships. Depending on the coachee's reasons for returning to coaching, it may be advisable to consider all the available options – there are many good coaches out there.

The purpose of completion

When completing the coaching assignment, the coach aims to:

➡ Leave the coachee feeling that the coaching has been worthwhile. In addition, where someone else has sponsored the coaching, the sponsor should also feel that they have received value from their investment.

➡ Identify ways in which the coachee may continue to learn when the coaching sessions end.

➡ Make sure that the coachee understands other ways they might be supported in future, e.g. which friends, which colleagues, which books, courses, seminars, etc.

It's no good having a wonderful coaching relationship with someone for several months if the coachee is left feeling cast adrift or unsupported a short time after the assignment has ended. We want to encourage the coachee to continue learning, building and developing the insights and ideas that arose during the coaching sessions. That way, the coachee is still getting value long after the last session has ended.

Begin with the end in mind

Strangely, preparing for completion begins right at the beginning of a coaching relationship. The coach must operate from an assumption that the coaching will have an end to it and that end should fulfil the above criteria. Throughout any coaching assignment, I will be looking for ideas that might support the effective closure of the assignment. For example, I might encourage the individual to create a personal development plan to focus on longer-term learning. Alternatively, I might look for book recommendations or explore possible ways that the coachee may gain more support from individuals that they know or work with.

Leave people feeling good about the coaching

Where the coaching has gone especially well, completion becomes really easy. For the coachee, the review processes have identified benefits and these have been confirmed. The coachee knows that the coaching has really worked for them and, specifically, knows *how* it has worked for them. If there was a business sponsor involved, again the review processes will have identified positive gains for them or the organization.

Where the coaching hasn't achieved the results that were desired or expected, we can use the opportunity of completion to reconcile the situation. For example, additional activities or ideas can be implemented to encourage change. Perhaps the individual requires some training or additional experiences in order to progress. By acknowledging the situation, a coach can do something positive about it.

Occasionally a coach will choose to perform a feedback exercise some time after the coaching has ended. This can be valuable both to confirm benefits and also to pick up any residual issues that need taking care of. For example, if the coach has agreed that the coachee find a friend or colleague to help support their development plan, the coach can hear how this is going on. Maybe this isn't working for the coachee and they simply need a discussion with the coach to realize why.

Wherever the coachee, or sponsor, is left feeling uncomfortable about some aspects of the coaching, I would hope that the coach would work to resolve that discomfort. Maybe the sponsor was left feeling unclear as to what should happen next, or perhaps the coachee doesn't feel able to take their learning forward. Whatever is incomplete about the coaching can be identified, discussed and made complete. After all, a coach's success is reflected in what clients and coachees say about them. Most coaches rely on referrals or recommendations for continued business. How a coach handles aspects of review, affirmation and closure within a coaching assignment can have a great impact upon people's impression of their services.

A coach's success is reflected in what clients and coachees say about them.

Personal development plans

A personal development plan identifies areas that the coachee wants to develop further once the coaching has ended. Goals tend to be over a longer period of time, e.g. months or years, rather than weeks. This might typically include gaining new experience or qualifications, hitting targets of earnings, health, fitness, etc. It may also include commitments that the coachee wants to maintain, like using a daily plan, or making a weekly phone call to someone.

Personal development plans are especially useful in business when used by the coachee to focus specifically on their career development. They form a record for the coachee of the main areas they want to improve in or goals they want to focus on. Also, these plans can be used to request further training or support from colleagues, managers, training functions, etc. Once developmental goals have been met, the plan can be used to demonstrate progress to others. This might be especially important where an organization has a formal appraisal process where financial reward is linked to performance.

Checklist	Key elements of a personal development plan (PDP)

The following are suggested headings (or columns) within a PDP document:

1 Area of development

This is the general skill or competence, e.g. time management, financial awareness, health/well-being, etc.

2 Development objective (goal)

This is what specifically the individual wants to do, e.g.:

➡ Reduce my working day to eight hours.

➡ Be able to read and understand financial information relating to my project.

➡ Improve my intake of food and drink during working hours.

3 Behaviours to develop and demonstrate competency

This is what the individual will be doing more of, when they start meeting their objective, e.g.:

➡ Use a weekly and daily diary to prioritize and schedule activity, and review these plans regularly with one other person.

➡ Regularly review financial reports relating to project area, spend compared with budget, etc.

➡ Eat a healthy lunch every day, drink one glass of water for every tea or coffee.

4 Actions to create progress

This is what the individual must do to really get into action on their objective. For example, book on a course, arrange a meeting, find a mentor, etc. Agree on a date by when these arrangements should be completed. Using the three categories above, we might choose:

➡ Arrange meeting with Jo to agree what my current priorities really are (10/07).

➡ Arrange to see project accountant to understand what's important for me to focus on (03/07).

➡ Share my goal re food and drink with at least three other people and request support (05/08).

5 Date to complete or review the objective

Here we record the relevant dates for completion or review of the initial objective, e.g. 'Reduce my working day to eight hours'. It's often a good idea to put a review date in before the final date, in order to check progress. For example, if my goal is to reduce my working day to eight hours within a three-month period, a review point after a month would make sense.

Other ways to encourage ongoing learning

If a personal development plan is not appropriate/possible, there are a variety of other ways a coach might suggest for a coachee to continue learning, including:

➡ Book recommendations: titles, authors.

➡ Record the coaching sessions and give the recording to the coachee.

➡ Home study courses.

⇒ Night school.

⇒ Start a personal development group – a community of like-minded people.

⇒ Attend courses.

⇒ Listen to training audio programmes.

⇒ Get a colleague or friend to help focus the coachee on their ongoing learning.

⇒ Ask for regular feedback from friends or colleagues.

The list is probably much longer and a coach is limited only by their imagination. I would suggest that the option be both pragmatic and desirable for the coachee. It's no good suggesting books to people who don't like reading, or night school to someone who has to look after children each evening. Simple things work best, as they are most likely to happen. For someone with a regular drive to work, maybe audio programmes for the car are good or, for a long train journey, a book might be a welcome distraction.

Make sure an individual feels supported

What's really great about a coaching relationship is the level of involvement and support that a good coach can create for the person they are working with. When that's gone, an individual may sometimes experience that as a sudden withdrawal of support. To avoid this happening, the coach needs to:

⇒ Prepare the coachee for the sessions ending.

⇒ Identify other potential ways the coachee may get support if that's needed.

⇒ Check back on the coachee shortly after the coaching has ended.

The preparation for the assignment to end will normally have happened long before the final coaching session. This begins by initially setting goals for the coaching assignment, reviewing progress, affirming learning, preparing for ongoing learning, etc. However, when it is actually over and the coach doesn't turn up the following month, some sense of withdrawal may still be felt. One simple option is for the coach to make one or two phone calls a little time after the coaching has ended. These don't have to be coaching conversations, although there is an obvious opportunity to offer a little reassurance, guidance or encouragement if needed.

Where the individual still wants and perhaps needs support, then the coach might consider other ways in which they might have that. Options of finding a 'buddy' or mentor can sometimes work, especially where the coaching has been done in a business environment. Where the sponsor of the coaching is the coachee's manager, perhaps they might be willing to meet with the coachee on a regular basis to discuss their performance or progress. This option has some advantages, in that the manager becomes more involved in what's happening with the individual who works for them. One disadvantage might be that the boss simply isn't the right person to listen to the coachee; maybe they're too busy, or perhaps the coachee doesn't feel able to discuss certain topics with them. Other alternatives within work might be a friend or colleague, or perhaps someone in the training or personnel/HR department, etc.

Checklist Are we complete?

At the closing stages of a coaching assignment, ask yourself the following questions to make sure the sessions are complete:

- **Q** Have you had a conversation with the coachee to find out what they thought of the coaching?
- **Q** Is the coachee comfortable that the coaching is coming to an end?
- **Q** Does the coachee now have other goals or learning objectives, e.g. how they might improve even more at something?
- **Q** Is the coachee clear about how their learning can be supported from now on, e.g. asking for regular feedback from colleagues, finding a mentor, etc.?
- **Q** Are there any other stakeholders you need to update or complete the coaching process with, e.g. managers, training department, etc.?

A framework for coaching

Figure 7.6 summarises our framework for a coaching assignment and may be useful both as an initial overview and as a subsequent checklist. All activities are intended to occur in most coaching assignments in some way. For example, whether an assignment is two sessions long or ten sessions long, it's still possible to have some form of review or confirmation of learning, etc.

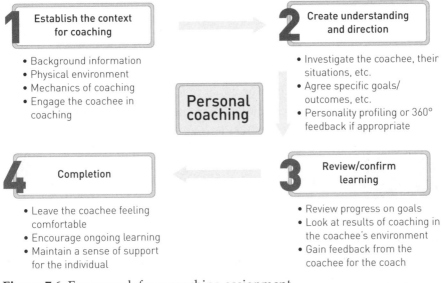

Figure 7.6 Framework for a coaching assignment

Separate selling from coaching

You will notice that the activity of selling coaching services, agreeing fees and payment terms, etc. does not form part of the coaching framework here. This is because selling coaching as a service would normally happen before any coaching session takes place. As much as possible, the coach should endeavour to keep any conversations to negotiate fees or services separate from actual coaching conversations. The coach and the coachee might struggle to concentrate on coaching goals and objectives if they have just been agreeing details relating to money or conditions of a contract.

When coaching in business, financial considerations rarely intrude on the coaching relationship. The individual enlisting the coach's services is often different from the person receiving them. For example, an HR or training manager might easily purchase coaching services for senior managers within the organization. Consequently, all matters of a financial nature will normally remain separate from the actual coaching sessions.

The order of coaching stages/activities

The sequence of coaching stages as shown in Figure 7.6 is based on what seems to make sense, but it is not what always happens. After all, a coach might decide to establish ways that the coachee can obtain further support for their learning from the very first session. While this normally is part of closure activity, it can also be valuable to promote from the outset.

Please note that one stage or activity does not necessarily equal one coaching session. For example, the initial coaching session will see the coach working on engaging the coachee's commitment, plus activities related to understanding the coachee and their current goals.

Checklist **How much structure do I need?**

Here are questions that a coach might consider to decide how much structure is needed:

Q What do I already know of the objectives for this coaching assignment?

Q How many coaching sessions will there be with this person and over what duration, e.g. five sessions over six months?

Q Where will the coaching take place?

Q Who is the true sponsor of this assignment – how should I involve them?

Q Is anyone else involved in this assignment – how should I involve them?

Q How long should/can each session last?

Q What experience of coaching or training might this person have had previously?

For example, if an individual has no experience of either coaching or training, I might choose to spend a little more time explaining coaching, or have them read an overview of coaching as preparation. Or, if they have had personal training or coaching before, I'd want to ask them about that. Then we could acknowledge any differences we might expect from the coaching approach I'm using.

Chapter summary | **Coaching assignment: structure and process**

Any coaching assignment benefits from some advance preparation by the coach. For some assignments, that demands a fairly rigorous assessment of the nature of and objectives for the relationship. The coach may decide on formal checkpoints or reviews, use of 360° feedback, shadowing in the workplace, etc. All of this must be planned for and organized.

For other assignments, it simply means thinking through some options, looking at the general nature of the situation and staying open and flexible as to how to progress the coaching sessions. In the end there's no right or wrong, only choices to be made. What's important is that a coach makes that choice in the knowledge of their options and the potential outcomes involved.

A well-structured coaching assignment has many benefits. By spending a little more time planning how you want your assignment to work, you can increase not only your enjoyment, but your effectiveness as well.

chapter

8

Emotional maturity and coaching

One of the benefits of effective coaching over time is the overall development of a coachee's emotional maturity. This chapter will explain the term 'emotional maturity' and its fundamental link to coaching. It will also consider how we can develop emotional maturity as coaches; for if our coaching conversations are supporting change for others, then our own emotional maturity is a constant enabler of that change to happen.

What is emotional maturity?

Emotional maturity relates to our capacity to deal with our emotions. Our ability to interpret emotions, express emotions and 'let go' of emotions are all functions of our emotional maturity. When we are able to do this effectively, we are described as emotionally mature. More generally, our maturity is our mastery of the skills of 'life', e.g. our ability to create conditions of happiness, success and fulfilment. It is demonstrated in how we think, what we choose to believe and what we ultimately do as a result of that.

Our emotional maturity (or lack of) is often demonstrated by our manner or moods, as well as our behavioural responses. Table 8.1 illustrates how we might describe ourselves when we are being either mature or immature.

Table 8.1 Indicators of maturity and immaturity

Indication of maturity	Indication of less maturity
We are able to stay generally calm and relaxed. We can be flexible in attitude and approach. We are typically less defensive.	We are uptight or tense more of the time. We have difficulty being flexible, perhaps seeming rigid. We can appear defensive.
We take responsibility for own self and own circumstances.	We blame others for our problems or situations, refusing to acknowledge our own influence in situations.
We have an appetite for learning, we evolve through our situations. We seek alternative views and information.	We appear resistant or slow to learn, either by rejecting new ideas, or refusing to consider alternatives. We rarely change attitudes or behaviour over time.

Our good humour is never far away, we can laugh at ourselves as well as our circumstances. We are comfortable with our self.	We use less humour, or perhaps only direct humour outwards. We find personal embarrassment very difficult to cope with. We are more self-conscious, or less comfortable with our self.
We have a 'live and let live' approach to other people. We rarely criticize others.	We may take issue when people don't think and act in the same way as we do. We criticize others frequently.
We are able to deal with life's difficulties and setbacks, perhaps by expressing disappointment and moving on.	We struggle to cope with disappointment, failure or setback. We may get 'stuck' in the negative emotions of a situation, which inhibits our progress forward.
We are generally easy to deal with on a personal level. We build and maintain relationships easily.	We can be 'difficult' to get along with, e.g. people may describe us as 'high-maintenance'.
We have learned optimism as something which sustains us through life. For example, we look for opportunity because we believe it exists.	We are determinedly pessimistic, sometimes refusing to acknowledge potential. We can sometimes 'filter out' or miss opportunity through an assumption it doesn't exist.

This is obviously an incomplete list, and it is important to recognize that we do not have to occupy one fixed place: sometimes we are relaxed and resourceful; sometimes we are uptight and critical. To be an effective coach, we want our general levels of emotional maturity in most circumstances to stay healthy. By 'healthy' we mean that our thoughts and behaviours create a generally constructive effect over time.

Before we begin to help support the success and fulfilment in others, we need to consider our own emotional maturity. The questions overleaf will help your own reflection, before we look at the topic more closely.

Try it yourself	Where can you improve your emotional maturity?

Answer the following questions for yourself. Then get someone who you know really well and whose judgement you value to answer them about you. Compare your answers and reflect on the differences.

Q How self-aware are you?

Q How well do you express and deal with your emotions?

Q How well do you handle yourself in difficult situations?

Q How good are you at relating to other people?

Q How well do you get along with other people?

Q How effective are you at influencing others?

Q How much do you operate from a principle of interdependency?*

What's in a name?

Although I prefer the term emotional maturity, it is important to mention that the same concept is also known as 'emotional intelligence', as formed by psychologists John Mayer and Peter Salovey. In a similar way to the assessment of IQ (intelligence quotient), emotional intelligence can be measured to produce a score known as EQ (emotional quotient). The studies to distinguish emotional intelligence, to measure it and to understand it have created a wealth of information and the body of research in this area is now extensive. If you are interested in the formative work, look for titles by Daniel Goleman, including *Emotional Intelligence* and *Social Intelligence*. Alternatively, as a taster, try *The Emotional Intelligence Quick Book* by Travis Bradberry and Jean Greaves.

The value of emotional maturity

We are all aware that our intelligence (IQ) has an impact on our ability to be successful in life. Yet research suggests that IQ might actually account for just 20 per cent of your career success. The rest is down to your basic

*When we are interdependent, we are effective by working *with* other people. Instead of being dependent or independent, we view ourselves as part of a system.

personality (preferences, attitudes, postures, etc.) and, of course, your emotional maturity.

Studies into EQ show that our level of emotional maturity will have more impact on our success and fulfilment than our IQ. This is great news because, although personality and IQ remain pretty fixed over time, our emotional maturity is something we can continually work on to develop and improve. A simple way to do this is to focus on the four key 'skills of life' that make up emotional maturity, namely: how self-aware you are; how you manage yourself in situations; how much you understand others; and how you good you are at building effective relationships with others.

Our emotions: what are you feeling – and why?

Emotional maturity relates to our ability to process our experiences, our emotions and our learning. When we have this maturity we are able to distinguish our emotions and express them appropriately. This obviously relies on our ability to recognize 'what's going on'.

> To go through life not dealing with emotions may mean that emotions deal with you.

Our emotions are not always easy to recognize. Sometimes it is as simple as noticing 'I'm a bit fed up about this really', while more significant feelings may take more thought in order to understand them properly, e.g. 'I should be delighted with this job offer, but somehow I'm not'. Sometimes you'll consider your feelings on your own and sometimes you'll decide to share how you're feeling, e.g. with people around you. It is a symptom of less mature people that they often get 'stuck' in emotions; for example, they stay angry so that 'anger' is never far away and they lose their temper easily. By learning to acknowledge our emotions and express them, even just to ourselves, we can release them and free ourselves to experience something different.

To go through life not dealing with emotions may mean that emotions deal with you. In a mild way it may simply be that we 'redirect' emotions that we have suppressed from elsewhere, such as staying tolerant during a difficult day at work and then going home and 'taking it out' on our partners, children or pets. This is probably 'healthier' than never expressing frustration at

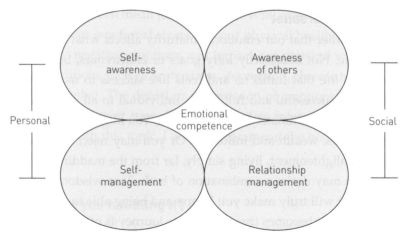

Figure 8.1 The four elements of emotional competence (with acknowledgement to Daniel Goleman)

someone takes your parking space just as you were about to pull into it you may just explode. I would offer that we are all capable of maturity and we are all capable of immaturity.

I've mentioned briefly how emotional maturity can be good for the coach and also good for the coachee. For the coach, emotional maturity gives stability to their decisions and reflections, making them more effective in their role. For the coachee, the development of emotional maturity will allow them to deal with future situations, long after the initial situation that required a coaching relationship has been dealt with. Let's look at each area of competence with these two outcomes in mind.

Emotional competence: self-awareness

This first competence is summed up by the phrase 'know thyself'. It relates to your ability to accurately understand yourself either in the immediate moment or in general, e.g. your ability to interpret and describe your feelings accurately. This could enable you to give an accurate response to the question – how do you feel right now? Or, more generally, how are you feeling about a certain subject, such as your career, your social life, a certain relationship, etc.? It is reflected in our knowledge of ourselves, from our strengths to our weaknesses, our likes and our dislikes, our features and our faults.

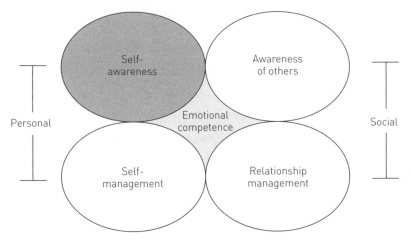

Figure 8.2 Emotional competence: self-awareness

Self-awareness: the link to the coach

As a good coach, you need to constantly develop your own level of self-awareness if you are to be effective. Your ability to express yourself clearly, make decisions and know your own mind all demand you be self-aware. Within coaching sessions, your ability to stay flexible is also related to your own awareness. For example, in a session, your self-awareness will help you understand what you are feeling, e.g. 'I'm nervous – I need to relax'. That's pretty obvious to most of us. But it may be more subtle, e.g. 'I'm being controlling, I need to listen more'. Many of the barriers to coaching we mentioned in Chapter 5 require self-awareness to avoid them, such as 'playing fix-it' or 'strategizing'. If you don't know you are doing those things, how can you stop doing them? The other reason for a coach needing to be self-aware is so that they can be more appreciative of the effect they have on their situations and conversations. Self-awareness will also inform us of our strengths, weaknesses and development needs. The questions below will help you consider this area further:

Try it yourself   **How self-aware are you?**

Answer the following questions for yourself. Then get someone who you know really well and whose judgement you value to answer them about you. If you have someone you've been coaching already, it might be a valuable way of getting some feedback. Compare your answers and reflect on the differences.

Q What are my strengths?

Q What is it that people really value me for?

Q What are my weaknesses, what do I need to get better at?

Q How do people experience me generally, i.e. how might they describe me during coaching sessions?

Q How am I different when I'm under pressure, e.g. during interactions or conversations with others?

Q What three things could I stop doing that would make me more effective?

Q What three things do I need to start doing, or do more often?

Of course, when you lack self-awareness it can work in different directions. You may believe you're better at something than you are, or not realize that actually you're very talented. Be open to the possibility of both!

Developing self-awareness

Ways to increase your self-awareness include:

→ To complete a personality profiling exercise yourself, e.g. Myers–Briggs, Belbin, the Enneagram, DISC, etc. – there are many. Be sure to have your profile explained by someone who is able to help you get the most from that process, e.g. a qualified practitioner.

→ To seek feedback on a regular basis, e.g. from clients, colleagues and other important relationships. But remember, feedback is just another person's perception, it is no more valid than your own perception: what you choose to do with the information is up to you. What's valuable is the additional information.

→ To attend developmental courses that will help you reflect on both how you are now and how you might be. I encourage you to choose courses that intrigue you, interest you and that you believe will have a positive impact on who you are.

→ To keep a learning diary. This can be a powerful learning tool over time. Write a few pages of reflection on a regular basis, to help you focus on your experiences, thoughts and feelings. Notice how your natural attention and behavioural responses can be shaped by this simple habit of writing.

➡ To read books and material that relate to practical psychology or human behaviour. Again, choose titles that you are naturally interested in as a way of enjoying this process. Reading is another activity that causes us to reflect. Reading also helps us view ourselves objectively in comparison to the thoughts and ideas we are being offered. Over time, our self-awareness increases. For a recommended reading list, see www.starrconsulting.co.uk.

Self-awareness: the link to the coachee

As a coach, self-awareness is something you are nurturing and encouraging in the people you are coaching. By the process of enquiry, exploration and challenge we are stimulating increased awareness in the coachee. That self-awareness may include what they really think, how they really feel or what their true values in a situation are. For example, when you ask someone 'What's really important to you about this situation?' the answer the coachee gives may have previously lain buried under a stack of other information or emotion. This is when you might see a coachee struggle to answer your question. So we must give the coachee time and space to consider what they really think. Then the thoughts and feelings they surface will help both their sense of clarity and also their self-awareness in relationship to the situation.

> **We must give the coachee time and space to consider what they really think.**

As you work with a coachee over several sessions, their overall self-awareness tends to improve. For example, they might shift from feeling that they have few development needs, to realizing that there's quite a lot they can get better at. Alternatively, they may begin to appreciate some of the finer qualities and talents they have. The ways in which effective coaching raises a coachee's self-awareness include:

➡ Through the process of enquiry into what the coachee thinks, the coachee realizes what they really think (rather than what they've been saying automatically). For example, a quick response of 'Oh, I'm not really worried about the changes at work' becomes 'Actually there is quite a lot about it that's an issue for me'.

→ As the coach uses tools of summary, reflection and feedback, the coachee gains a fresh perspective on themselves. For example, the coach reflects 'You're spending a lot of time describing the problem, but appear reluctant to make a decision – what's causing that?' Over time the coachee may realize a tendency to procrastinate, as a way of avoiding the tougher challenge of productive action.

→ Through the experience of being coached, the coachee realizes a better appreciation of who they are, who they are not and what they are capable of. For example, prior to coaching, the coachee may never have envisaged themselves as someone who might enjoy being self-employed. And they might be even more reluctant to imagine they could ever be very successful as a self-employed person. Or vice versa, that they might return to an employed status and actually enjoy that even more than being a lone operator.

The early stages of the coaching assignment structure in Chapter 7 are designed to accelerate self-awareness, through the use of tools such as personality profiling and feedback. The tools of profiling and feedback help the coachee to appreciate different views of themselves, which all help build a fuller picture of who they are, and who they might become.

Emotional competence: self-management

Self-management is the ability to influence ourselves: to choose our responses and behaviour. This relates to the short term and longer term; for example, your ability to:

→ Make a tough decision and stay with it.

→ To adapt your natural behavior for a 'greater good' e.g. for the longer-term benefit of yourself or others. For instance, staying patient with a naughty child.

→ To do something you don't 'feel' like doing, e.g. say 'no' to a dessert in a restaurant, go for a run when you'd rather watch TV, or stay silent when you'd sooner speak your mind.

Self-management builds on the previous competence of self-awareness perfectly, because it's one thing to be aware of your natural feelings or tendencies, but it is another to be able choose consciously what to do in a situation. Sometimes that means we'll choose to act 'in flow' with our feelings and sometimes it means doing the exact opposite, i.e. what we don't 'feel like' doing.

Self-management: the link to the coach

As a coach, your self-management affects many areas of the quality of service you deliver to your clients. For example, outside of coaching sessions, your ability to influence yourself includes:

⟹ Your basic self-discipline, such as your ability to work to consistent standards and quality, e.g. keeping appointments and agreements, staying focused and organized.

⟹ Your ability to stay resourceful, e.g. your ability to motivate yourself to keep going when things get tough – maybe business isn't booming and you need to stay optimistic and creative.

⟹ Your ability to act on your own decisions and insights, e.g. 'I need to find more work', which means getting into action and contacting people.

⟹ Your ability to handle pressure, e.g. you are really busy and you need to find ways to accommodate all the demands upon you.

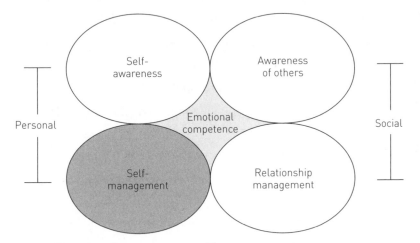

Figure 8.3 Emotional competence: self-management

➡ Over time, your ability to develop character traits that you value, such as patience, tolerance, humour or joyfulness (sometimes being happy is just a question of practice).

Inside coaching sessions, as a coach, the ability to influence ourselves enables the following:

➡ To stay focused on the coaching conversation, e.g. to maintain concentration even through a long session.

➡ To avoid displaying inappropriate characteristics to the coachee, e.g. frustration, nervousness, boredom.

➡ To avoid some of the barriers to effective coaching, e.g. talking too much, poor listening, seeking the 'perfect solution'.

➡ To display characteristics you know will be supportive of your coaching ability, e.g. patience, flexibility, non-attachment to your own ideas or views, openness, warmth, generosity.

➡ To develop yourself as a better coach, e.g. respond to feedback, learn from mistakes, push yourself to try new things, etc.

Try it yourself	Where do you need to work at self-management?	

Answer the following questions for yourself. Then get someone who you know really well and whose judgement you value to answer them about you. Compare your answers and reflect on the differences.

Q What were the three things you identified in the previous list of questions that you wanted to *stop doing*?

Q What is it going to take for you to stop doing those?

Q What were the three things you identified that you want to do *more of* to improve your effectiveness?

Q What is it going to take for you to do those three things more often?

Q If you decided you wanted those two sets of three things as goals – how likely would you be to reach them?

Self-management: the link to the coachee

For the coachee, being coached will often increase their own ability to be self-managing around areas they want to improve. Just the simple act of focusing on issues, deciding on solutions and making the commitment to take action between sessions helps. We might call the experience of being coached in this way 'motivational'. What we're referring to is an increased sense of wanting to act, perhaps against some of our more usual tendencies. Also, when we fail to act upon the insights and decisions we surface during coaching, our coach can support us to overcome unseen barriers to progress.

Perhaps we've decided we need reshape our approach to our work in order to create more free time. We decide we spend too long talking about what we're going to do instead of simply getting on and doing it. Sometimes that discussion is with other people; sometimes it's simply discussion with ourselves (procrastination). After our initial coaching session we attack the situation with relish, making decisions, getting into action and staying in action. The initial results are tremendous. Our personal productivity and effectiveness go up, while our time spent at work goes down. Success! But by our third coaching session, we find that the situation has returned pretty much to the original situation. We seem to be 'bogged down' by a mountain of tasks and feel like we are pretty much out of control again. Our work hours are back to their original length and we're frustrated with ourselves. Here's how the coach can help:

➡ The coach can act as a barometer or measure of the coachee's progress over time. By creating a constant focus on progress, the coach keeps productivity in the awareness of the coachee. By celebrating success, the coach encourages further success. By gently surfacing the issue of lack of progress, the coach is another source of commitment to the coachee's goal.

➡ The coach can explore what is causing the apparent 'regression', i.e. surface other values or motivations affecting the coachee's behaviour. For example, maybe the seduction of the old 'comfort zone' of spending time in thought or discussion about tasks is too easy to return to. Or maybe the coachee struggles to maintain concentration for long periods of time and is fatigued by the process.

➡ The coach can revisit the original benefits of improving productivity or reminding them of the cost of poor productivity. By increasing the coachee's awareness of both the 'cost' of poor productivity and the benefits of great productivity, the coachee's natural motivation is encouraged.

➡ The coach can help find ways to return to a productive state: perhaps ask the coachee how they might regain focus when they begin to procrastinate, or help them find a natural balance, e.g. the coachee may decide they'd prefer to finish one task and then take some kind of brief rest or reward.

➡ Over time, the coachee learns what drives them, what motivates them and what it's going to take for them to be more powerful at managing themselves in their work. Through intention, commitment and practice, they develop the 'muscle' of self-management.

Emotional competence: awareness of others

Awareness of others refers to our ability to observe other people and appreciate what is going on with them. This competence is linked to our ability to empathize (empathy is different from sympathy – see Chapter 5, 'Barriers to coaching') and demands being able to understand other people's emotional states and process that information appropriately. It can be quite a sophisticated skill. For example, to notice that someone is angry because they are shouting is fairly easy. But to notice someone is angry when they are apparently 'not angry' (e.g. quietly nodding, even smiling) is more demanding of us.

Awareness of others: the link to the coach

When coaching, your awareness of others will assist your ability to relate to them. Your ability to notice and accurately interpret signals and behavioural cues from the coachee is significant; for if you cannot create and demonstrate understanding, you are less likely to build rapport or relationship. Imagine it is your first coaching session and you completely mismatch the coachee's emotional state. Maybe they are cautious, mistrusting and fairly cynical about the process, but maybe your focus and attention is on 'getting started' and so you begin describing the coaching process, gathering initial

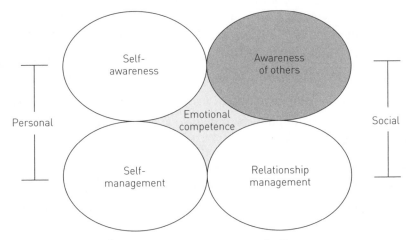

Figure 8.4 Emotional competence: awareness of others

data from them, etc. While you are focused on the 'task', you miss signs of their emotional state, i.e. they are cautious and slightly worried. This would have been more noticeable if your attention was more on them than on what you were doing. Maybe there were behavioural clues that you missed, e.g. their clipped, business-like tonality; their expression was watchful; they were fiddling with a pen, etc.

It's difficult to describe how anyone displays an emotional state like 'worried' – we all do that differently. But to notice what happens with other people and be able to interpret them as an individual is a skill you already have. Not only that, it is a skill we can all hone further. For a coach, the benefits of this are tremendous: when you can judge or 'read' people more accurately, you are able to communicate with them so much more easily. Through your ability to empathize and relate to others in their own terms, you gain more access to their world. Here are some of the benefits when you develop your awareness of others:

➡ You are able to interpret their thoughts and feelings quickly and respond in direct relationship to them, e.g. they are not comfortable with this/they are comfortable with this.

➡ You are able to demonstrate understanding, which helps build rapport, trust and openness, e.g. 'I wonder if that's frustrating you?' When we do that accurately, the coachee feels 'understood'.

➡ As real understanding is surfaced more quickly, the direction of the conversation can be navigated more accurately and effectively. This leads to fewer 'blind alleys'. For example, 'OK, it seems like that's something that's important to you, can we explore that more?'

➡ You are able to acknowledge and respect the coachee's thoughts and feelings, perhaps adapting your own style accordingly, e.g. increasing or decreasing pace, taking a break if they appear fatigued, etc.

➡ When you are able to interpret how someone is feeling, you are more able to help them deal with that feeling. For example, if you suspect your coachee is really worried about something, you can express that and look at ways to support them with that.

| Try it yourself | Where do you need to work at your awareness of others? | |

Answer the following questions for yourself. Then get someone whose judgement you trust and value to answer them about you. If you have someone you've been coaching already, it might be a good way of getting some feedback. Compare your answers and reflect on the differences.

Q During conversations, how well are you able to interpret the emotional state of the person you are talking to?

Q How well do you 'read' people, i.e. gauge them correctly, interpret their meaning, etc.?

Q During conversations, how much of your attention is focused on the words or content of the discussion, i.e. comprehension and how much is focused on the person themselves, e.g. their expressions, tonality, how they 'seem'?

Q How quickly can you gain a true understanding of someone, e.g. what's important to them, what's not important to them, their temperament, typical attitudes and behaviours, etc.?

Q How accurately do you empathize with others, e.g. demonstrate an understanding of how things are for them or how they are feeling?

Developing awareness of others

Judging ourselves in relation to our competence is obviously subjective. What is useful is that we create attention on the topic and develop our intention to improve our competence in this area. In coaching, ways in which we can develop our awareness of others include:

➡ Write a 'reflection' note after your coaching sessions, focusing on what was happening with your coachee. For example, try to guess their 'emotional journey' during the session: perhaps they arrived calm and engaged, surfaced some frustration, expressed discontent, got clearer, left brighter, etc.

➡ Engage in the process of being 'supervised' by an experienced coach. Tell them that one of your goals includes improving in developing this awareness. Work on the subject together. The other coach will help you judge your ability to read or 'calibrate' the people you are working with.

➡ Acquire the knowledge or qualification of an assessment tool, which will help you notice and interpret the behaviours of other people more accurately. Something built on robust research and based on known character types is particularly useful. For example, Myers–Briggs, LAB Profiling (Language and Behaviour), DISC. By having a thorough knowledge of an objective model, you will again develop your attention. In addition, you may become more skilled at predicting other behaviour or noticing important 'clues' or responses. As a cautionary note, ineffective use of these tools may do the exact opposite and have you jumping to hasty conclusions!

Awareness of others: the link to the coachee

Within coaching, the coachee can be encouraged to increase their awareness of others. There are many different ways we can do this, see overleaf:

An effective coach will often encourage a coachee to pause and reflect on what is happening with other people, either by enquiring into the coachee's awareness of others, or by challenging them. For example, if a coachee protests that someone is 'bullying' them, a coach may offer an alternative perspective, e.g. 'Maybe they simply aren't aware of how you feel ...' or

Objective/Purpose	Question
Encourage the coachee to reflect on someone's thoughts or feelings in the past.	'What was Sally feeling/thinking at that point?'
Help the coachee develop their ability to interpret the responses of others.	'How did you know that you'd upset Sally?' or 'When have you seen her do that before?'
Reflect on the views of others.	'If Sally were here in the room now and I asked them what they really thought – what do you think she'd say?'
Reflect on the values or motivations of others.	'What's really important to her about this situation do you think?'
Help the coachee consider a future event in the same way.	'How might Sally react to that offer do you think?'

'How aware are they of your feelings about this?' Over time, it becomes more natural for the coachee to consider the thoughts, views and feelings of others. During coaching, they have learnt the skill and also the value of doing it.

Emotional competence: relationship management

This fourth competence brings together the previous three by building upon them. Relationship management refers to social abilities such as building relationships, harmonizing relationships and sustaining relationships over time. It affects our ability to communicate clearly with others; collaborate with others; negotiate; deal with conflict; motivate and manage others, etc. When we demonstrate this competence, the other three competences are brought into play. Our ability to remain self-aware, self-managing and aware of others governs our ability to influence those around us, whether that's getting someone to make you a cup of coffee or help you win the hottest deal in town. And your ability to 'manage others' may not be as obvious as 'getting someone to do something'. It may be how people feel about you, or understand and appreciate you. Relationship management describes how you are able to engage with and interact with others.

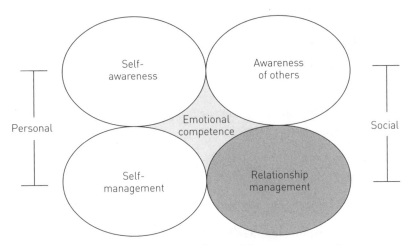

Figure 8.5 Emotional competence: relationship management

Relationship management: the link to the coach

Any successful coach needs to be good at interacting with others. Whether employed, self-employed or a volunteer, we rest on our ability to engage others in what we do and have them be supportive of us. If we are to build a successful coaching practice, we need to build and foster goodwill within our business relationships. For example, we need others:

➡ To listen to us as we explain our services.

➡ To choose us over any other coach.

➡ To value us and recognize the quality of service we deliver.

➡ To encourage us to succeed, perhaps advising us, or offering constructive feedback.

➡ To stay committed to use us as a coach over time (even if we make mistakes).

➡ To recommend us to others and champion our services.

In coaching sessions our ability to interact with the coachee is at the heart of an effective session. Just a few of the benefits include:

⇒ The coachee engages with us and commits to our coaching relationship.

⇒ The coachee appreciates what we do and understands the value we add to them.

⇒ Our relationship with the coachee over time is warm and enduring.

⇒ The coachee trusts us and feels they can be open with us.

⇒ The coachee understands us, and we create clarity between us.

⇒ The coachee will work with us, as a team, to make the coaching successful, e.g. tolerate mistakes, or temporary lapses in quality, due to a broader appreciation of the overall quality we deliver.

⇒ The coachee is more motivated to keep agreements between sessions, as a reflection of their commitment to the coach.

⇒ The coachee becomes an advocate of the coach and their business.

Of course, an important benefit of the above list is for the coachee. Ultimately, if the above is true, then the coachee will gain more from the coaching. Their commitment to the relationship over time will increase their investment and effort. The results they produce are likely to improve and the rewards they reap will mirror their own efforts.

Try it yourself	Where do you need to work at your influence of others?

Answer the following questions for yourself. If you have someone whose opinion you value, maybe ask that person to answer them for you as well. Compare and reflect on the answers afterwards.

Q How easily do you build new relationships?

Q How good are you at sustaining relationships over time?

Q How good are you at handling conflict?

Q Can you naturally get other people to support you?

Q How good are you at working within teams?

Q How good at influencing others are you? For example, if you make a request of someone – will they do it for you?

Q How good are you at negotiation?

When we consider these types of questions, we obviously need a good level of self-awareness. That's why it is often helpful to ask the views of a valued colleague or friend.

Developing relationship management

Here are some ways to increase our ability in this area:

⇒ Learn more about humans and how we interact, e.g. principles of communication, or motivation, or relationships. Take more time to consider what's 'behind' our interactions and consider yourself in relationship to others. Find books or courses that interest you, e.g. negotiation skills, conflict resolution, influencing skills, or perhaps a broader study of psychology.

⇒ Seek regular feedback on how people experience you, to appreciate better the perceptions you create with others, based on your interactions with them.

⇒ Consider two relationships you have had in the past. Pick a 'good' relationship and one where you have experienced issues. Find a way of reflecting upon them that helps you appreciate a broader perspective if possible. For example, write about the relationship, the nature of that relationship, how it developed, what caused it to develop in that way, etc. Try 'standing in the other person's shoes' where possible, to gain a more objective view. Try telling the 'story' from someone else's perspective. Get help from someone you trust if that feels appropriate. Reflect on yourself in the two scenarios, e.g. how were your thoughts on behaviour different in each relationship? Consider how you were around each person and how that affected things. What would you do differently next time?

Relationship management: the link to the coachee

An effective coach will use techniques of enquiry, summary, reflection and feedback to encourage the coachee to improve their ability to relate to and influence others. The ways we might do this include:

⇒ Help the coachee cope with other people's reactions more effectively, e.g. 'If your customer is frustrated by the news, how might you deal with that?'

➡ Help the coachee plan to negotiate, e.g. 'What is going to convince them do you think?' or 'What's most important to them?'

➡ Help the coachee maintain commitment from others, e.g. 'What do you need to do to sustain this relationship over time?'

➡ Help the coachee to recognize their patterns of behaviour, e.g. 'Have you had a situation like this before?' or 'How similar is this relationship to the one we discussed earlier?'

➡ Help the coachee influence constructively, e.g. 'How will you gain the team's support for your plans?' or 'How will you sustain support for your plans over time?'

➡ Help the coachee deal with conflict, e.g. 'What caused the argument?' and 'What options do you have now?'

➡ Encourage ongoing learning, e.g. 'What decisions are you making about your leadership style?' or 'How does your style of leadership need to develop going forward?'

Chapter summary **Emotional maturity and coaching**

Emotional maturity refers to our ability to deal with emotions, e.g. interpret emotions, express emotions and process emotions. More broadly, our emotional maturity helps us cope with life. Our ability to stay resourceful, to manage ourselves, to build and harmonize successful relationships are all life skills that are embraced under the heading of emotional maturity. Our emotional maturity will have a major impact on our ability to create the conditions of success, happiness and fulfilment over time. Another common term used for this concept is 'emotional intelligence'.

Signs of emotional maturity, or immaturity, can be reflected in our typical behavioural responses. Instinctively, when we describe someone's behaviour as 'mature' or 'immature' we are often referring to their apparent levels of emotional maturity. Like intelligence (IQ), we can measure emotional maturity (EQ). Unlike our rating of

IQ, emotional maturity is something we can nurture and develop over time.

Emotional maturity has four main areas of competence:

➡ Self-awareness.

➡ Self-management.

➡ Awareness of others.

➡ Relationship management.

The first two skills are in the area of personal competence, while the second two skills are described as social competences. It is our mastery of all areas that develops our overall emotional maturity. And it is our emotional maturity that enables us to foster and encourage maturity in others.

Emotional maturity is a requirement of any coach as it impacts on our ability to be effective as a coach. Effective coaching encourages self-development of the coachee, improving their emotional maturity. The benefits of increased maturity for the coachee include an increased ability to create the conditions of success and fulfilment. As the coachee learns these 'skills of life' they can continue to use them long after the coaching has been completed.

9

Becoming a coach

There are many reasons why you may be reading this book. Your reasons may include a consideration of coaching as a career (a way of providing income), or it may be that you want to add coaching to what you already do. If either of these reasons relate to you, then this next chapter is designed to help. I'd like to offer you some questions and perspectives that might assist with your decision to become a coach and also how you make that happen. The questions that follow are designed to help you 'coach yourself' to become clearer about your situation and what changes you may need to make. This chapter will focus mainly on your internal thought processes, so, to gain the most benefit, I encourage you to work through the groups of questions or 'mini-assignments' in a calm state of mind. That might mean going somewhere quiet, switching off the telephone and giving yourself the gift of enough time and space to consider your thoughts carefully. You will get maximum value by writing your answers down. It's always tempting just to read through the questions and form mental answers, isn't it? That's fine but you are likely to get less of a result – you will know what's best for you.

What this chapter will not do is tell you how to write your business plan, what to charge or how to agree charging mechanisms. Our focus here will be on whether coaching is right for you and making the most of your internal sense of how to move forward. For those of you interested in the commercial elements of coaching, such as marketing, money management, etc., I'd encourage you to find a specific title on this topic, such as *Getting Started in Personal and Executive Coaching* by Chris Stout and Stephen Fairley.

What do we mean – 'become a coach'?

First, let's begin by saying that you don't have to declare yourself as a coach to the world in order to engage in the activity of coaching other people. However, if you want to be frequently engaged in coaching, as an activity, then you will benefit from having your own personal sense of 'being a coach'. It's as though part of your identity (who you think you are) is a coach. Over time, this aspect of who you are develops; you know you're a coach and for you to coach others is a natural form of self-expression. This self-concept will sit alongside other aspects of your identity, e.g. a mother, father, partner, financial advisor, police officer, doctor, etc. When part of your identity includes being 'a coach', it will strengthen and support your ability to coach others. During coaching conversations, your confidence and natural ability is what sustains you, as well as skills, principles and operating beliefs, of course. When you have the inner sense of alignment that comes with being a coach, your confidence, your surety and your energy will all flow more naturally. The questions that follow may help you begin to notice the part of your nature that can be called a coach. Please reflect upon, and then write answers to, each question. Why not keep them to read in a few years' time?

Try it yourself **Becoming a coach**

Q How have you been drawn towards coaching? For example, what are the events, people, or circumstances that have brought you to this point?

Q How would you describe coaching? For example, what difference does it make to people? Why is it valuable? How do you feel about it?

Q What will becoming 'a coach' do for you?

OK, so that's got you thinking. Please know that, whatever you write, it is relevant and useful. The 'right' answers are whatever is true for you. Pause a while and look at your answers before continuing.

So you want to be a coach?

There are many reasons why you might consider becoming a coach. While no reason is right or wrong, some reasons are better than others. For example, if you've recently quit your graphic design job in anger and are looking to get rid of having a boss, you may want to think your decision through a little more. If, however, you've felt drawn to coaching for some time, find yourself naturally supportive of others and find the idea of becoming a coach both interesting and challenging, then the path to becoming a coach might be more in alignment with your values and goals. But not necessarily! The following questions are intended to help with your thoughts and decision making. Please reflect upon, and then write answers to, the questions overleaf.

Try it yourself | **Your values and goals**

Q Think about your previous occupations, e.g. jobs or roles that you've had. Think about what you've enjoyed, been good at, not enjoyed, not been good at, etc.

Q For you to enjoy and be fulfilled by your work, what has to be true about the work that you do? For example: it's creative, it's got variety, travel, etc.

Q What are the special talents you think you offer? What abilities do you have?

Q What do people really value you for?

Q Spend a few minutes imagining yourself as a coach: either as part of what you already do, or as something different. As you think about how that might be, what might you be doing, seeing, thinking, etc.? How does it make you feel?

Q How will things be different for you when you're a coach? Think about your day-to-day life, the effect on people around you, etc.

Q How do you feel about becoming a coach now?

These questions are intended to increase your level of self-awareness, and have you blend your experience to your expectations. As you reflect on your answers, you will, it is hoped, see yourself in relationship to this decision, e.g. is coaching a good way forward for me now? Coaching as a profession needs to align with your values, your talents and your interests. If coaching contradicts what's important to you, then you need to consider what you want to do with that lack of balance. For example, if you love working in teams, can you still do that? Or if what people value you for is as an 'expert' and you *love* being 'the expert', you may want to reflect on how becoming a coach will impact on that. Let's continue with the process.

Paid coach or unpaid coach?

In the process towards becoming a coach, you have several decisions to make. These decisions include choosing to make coaching something you receive payment for, or not. Before we consider that further, let's revisit our definition of coaching:

> Coaching is a conversation, or series of conversations, one person has with another. The person who is the coach intends to produce a conversation that will benefit the other person, the coachee, in a way that relates to the coachee's learning and progress.

I know you'll have some life experiences that fit into the above description, where you have positively influenced someone through conversation and they have valued you for that. So clearly it's possible to 'coach' others without giving up anything else that you do, or making any radical life changes. Maybe you simply want to develop your ability to adopt a coaching style of response more often. Remember, coaching can be both a distinct activity and also a style of behaviour. For you, becoming a coach may simply mean shaping your general day-to-day behaviour using coaching principles and guidelines. Maybe you will develop a tendency to listen to people more deeply, use purpose-based questions, offer reflective feedback more often, etc. And these forms of coaching may happen while you're employed in a job that's unrelated to coaching, or maybe you're not employed at all.

Coaching can be both a distinct activity and also a style of behaviour.

For example, you may run a small theatre production company: while you're pursuing the business of keeping the theatre running smoothly, you may also be coaching your colleagues as they continue their work around you. In this instance, I would call you a coach, just as I call myself a coach. In addition, while you are running your theatre company, you may choose to hold formal coaching sessions in a quiet setting with people who are happy to receive coaching from you. Those relationships may develop over time and you may enjoy being recognized as that person's 'coach'. It may not say 'coach others' on your job description, but that's not going to inhibit you from doing what you feel is worthwhile. You're choosing to coach anyway; getting on with your everyday life, whilst adopting a coaching approach.

It's a tremendous contribution to make: for in that simple decision to 'be a coach' you are committing to making an ongoing contribution to the people around you. You are making the well-being and development of others important. It's a contribution based on nothing more than a personal sense that it's the best way to be. I often wonder if that's where the potential of coaching really lies: imagine a world where we all encouraged each other to be the best we could be. Using the powerful principles that underpin coaching, we might support each other to do better, be better and create more. What an encouraging world we might live in.

Use the following questions to help you become clearer about the question of becoming a professional coach or a coach who coaches within their current professional occupation:

Try it yourself   **Paid or unpaid coach?**

Q What are your current thoughts and feelings on this? Do you see yourself charging for your coaching or not?

Q If you did want to coach professionally (with charges), what changes would you have to make to your working life to allow that to happen?

Q Take a moment to imagine choosing to coach people professionally – how does that feel?

Professional coaching – 'just coach' or 'coach and also …'?

You may have decided that you want to become a professional coach. That is, someone who performs coaching for part or all of their income. So now your decisions include whether to be a full-time coach (just coach) or a coach that practises coaching as just one part of the paid work that you do (coach and also …). I'd like you to consider first becoming a coach who also does other things, for I suspect that any professional coach benefits from having a varied career that includes other activities, occupations and work experience. Part of the contribution a coach brings is themselves, their nature and true self. I think as people we are enriched by diversity, or shrunk by stagnation. So it seems healthy to engage in work-related activities that are not coaching. It doesn't have to be a feat of super-human endeavour, just something to broaden your horizons. Maybe you perform coaching during some of your working week and sometimes you help out at the local restaurant. Or maybe in between coaching sessions you design and deliver training, or write music, or sing. Whatever enlivens you will be an asset to your coaching. Here are some potential benefits from thinking more broadly about your involvement as a coach:

→ Coaching people is an intense thing to do that requires recuperation time to enable the coach to stay mentally alert and well-balanced. Doing 'nothing' is one way to help yourself rest and recuperate. Doing something completely different is another way to stay resourceful over time (not better than doing nothing – just different).

→ Any coach benefits from a rich life experience, filled with personal challenges, creative endeavours and collaborations; just as anyone is enriched by such a life. The added benefit for a coach is that they develop a 'broader' viewpoint on the world, which can inform their coaching conversations.

→ A sole focus of one-to-one interaction with others may prove limiting over time, either through lack of personal stimulation, learning or having more varied challenges.

I recognize that some coaches decide that 'only coaching will do' and want to dedicate themselves solely to that task. They commit to build a client base that will sustain both their income and their time. Their sole professional occupation becomes coaching and they spend the majority of their working week in personal coaching sessions. I can imagine it's very possible that for some people that's a perfect choice. If that is you, I wish you luck and good fortune. I'll also observe that such a focused occupation may be very demanding upon you and your system. Sitting in one-on-one sessions concentrating for hours on end can be both draining and dulling for the senses. Of course, it is frequently energizing and rewarding – as usual, the art is in achieving your own balance. Depending on how much you 'put in' to your sessions you may find that repeatedly coaching others may reduce your vibrancy over time. For example, if I were engaged in back-to-back coaching sessions, each day for a five-day week, I'm not sure how I would ensure full competency right through until the final session on Friday. It's not true for everyone, and resilience comes with experience, but you may

259

want to consider yourself first. For example, how will you stay fresh and resourceful for your clients? What do you need to maintain your own sense of balance? Of course, there are ways and I'm sure that successful (happy) full-time coaches have found what works for them. Here are some ways that anyone deciding to 'just coach' may balance any negative effects:

→ Schedule appropriate breaks between sessions, e.g. 15–20 minutes between a two-hour session. If you're coaching all day, make sure you have a lunch break of at least 45 minutes.

→ Reduce your travelling time – especially driving time – as much as possible, e.g. arrange to meet halfway, coach from your home, travel the night before.

→ Consider the benefits of coaching supervision, e.g. getting your own expert mentor or coach to talk through your assignments confidentially, giving you guidance and support with issues or challenges.

→ Maintain a strong focus on your own personal development, e.g. attend courses, seminars, read developmental books.

→ Ensure a healthy work–life balance: rest a lot, play a lot, engage in hobbies or interests that you find relaxing, stimulating, creative, etc.

Interestingly, the above list also provides a great set of principles for anyone, whether we're in the category of 'just coach' or 'coach and also ...'.

What kind of coach are you?

There are many different styles and types of coach. It's important that, over time, you develop your own style and approach to be an authentic expression of you. By authentic I mean that the type of coaching work that you do, and the way that you do it, suits you as a person. If you are going to coach, I would hope that you enjoy it and are good at it. And for you to enjoy and be good at something, that activity will need to blend with your personality and talents. And, of course, when offering or selling your services formally, you will want to distinguish yourself from other coaches. It's important to know what circumstances are best suited to what you offer and what value you will add. Being clear about who you are as a coach will help with both your confidence and also your ongoing success as a coach. When you're describing your coaching services with potential clients you will sound clear and aligned about what you're going to do. That gives your client the assurance that they are in 'safe hands'. And that's one of the main reasons they will buy from you. Obviously your awareness of yourself as a coach will develop over time, as your coaching identity emerges. In the meantime, you'll want to spend a little time constructing your own picture of the type of coaching that might suit you.

Begin from where you are now

In developing this sense of yourself as a coach, I would recommend that the place to begin that journey is from where you already are. In other words, don't look into the distance at some other professional coach and decide you need to model yourself entirely on what they do. Indeed, you may learn from other coaches, but please let any changes you make to your style or approach be something you feel is right for you. For example, you may see another coach accessing lots of government-funded work by coaching young

> Let any changes you make to your style or approach be something you feel is right for you.

people who want to get into full-time employment. If that 'speaks' to you as something you'd love to do, and you feel you've got something to offer those young people, then great. But if in truth you'd be frustrated at the nature of the conversations, or don't relate to the challenges of that community, then perhaps reconsider. Based on your background, what you enjoy and are good at, you may find that there is better work waiting for you. And, of course, in the meantime you might decide to try working with the youngsters – who knows, you could find that actually you enjoy making a difference to them.

Build from what you have now

I sometimes hear from people wanting to 'get into' coaching who are in danger of ignoring all their existing talents and experience, by assuming they need to make radical changes to become a coach, such as change the industry they operate in, or their professional profile in some way. Some people put themselves out of work in order to focus themselves totally on building a coaching profession. It's quite a commitment to make and I'm not qualified to judge the wisdom of that for the individual. What I do try to encourage is that people see the potential of their existing resources, e.g. skills, experience, relationships, network of contacts, etc. I do wonder if sometimes people 'throw the baby out with the bath water' and disregard resources that may form the perfect foundation for them to move forward into coaching. Maybe you're operating in a sales profession, maybe you manage IT projects, or maybe before you had children you worked in recruitment. Look at your existing skills and experience. That's often the best place for yourself as a coach to emerge from. It's also a potential source of immediate work opportunities. Maybe you can coach salespeople. Maybe you can coach other project managers. Or maybe you can find agencies who want some coaching for their recruitment agents. It may be that there are coaching opportunities that are looking you right in the face, if only you stopped searching the horizon!

As before, please take some time to reflect on the following questions, writing down your responses:

Try it yourself   **Your resources**

Q What professional experience do you have? For example: what type of businesses and situations have you worked in?

Q What type of roles have you had? For example: administration, selling, training.

Q What are the common themes that seem to run through your professional experience? For example: my role is often about getting people to work together, or about introducing change, or day-to-day running of small businesses.

Q What other life experience have you had? For example: raising a family, organizing a household, arranging large events. Please think of everything; look in every corner, uncover every formative period of your life.

Q List all the people, companies or communities you know of, who might benefit from your services as a coach. Some people might be potential clients and coachees, others may sponsor your coaching assignments. Think carefully about your existing network of contacts and also those individuals or groups just outside your network.

Q Let's assume that the design of your previous experience provided the perfect foundation on which you're going to build yourself as a coach. How does your experience and skill affect the kind of coach you might be?

Q What kind of coaching would you be good at? For example, what kind of people, with what kind of objectives and goals? In what kind of environment or circumstance?

These questions are intended to help you appreciate all the resources you already have and the opportunity that they create for you now. They are also designed to encourage you to realize how the steps you might take forward can be simple, logical steps, rather than dramatic 'giant' strides. Finally, spend a few minutes reflecting on both your responses to the previous sets of questions and also those on this list. What thoughts are you having now?

Let's also acknowledge that it's not possible to know all the answers. A world of possibility exists in front of you and, of course, there's an element of the unknown that you are venturing into. But I do believe that, as you journey into this uncharted territory, it's useful to remind yourself how capable you already are, and how you may be better prepared for the journey than you perhaps thought.

How do you equip yourself to be a great coach?

When you describe yourself as 'a coach', you need to feel confident and clear that you have authority to declare that to be true. Ultimately, the person who decides if you are fully equipped to begin coaching others (formally or informally) is you. A combination of study and experience will foster your ability as a coach and you need to consider what development path might be best for you.

There is a permanent discussion within the field of coaching that relates to the 'qualification' needed for a person to be able to coach. As yet, no single organization has any universally accepted authority, and I'm not sure if they ever will. There are a few players who appear to be central to the debate. Most seem fairly well-intended, others seem more commercially motivated. Spend a little time surfing the internet and I'm sure you'll find them all.

Personally, I applaud anyone who can help coaches develop high personal standards. I'm less enthusiastic at the idea of the coaching field appearing exclusive and daunting to potential coaches. Ultimately, your reasons for gaining a formal qualification will relate to the benefits of that for you; for example, if you think your clients may want you to have a formal qualification, or if your ability or confidence will increase.

So rather than engage in a discussion of 'What's the best coach training course?' I'd sooner pose the question, 'How are you going to equip yourself to be a great coach?' My question has a different intention and purpose. At this stage in your thinking, I'd encourage you to think of the various considerations that may help you progress. The following questions may take a little more time for you to answer, but I believe you'll find that worthwhile:

Try it yourself **Equipping yourself**

Q What skills do you still feel you need to develop?

➡ Which skills are things you need now? And which can you develop over time?

➡ What are the various options you have to obtain those skills?

Q What further experience do you need?

➡ How could you gain that type of experience? What coaching opportunities are right in front of you?

Q What are the practical 'tools of the trade' you might need?

➡ Personal vision and action plan, descriptions of your services, website, business cards, pricing list, etc. (remember – you decide what you need).

Q What support/advice/challenge do you need going forward?

➡ Who or what do you know of, that might provide the support you seek?

Q How are you going to maintain focus and motivation over time?

➡ Who and what will help you stay on track?

Q What is it going to take before you feel really equipped to coach other people?

➡ For example, a certain number of sessions or assignments, some kind of qualification, a stronger sense of self-belief, etc.

Q How else might you develop yourself as a person, to equip yourself to coach others?

➡ For example, life experiences, self-development courses, specialist study in the type of situations or challenges your coachees may raise with you, etc.

For some people, a training course specifically focused on coaching may be a good idea. But you do have other options. For example, you might study counselling first, or learn more about personality profiling, language patterns, or motivational theory. There are lots of specialist skills that you may feel interested in or drawn to, which might enhance you as a coach. Instead of focusing on skills, you may choose the 'self-development' route, by focusing on yourself as a person: how you think, why you are like you are, how you want to be instead. You may consider getting coached yourself, or studying an area such as NLP (neuro-lingustic programming). Both these routes will help you develop your self, while improving your coaching ability.

This book is obviously intended to equip you and support you as you develop as a coach. You may also find useful resources in the free downloads area of our website: www.starrconsulting.co.uk. Of course, reading will only help you so far and there's no substitute for real coaching. What you will also need is the intention to succeed and the emotional maturity to sustain you through your own personal journey. While my own journey to becoming a coach has been a challenge, it's also been a worthwhile adventure. What's always sustained me is the belief that I am both 'enough' and also still capable of more – and I know that's true for you too.

Chapter summary — Becoming a coach

Anyone who aims to coach others will benefit from a clear sense that part of who they are is a coach. There are different expressions of being a coach, including:

➡ Someone who simply adds coaching as a style of behaviour to their existing occupation or role, i.e. the job they already do.

➡ Someone who wants to perform professional coaching for a living – and have no other paid occupations.

➡ Someone who wants to perform formal coaching sessions and get paid for it, as an additional source of income or service that they offer.

No choice is better than any other. What's important is that you work through the facts of your situation in a way that is logical for you. By surfacing your own thoughts and feelings about the options available to you, you can decide what is best for you.

Too often people disregard all that they already are. So take time to consider what existing resources you have, such as skills, experience, contacts and immediate opportunities to coach. Also reflect upon what resources you may need to create a basis for a successful coaching practice. These resources might include professional tools (website, brochures, etc.) as well as new skills, support from others, or simply more experience of coaching. Whatever you decide, I wish you good fortune.

chapter

10

Summary and close

Key points of learning
Collaborative coaching is an effective, respectful approach

Collaborative coaching is effective because of the underlying principles that support it, namely:

➡ The coachee appreciates being really listened to and the effort the coach makes to understand them.

➡ The relationship is based on equality, which encourages openness and trust. The coach is not claiming to have all the answers and the coachee feels their contribution is valuable.

➡ Insights, perspectives and ideas are highly relevant to the coachee and they relate to them with both ownership and responsibility.

➡ Most ideas and actions come from the coachee, which means responsibility for completing actions also stays with the coachee.

➡ Solutions emerge from the understanding of the person experiencing the situation. As a result, solutions are normally of much higher relevance and effectiveness.

➡ If an idea doesn't get the result the coachee wanted, the coachee still feels ownership of the idea and so will be more willing to work to get a better result.

➡ Thoughts and ideas provoke ongoing learning in the mind of the coachee. Like a pebble thrown into a pond, good coaching will trigger a reaction. Sometimes responses are immediate, whilst others are delayed. Coaching conversations can create benefit long after the session has ended.

By adopting a less directive style of conversation, we focus more on the internal learning processes of the coachee. We respectfully maintain the responsibility of the coachee for their situations and retain a sense of equality within the coaching relationship.

A good coach is defined by the principles they operate from as much as what they actually do

The principles a coach operates from create a foundation for everything they do. The following are key within a collaborative coaching approach:

➡ To maintain a commitment to support the individual.

➡ To build coaching relationships on truth, openness and trust.

➡ To remember that the coachee is responsible for the results they are creating.

➡ To believe that the coachee is capable of much better results than they are currently generating.

➡ To maintain our focus on what the coachee thinks and experiences.

➡ To believe that coachees can generate perfect solutions.

➡ To assume that coaching conversations are based on equality.

Use of these principles can sometimes have more impact than technical skill. For example, operating with a commitment to openness, honesty and trust can often do more for the coaching relationship than conscious rapport-building techniques.

Core skills can be identified and developed

The skills and disciplines needed to be a successful coach do not come naturally to most of us. Instead, they are skills that we learn and develop constantly. The core skills of a collaborative coach are highlighted again in Figure 10.1.

Some coaches have some of these skills naturally, either because of their basic personality, or as a result of previous experiences and learning. Some skills require more technical competence, such as asking questions, and gaining these skills requires a more focused, disciplined approach. Once acquired, these skills must be practised. Many everyday situations present opportunities to develop or maintain these skills, e.g. natural conversations with colleagues or friends.

What a coach doesn't do is often as important as what they do do

Certain behaviours or principles of behaviour form barriers to the development and flow of great coaching conversation. They include:

➡ Talking too much.

➡ Giving too much sympathy.

Figure 10.1 Fundamental coaching skills

⇒ Seeking to control or dominate the conversation.

⇒ Needing to be 'right'.

⇒ Playing 'fix-it'.

⇒ Assuming your experience is relevant.

⇒ Looking for the 'perfect solution'.

⇒ Trying to look good in the conversation.

⇒ Strategizing in the conversation.

⇒ Focusing on what not to do.

Some of these behaviours are simple traps to fall into, for any coach, no matter how experienced they are. Many arise from natural human tendencies such as being enthusiastic or enjoying solving other people's problems. So when we're coaching, we're looking to develop a three-step process:

1 Become aware that we're doing or thinking something that's not working.
2 Acknowledge that – and give it up, i.e. let the thought go.
3 Substitute or refocus with another more effective intention or behaviour.

The coaching path can support most formal coaching conversations

The coaching path can support most typical coaching conversations, whether they are planned or unplanned, formal or informal. The coaching path is illustrated in Figure 10.2.

The different stages along the coaching path are activities to focus on, rather than tasks to be completed. The coach must fulfil the broader purpose of each stage, while staying aware of the needs of the coachee. Some activities may occasionally be revisited, such as the coachee's goals for the conversation, e.g. if the direction of the discussion changes course.

The role of the coach is to navigate through to conclusion, while facilitating a less directive style of conversation. That demands an awareness both of where the discussion has reached on the coaching path, and of where the coachee needs to be guided towards next. The coachee needs to feel they are in safe hands, so that they can focus on the content of the discussion, rather than the process of the session.

While the structure may require concentration and focus initially, with practice, it will help the coach develop a style that is effective and also naturally their own.

Figure 10.2 The coaching path – structure for a conversation

Thinking about structure and process helps make coaching effective

An ongoing coaching relationship is made more effective by planning and preparation. By considering the key stages or components of the coaching process, we are able to balance the amount of time we spend on these activities. These stages are highlighted in Figure 10.3.

It makes sense to consider these stages in the logical order they are indicated. That's not necessarily how they will occur though, and the sequence of activities may need to be changed. Once these stages have begun, they become themes that are developed throughout the coaching assignment. For example, once we've defined initial goals and a sense of direction for the assignment, we must maintain these over time.

A good coach is emotionally mature

Emotional maturity refers to our ability to deal with emotions, e.g. interpret emotions, express emotions and process emotions. More broadly, our emotional maturity helps us cope with life. Our ability to stay resourceful, to manage ourselves, to build or harmonize relationships are all life skills that are embraced under the heading of emotional maturity. Our emotional

Figure 10.3 Framework for a coaching assignment

maturity will have a major impact on our ability to create the conditions of success, happiness and fulfilment over time. Another common term used for this concept is 'emotional intelligence' (EI).

Signs of emotional maturity, or immaturity, can be reflected in our typical behavioural responses. Instinctively, when we describe someone's behaviour as 'mature' or 'immature' we are often referring to their apparent levels of emotional maturity. Like intelligence (IQ), we can measure emotional maturity, in a rating called EQ. Unlike our rating of IQ, emotional maturity is something we can nurture and develop over time.

Emotional maturity has four main areas (see Figure 10.4):

➡ Self-awareness.

➡ Self-management.

➡ Awareness of others.

➡ Relationship management.

It is our mastery of all areas that develops our overall emotional maturity. And it is our overall emotional maturity that enables us to foster and encourage maturity in others.

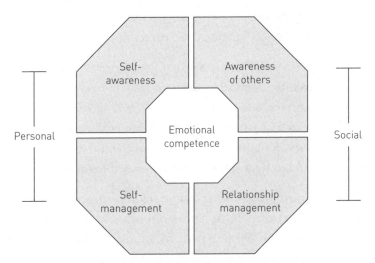

Figure 10.4 The four elements of emotional competence (with acknowledgement to Daniel Goleman)

Emotional maturity is a requirement of any coach as it impacts on our ability to be effective as a coach. Effective coaching results in an increased emotional maturity of the coachee as they learn new principles of thought and behaviour during coaching. As the coachee learns these 'skills of life' they can continue to influence them long after the coaching has ended.

Becoming a coach

Anyone who wants coaching to be something they are good at, and recognized for, would benefit from a personal sense of being a coach. Someone may declare themselves a coach whether or not they charge for their coaching services. A 'professional coach' is someone who earns an income from coaching. That income may derive from formal or informal coaching. There are three main expressions of 'being a coach'. They are:

➡ To integrate coaching as a style of behaviour that enhances your current job or role, so that what you do remains broadly the same, but how you do it is sometimes in a less directive, coaching style.

➡ To avoid any occupations other than coaching, and devote yourself to earning an income purely through coaching.

➡ To supplement or combine your current methods of earning income with coaching. For example, declare yourself as offering coaching services, and charge people for those coaching services. At the same time, maintain other occupations and professions.

There is no 'right' way to become a coach. Each individual must reflect on their own circumstances and objectives, to find the best way forward for them. What's important is that a coach develops their own style and application of coaching in a way that is aligned with who they are as a person. In that way, they develop their coaching as an authentic expression of themselves, which is guided by a set of universal principles and skills.

When we first venture into professional coaching, we sometimes disregard all the resources we already have. Those resources include skills, qualifications, experience, and our existing network of relationships and contacts. It is likely that we have immediate opportunities to coach all around us. Once we have reflected upon our existing resources, we can focus on what other resources we also need, e.g. skills, experience or support from others. As a guiding principle, the idea that we are 'enough', and can also be so much more, will help sustain us as we embark upon the journey ahead.

The future of coaching

The personal coaching field has grown significantly during the past 30 years, and it continues to grow. No longer do we think of coaches as being associated only with the field of sports. We've got coaches in business, life coaches, coaching for presidents and politicians – wherever people strive to attain success and fulfilment, coaches are often at work. Clients are becoming more aware of the potential benefits of coaching, and more aware of what they are looking for in a coach.

So, the field of coaching is firmly established and is growing. It still needs to become more clearly defined. Too much of what distinguishes quality coaching remains a mystery to both clients and coaches alike. Where a lack of clear definition exists, coaches waste valuable time and take unnecessary risks with coachees, trying to learn for themselves what works and what doesn't.

Clients need to know what to look for when securing the services of a good coach. They need to know what to expect and what constitutes good coaching practice. They need to feel that their investments of time, effort and money are resources well spent. Great coaching can literally be transformational, causing dramatic improvements in both professional and personal situations. Poor quality coaching does no one any good, least of all the coaching profession itself.

> Great coaching can be transformational, causing dramatic improvements in both professional and personal situations.

Anyone interested in coaching as an activity or profession needs clear guidelines and principles to operate from. Coaches need the support of structure, process, tools and techniques upon which they can build a really great coaching practice. I'll add that what they don't need is an inhibiting, exclusive set of rules and regulations that have them decide against coaching as something they will enjoy. As in life, achieving balance is the key. The balance we must find is to establish principles and guides that support both coach and clients. While great strides forward have been made, we still have work to do.

Taking your learning forward

The person who ultimately benefits most from your learning and development as a coach is you. The skills gained within coaching – of awareness, communication, analysis and insight – are incredibly fulfilling. They're also invaluable life skills and help all of us in our own situations and relationships.

As a profession or simply as part of what you already do, coaching offers you an opportunity to make a real contribution to others. Good coaches can make a great difference. And no matter how experienced or skilled a coach is, there's always more to learn. New approaches and principles constantly emerge to keep us fresh and aware of the options available to us. So I hope this book has added to your own learning (I know it's added to mine). I encourage you to stay committed to your own self-development and I wish you enjoyment and success with that.

Chapter summary   **Summary and close**

Coaching is ultimately a journey of discovery for both the coach and the coachee. In coaching, I'm sometimes profoundly affected by the conversation I've just had. Either I've had insights that were relevant to me, or I've simply been touched by what has occurred. While it is never the purpose of the conversation, a coach can sometimes benefit from the coaching as much as the coachee.

So coaching is no ordinary work but a labour of love; often demanding, sometimes frustrating – always worthwhile. And if you accept the challenge of coaching, it's a lifelong journey of learning, where you'll experience the circle of giving and receiving often. And if you've got this far, I suspect you're already a traveller on that journey ...

Toolkit – Practising Coaching Behaviours and Building Assignments

This section provides you with ways of practising coaching behaviours and also short pieces intended to help you build your coaching assignments. The first part, 'Strengthen your skills', consists of activities that will help increase your coaching ability, or enable you to revisit core principles of behaviour in the future if that's useful. They are more detailed exercises than in the previous chapters of this book. The second part, 'Building blocks', consists of items to help you get started with more formal coaching and will help you begin a coaching assignment. Use the following overview to help you select what you need:

Part 1. Strengthen your skills

Activity	Purpose
1.1 Help someone else find their answer	Practising a core coaching principle of helping someone else surface their own ideas and conclusions.
1.2 Meditation for non-judgement	Helping you develop a 'still mind' needed to coach effectively.
1.3 Developing deep listening	Helping you develop the attention you need to coach effectively.
1.4 Get some feedback	Learning the principles of giving constructive feedback, by receiving some.
1.5 Building a clear goal	A structured tool that helps someone get really clear about what they want in a situation, and become motivated towards it.

Part 2. Building blocks

Building block	Purpose
2.1 Coaching overview document	A document you might give to a new coachee or client, to help begin an assignment.

2.3 Preparing for a first session	A quick checklist to help you plan and prepare for a coaching session.
2.3 Summary of a first session	An overview of what happened in a first coaching session, to help you orientate to a typical conversation.
2.4 Feedback interview document	An overview of a conversation a coach has had with an individual nominated to them by their coachee, in order to gather feedback on their behalf (as input to a coaching assignment).

Online resources

For more coaching information and resources see our website, www.starrconsulting.co.uk. Here you can register to become part of our coaching community and access free downloads, watch video clips or ask us a question relating to coaching or building a coaching practice. We welcome feedback and we'd love to hear from you.

PART 1. STRENGTHEN YOUR SKILLS

Activity 1.1 Help someone else find their answer

What is this?	Guidelines on how to have an informal conversation with someone that will help you practise being 'less directive'.
When might I use it?	When you want to begin coaching and aren't sure how to. Or when you have realized that you are still giving your coachees too much advice, or controlling the direction of conversations.
Why would I do this?	To reveal the simple power of this technique for yourself, to prove that you often don't need to

tell anyone what to do, or even how to do it. That people normally have the best answer for them, they just need help to surface it.

To help let go of any cynicism you might have, about the potential of coaching.

To get better at coaching and facilitation generally.

For this exercise, you'll need to have a casual conversation with someone where they are discussing a problem or frustration. You can have this conversation by asking someone to do this, or you could wait for the next time this occurs naturally. It will be a conversation where the other person is not asking you to solve their problem; they're just talking, or complaining about it. For example, perhaps they're too busy, or in conflict with someone, unhappy with their job, etc.

Rules for you

During the conversation, you *must not* give them any advice or suggestions for a way forward. No matter how great your ideas or advice, just pretend for a while that you don't have an answer – and they do.

Stage one – Display the relevant facts

Ask them questions until you've (both) heard what you feel to be the 'key' or the relevant facts about the situation, e.g. 'What's actually happened? What is causing that?' 'How supportive is your boss?' 'What's the real issue for you?' If observations work better than questions, then use them, e.g. 'You seem to be spending a long time out of the office'.

Stage two – Discover their answer

When you feel you've got enough information for them to answer the following questions, use whichever seems appropriate:

➡ 'What are you thinking of doing then?'

➡ 'What needs to happen, do you think?'

➡ 'What could you do then, to improve the situation?'

➡ 'What options do you have?'

➡ 'What have you decided then?'

Or any other question that requires them to think of their own solution to their situation.

Stage three (optional)

If you are still 100 per cent convinced that you have a better answer, the right answer, and that they will benefit greatly from hearing it, then tell them. Perhaps use one of the following phrases to link to the previous part:

➡ 'Can I offer an idea?'

➡ 'As you were talking, I've thought of something that might help. What if ...'

➡ 'You know, I'm wondering if another answer might be to ...'

What if it doesn't go well?

If the conversation isn't going well, for example:

➡ the discussion isn't flowing naturally;

➡ you can't think of the right questions or observations;

➡ they really (definitely) can't think of any ways forward;

give up, and have a go another day! Go back to having a normal, casual conversation, e.g. give your own views, experience, ideas, etc.

Alternatively, do stage one on its own, then add stage two when it feels right. Simply ask a few more questions than you would normally, before suggesting something. Before long, you'll find that feels more natural, as you feel less compelled to give your idea or advice. Then when that stage feels comfortable, ask them what their solution is, perhaps using some of the suggestions in stage two.

> Once we allow ourselves to detach from our own thoughts or judgements about another person, we can stop those thoughts getting in the way of something else we want to do, e.g. listening to the client.

Activity 1.3 Developing deep listening

What is this?	An exercise for listening to someone that creates a deeper understanding of them and their thoughts.
How would I use it?	You'll need someone to do this with you, who knows what you're doing and why. That way you can ask them for feedback and you'll learn faster. Once you're comfortable with this style of listening, you can use it anywhere you like. It's especially useful for coaches to be able to listen in this way during coaching sessions. Or use it anytime you want to give someone a really good listening to!
Why would I do this?	As the quality of your listening improves, you will benefit from:

- A clearer understanding of other people, their situations, thoughts and issues.
- An ability to develop better rapport or relationship with others.
- A more relaxed style of conversation with others.

How long will it take?	Approximately 45-60 minutes, depending on what the person you are working with wants to discuss.

Set-up

Ask your partner to think of three situations they'd like to create change around. These might be problems, minor frustrations, or goals and objectives they already have. If they can only think of a couple, that's OK – a third often pops up during the conversation. You are going to ask your partner to talk about each of the three situations or issues, one after another. Your role is that of listener, and your partner is the speaker.

The conversation – step by step

1 The speaker talks about their three things (problems or situations they want to change) with the listener. This might take about 30–40 minutes. During this time the listener may ask questions, acknowledge points raised, clarify information, etc.

2 The listener then takes about 10 minutes to summarize back to the speaker:

→ What the three issues or situations are.

→ How the listener feels about them.

→ What else wasn't actually said, but seemed relevant to the conversation.

3 Then the speaker gives the listener feedback, specifically:

→ How 'listened to' did they feel? e.g. How well did they feel you gave them their full attention as they were speaking, and how well did they think you understood them?

→ What effect did your 'listening' have upon the speaker, e.g. 'It made me talk more, made me feel like this …', etc.

→ How did the conversation affect how the speaker now feels about the three things?

During feedback, the speaker should give both their experience, e.g. what they felt, and what caused that experience. For example, the speaker might say, 'I felt listened to because you asked me questions to help you understand what I was saying.'

Your role as the listener

The primary aim of the listener is to understand what the speaker is saying. By a process of listening, questioning or clarifying, you should aim to:

→ Understand what the situations or problems really are, e.g. if the speaker is not happy with their job, identify some of the causes of that. If they want a closer relationship with their step-children, find out the driving factors behind that, what is currently in the way, etc.

→ Understand how they feel about the situations and be able to tell them afterwards, e.g. 'I think this situation is frustrating you and also perhaps upsetting you a little'.

⇒ Be able to fill in gaps in the conversation, i.e. what wasn't said. For example, 'I think maybe you're wondering how your step-children's mother might react'.

Ground rules for you as the listener

During the conversation, *do not*:

⇒ Attempt to give the speaker ideas, solutions or suggestions relating to the situations they are discussing.

⇒ Refer to or discuss any of your own similar circumstances, experiences or feelings.

⇒ Attempt to control the direction or content of the conversation.

⇒ Seek to look good or impress the other person in any way, e.g. by asking 'clever' questions, by offering impressive facts or information, etc.

⇒ (Do not) try to coach them ...

Toolkit summary **Developing deep listening**

The exercise is great for developing a different listening perspective. The listener's only motive is to really understand and relate to the other person, nothing else.

This exercise causes us to become aware of how much we are pro-grammed to want to put 'something of ourselves' into a conversation with another person. We might do this by solving their problems for them, showing them how much we know about what they're talking about, or even taking over the conversation completely.

Once this way of listening has been experienced, you can then practise this again and again, whenever you like. The other person doesn't have to know what you're doing, unless you want feedback. At some point during their practices, you are likely to experience a greater sense of what's really going on with the speaker, including those thoughts or feelings that aren't actually spoken. That's deep listening!

Activity 1.4 Get some feedback

A great way to learn about giving feedback is for you to experience receiving some. That way you can learn about what works and what does not work, plus how it actually feels to be focused on in this way. To do the exercise, choose someone who knows you well (whom you trust). As a word of caution, there can be no guarantees that you'll like what you hear, or agree with what's said. Remember, to give supportive feedback yourself you need to know what works and what doesn't.

Stage one – Set-up

You're going to ask this person for some feedback on a particular topic that you feel comfortable discussing, for example:

➡ What kind of manager am I?

➡ What kind of parent am I?

➡ How am I at giving presentations/running meetings, etc.?

Or any other area that you're interested in getting better at. If you're interested in a stretch, ask them to think about how they experience you generally, as a person.

Stage two – The questions

Ask them to consider the following three questions, with regard to the topic or area you've requested feedback on:

➡ What am I good at? / What do I do well? / What are my strengths, etc.?

➡ What am I not so good at?

➡ What could I do differently to improve?

When your partner has answers for each section, continue to stage three.

Stage three – Have a feedback conversation

Ask your partner to give you their responses to each question in turn. Make sure that you understand each response, and use questions to clarify if necessary, e.g. 'Can you tell me a little more about that?' or 'Can you think of an example?' Receive all feedback graciously, maturely, and don't contradict the other person's view – after all, it's just their view. If they say something that you don't like or disagree with, simply find out a little more about what may have caused this view. When your partner has finished, thank them.

Stage four – Take the learning

Now, on your own, sit down with a piece of paper and write answers/notes to the following questions:

➡ What did I learn about myself from that conversation?

➡ What will I do differently as a result of that conversation?

➡ What was good about the way they gave me feedback?

➡ What didn't work about the way they gave me feedback?

➡ What can I learn from that? e.g. what principles will I use when giving feedback now?

Think also about how the conversation was useful to you generally. What was it like seeing yourself through the eyes of the other person?

Stage five (optional) – Share your learning

If you feel it is appropriate and useful, share your answers to the above questions with your partner. Ask them first if they'd like to hear them, as a way of sharing your learning. Remember, you'll now be in position of giving feedback yourself, so please employ all your learning and care!

Toolkit summary   **Get some feedback**

This is an exercise where what you actually get from it might be something different than you imagined. For example, self-awareness or a desire to adapt some of your behaviour in some situations. Remember, one of the key benefits of coaching conversations is emotional maturity, and the giving and receiving of feedback demands emotional maturity in either situation.

Activity 1.5 Building a clear goal

What is this? A way of helping someone define a goal or objective they have more clearly.

What does it do? Helps someone gain a fuller understanding of their goal.

Explores the motivation behind their goal.

Either (a) increases their motivation towards their goal, or (b) helps them realize they don't really want it after all.

Identifies situations or barriers that might stop them from having their goal.

Agrees immediate actions related to the goal.

When might I use it? During initial coaching sessions, when discussing what goals the coachee wants to work on.

Any time that someone seems to have a vague goal or 'wish', e.g. 'I wish I had a better job'.

Parts of it may also be used in isolation, e.g. some questions work well on their own in general conversation.

Learning guidance

The stages described opposite deal with those aspects of the goal that need to be explored and discussed by the coach. The aspects can be covered in the order in which they are written here, or in a different sequence if needed. It's more important to create a conversation that flows naturally. The best way to learn the parts of the conversation is to write a checklist, i.e. make a note of the headings, then tick each one when you've covered it. You'll soon remember them and be able to hold the conversation naturally without the checklist.

Some stages might be covered quickly, while others require further discussion. For example, someone might know exactly what they want, but need help understanding why they want it.

The 'coaching questions' are suggestions you might find useful. Just use those questions that work for you and the situation you are discussing. Remain flexible during the conversation, e.g. if the person changes their mind about what they want, you may have to go back a few steps to create a clear view of the revised goal.

State the goal in positive terms

The goal must be stated in terms of what the individual wants, rather than what they don't want, for example:

➡ What they don't want: 'Stop losing my temper so often.'

➡ What they *do* want: 'Keep calm and relaxed in difficult situations.'

Coaching questions – be positive

➡ 'What *do* you want?'

➡ 'What would you rather have or be true?'

➡ 'What do you want instead?'

➡ 'What is it you actually *do* want?'

Get specific! What, where, when, with whom?

In order to be really clear about the goal, we begin to add more and more detail. For example, 'I want more energy' is too vague. We need to understand when, where and with whom, e.g. 'I want more energy to be able to play sports with my kids after work'. If there's a timescale involved, find out what it is, e.g. within three months.

Coaching questions – be specific

➡ 'When do you want more energy specifically?'

➡ 'What does having more energy mean to you?'

➡ 'When might you not need more energy?'

Remember to focus on what *they* want and not what *you* think would be good, e.g. 'Wouldn't more energy help you to play sports with your kids at the weekend?'

You may sometimes want to challenge the person a little, either to improve the goal, or their level of commitment. Please use care and judge wisely if you do. The person will normally know what is a stretch for them. Sometimes a simple question will identify whether the goal is challenging enough, e.g. 'How much of a challenge is that for you?'

Use imagination to pull it closer

Using other senses, e.g. sight, sound, etc. helps the individual to create images or ways of representing the goal, to enable them to understand the goal more easily. It is even more powerful to ask these questions from a position of assuming they already have the goal.

Coaching questions – pull it closer

→ 'How will you *know* when you have your dream job?'

→ 'Imagine you have your dream job – what do you feel like?'

→ 'How are things different now that you have your dream job?'

→ 'How does this affect the way you look?'

→ 'What are people saying about you now that you have this dream job?'

→ 'So, imagine you wake up tomorrow and you have this dream job – now tell me what that's like.'

The other benefit to these questions is that you may spot 'something missing', e.g. they don't seem as thrilled as you expected. Their response might be a prompt for you to recheck that they do actually want what they say, or seek to understand their hesitation.

Check their power to influence

A goal is more easily reached when it is within the natural influence of the individual who wants it. For example, I can't get my boss or partner to stop acting stressed around me, but I can have the goal of responding in a relaxed, resourceful way to their behaviour. I can control my own actions – not those of others. I can't have a goal for someone else. Also, when someone else has a goal for me, I need to want it as well in order to be really motivated to make it happen.

So we need to discuss the goal in a way which establishes a clear responsibility, or influence, over the goal.

Coaching questions – check influence

➡ 'How much influence do you have over this?'

➡ 'Are you responsible for making your goal happen?'

➡ 'What can you do to achieve it?'

➡ 'Is it within your power to influence this?'

➡ 'Who else wants this for you?'

Check that the goal is in balance

We want to make sure that it's 'OK' for the individual to have this goal, in relation to the rest of their life. For example, if someone wants to travel more with their job and they have young children, they need to look at the effect of travel upon their home life. By exploring the impact of their goal on other situations, we work to maintain balance. We are also respecting other parts of their life, relationships and circumstances around them, by considering any knock-on effects elsewhere.

Coaching questions – check balance

➡ 'What would the consequences of getting this goal be?'

➡ 'Are there any negative consequences of having this?'

➡ 'How would having this affect your home life (or your family, or your friends)?'

➡ 'How does this affect other people at work?'

➡ 'How does this affect other things which are important to you?'

Increase motivation

This is a way of referring to basic values and understanding our goal in relation to those values. By aligning with values that are important to us, we can better understand the priority of our goal. For example, if variety and challenge are important to you, you may notice that it doesn't 'feel good' to consider doing exactly the same job for the next three years. However, if security and stability are more important to you, you may view three years in the same job as perfect. In this check we also identify potential barriers, either internal or external, in order to shift those barriers.

Coaching questions – increase motivation

➡ 'What would achieving this do for you?'

➡ 'What higher purpose does this fulfil?'

➡ 'If you have this, what sort of person will that make you?'

➡ 'What else will you get if you have this?'

➡ 'What is stopping you from having this?'

➡ 'What might stop you from having this?'

➡ 'As you think about the journey towards this – what might stand in your way?'

➡ 'If you could have this right now – would you take it?'

That final question is a clever one, as it works with people's gut instinct. Ask someone who says they want to quit smoking that question, e.g. 'If I could make you a non-smoker right now – would you let me?' If they hesitate, that's usually because they have some doubt. Once you've identified the hesitation, you can explore the cause.

Identify action – do it now!

This check identifies the next logical action in relation to the goal and gains commitment to taking this action. We begin to move out of thinking and talking about it and into 'doing'. For example, 'I want to study for my degree' becomes 'I'm going to call three colleges to get their current syllabus'. You may choose to support the individual further by gaining a more formal agreement to taking this action, e.g. which colleges, by when – and agree to check in later to hear what progress has been made.

Coaching questions – identify action

➡ 'What can you do to achieve this goal?'

➡ 'What is the next/first step for you now?'

➡ 'What's the next logical thing you would do to achieve this?'

➡ 'What one (or two, or three) thing(s) could you be doing right now which would have tremendous impact on your progress towards this goal?'

Toolkit summary **Building a clear goal**

By talking through different perspectives on their goal, the individual will normally benefit. Hopefully they will be feeling clearer, optimistic and perhaps more determined or motivated as a result.

Alternatively, they might have discarded the original goal completely, having realized that it wasn't something that they really wanted or would benefit from. Maybe they've replaced it with a new goal, or maybe they need to go away and do some more 'thinking'. In either instance, the coach now knows much more about the person's thinking and can support them more effectively.

PART 2. BUILDING BLOCKS

Building block 2.1 Coaching overview document*

What is this?   An overview of coaching.

What does it do?   Gives someone an initial understanding of coaching, what it is, possible benefits, etc.
Establish mutual expectations, e.g. what your coachee can expect from you, what you will expect from them.
Encourages a coachee to begin thinking about any goals or objectives they might have.

*For a pdf download version of this document, go to www.starrconsulting.co.uk

When might I use it?   During initial discussions about the potential of coaching.

When beginning a new coaching relationship, to give a new coachee some background information or reading.

Introduction

This document is intended to:

⇒ Give an overview of personal coaching, what it is, how it works, and its potential benefits.

⇒ Describe what you can expect from your coach and what your coach will expect from you.

⇒ Encourage you to think about how coaching might benefit you.

What is personal coaching?

Coaching is a form of learning, where a person (a coach) supports someone else (a coachee) to create learning and self-development in a way that benefits them.

From early forms of transportation, i.e. stagecoach or rail coach, the word 'coaching' literally means to transport someone from one place to another. One thing that all forms of coaching seem to have in common is that people are using it to help them move forward in a certain direction.

Coaching is normally a conversation, or series of conversations, one person has with another. The coach intends to produce a conversation that will benefit the other person, the coachee, in a way that relates to the coachee's learning and progress. Coaching conversations might happen in different ways, and in different environments.

For example, coaching might consist of two people talking in a room about things the coachee wants to change. This is sometimes called 'off-line' coaching. It might also be one person observing another person doing something, e.g. chairing a meeting, then discussing that with them. This can be called 'on-line' coaching.

Why do people have coaching?

People enlist the services of a coach because they want to improve their situations and achieve goals. They want to learn new ways of thinking and approaching situations, in order to get better results. Common goals might be to be more organized and effective at work; gain confidence in certain situations; or simply interact with other people more effectively.

A coach uses a combination of observation, questioning, listening and feedback to create a conversation that's rich in insight and learning. For the coachee, they will experience a focus and attention that enable them to develop a greater awareness and appreciation of their own circumstances. In addition, they'll also create new ways to resolve issues, produce better results and generally achieve their goals more easily.

Common benefits people experience from coaching include:

➡ Improved sense of direction and focus.

➡ Increased knowledge of self/self-awareness.

➡ Improved ability to relate to and influence others.

➡ Increased motivation.

➡ Improved personal effectiveness, e.g. focused effort.

➡ Increased resourcefulness/resilience, e.g. ability to handle change.

What coaching is not

Coaching is none of the following:

Structured training, e.g. classroom learning

Structured training relates to a fixed agenda of learning and a prepared approach to making that learning happen. For example, if you were being trained in a classroom to use a computer, the trainer would often use a structured approach to making sure you learnt a certain amount of information, within a certain time frame.

Coaching follows a more flexible format, according to the coachee's objectives. Both the coachee and the coach influence the direction and content of sessions. Coaching also places real responsibility for learning on the individual and encourages learning to continue after the session.

Therapy, psychoanalysis, psychotherapy

While coaching is not therapy, and should not be viewed as therapy, it does provide a viable alternative to people who may have previously considered some form of counselling to resolve a situation. For example, coaching promotes a greater self-awareness, and fuller appreciation of our own situations and circumstances. Sometimes, change can emerge from a simple shift in perspectives. Barriers of self-belief such as 'I can't' or 'I don't' can be challenged in order to encourage fresh approaches and ideas.

A way of someone else solving your problems for you

Coaching is based on the principle that an individual is ultimately responsible for their lives and the results they're getting. If we acknowledge that we are responsible for something, it follows that we have power and influence over it. For example, if you're not getting the results at work that you want, a coach might encourage you to:

➡ Understand that situation more clearly.

➡ Develop new ideas or approaches for such situations.

➡ Take constructive action that gets you the results you want.

What a coach will not do is instruct you to go and do something specific, or go and do it for you. If they did, the coach would be taking responsibility – and so power – away from you.

What you can expect from your coach

The role of coach provides a kind of support distinct from any other. Your coach will focus solely on your situation with the kind of attention and commitment that you rarely experience elsewhere.

Your coach will listen to you, with a genuine curiosity to understand who you are, what you think and generally how you experience the world. Your coach will reflect back to you, with the kind of objective assessment that creates real clarity. During conversations, your coach will encourage you to rise to challenges, overcome obstacles and get into action.

A coaching relationship is like no other, simply because of its combination of objective detachment and commitment to the goals of the individual.

Because the relationship is based on trust and openness, the content of your discussions will be confidential. Where a third party has requested the coaching for you, your coach will agree with you the best way to keep them involved or updated.

What your coach will expect from you

In return, your coach will encourage you to stay committed to the coaching process. That means showing up for sessions, taking your own notes where appropriate, and keeping any agreements you make during sessions.

Your coach also needs you to be open to the potential of coaching. That means contributing to conversations honestly and openly. For example, if something isn't working, your coach needs to know. If you have concerns or problems, voice them. If you know why a problem is occurring, say so. The strength and power of coaching relates strongly to the level of openness and trust between you and your coach.

How might coaching benefit you?

The following questions will help you begin to form goals for a coaching relationship. They are not intended to identify specifics, but rather encourage thoughts or ideas.

Please take a few minutes to sit quietly with the questions, writing down your answers on a blank sheet of paper.

What current goals (if any) do you have relating to the following areas:

Your work, e.g.
- ➡ Personal performance/effectiveness.
- ➡ Career development, progression.
- ➡ Ability to lead/manage others.
- ➡ Motivation, fulfilment.

Your lifestyle, e.g.

➡ Work/life balance.
➡ Social life.
➡ Hobbies/interests.

Your relationships with others, e.g.

➡ Your partner.
➡ Your immediate family.
➡ Your friends.
➡ Your extended family, i.e. relatives.

Your learning/development, e.g.

➡ Life experiences.
➡ Formal training/development.

Your sense of contribution, e.g.

➡ At work.
➡ At home.
➡ In your community.

Your health/well-being, e.g.

➡ Health.
➡ Nutrition and eating patterns.
➡ Fitness, exercise, relaxation etc.

Thinking about your current circumstances:

➡ What would you like to do less of?
➡ What would you like to do more of?

If you could change one thing about your current situation right now, what would you change?

What's going really well for you right now, which you'd like to build on? For example, do more of it, or make it even better.

In what ways do you currently obtain learning?

➡ By experience, i.e. doing things.
➡ Formal study, e.g. taking qualifications.
➡ Through observation of others.
➡ Reading, listening to audio programmes, etc.
➡ Structured training, i.e. courses.
➡ Mentoring or coaching relationships, e.g. discussion, feedback.

How much does these styles of learning support your goals and objectives? What thoughts are you having now?

Toolkit summary | **Coaching overview document**

The important things to communicate in the initial stages of a first coaching conversation are:

- That you know what you're doing.
- That you're confident to do that.
- That the other person is in 'safe hands' (and so they can relax).

A little thought and planning ahead of time will help you to communicate those things, while helping you to be comfortable too.

Building block 2.3 Summary of a first session

What follows is a summary of the first session of a coaching assignment. It might have been written by a novice coach, to help them reflect on what happened during the session. The purpose of offering it here is to display the key points, the flow of the discussion and a little content from the discussion. It is not a 'scripted' account of the conversation, nor a guide to the 'perfect' first session. It simply shows what type of things might be discussed, to provide a foundation for later coaching conversations. Detailed facts of the discussion are intentionally reduced, to enable us to focus on the key points and general flow.

Coach: Carla Foster
Coachee: Jack Aston
Date of session: 3 May
Duration: 2½ hours
Location: Derby

Session objectives

➡ To learn a little more about Jack.

➡ To discuss how the coaching assignment might be structured over time (currently estimated at five sessions over six months).

➡ To identify some initial goals for the assignment.

➡ To discuss some of Jack's current issues and challenges.

➡ To agree a way forward following this session.

Background

➡ Joined Global Autoparts Ltd seven years ago (has over 20 years in manufacturing).

➡ 49 years old.

➡ Originally from Dublin, Ireland.

➡ Married to Elizabeth for fifteen years.

➡ Has two children, Frankie (seven years) and Chloe (ten months).

➡ Still has both parents, Donald (retired teacher) and Kath.

➡ Brother Matthew is older by three years.

➡ Sister Jolene younger by five years.

Jack is the Project Director of the Pyramid Programme, which is six months old. The Pyramid Programme aims to create environmentally friendly processes for the manufacture of car parts. It is a two-year project with a budget of £2.7m. This project is already the subject of media attention and represents a new direction for the company. This means the Pyramid Programme is both a high-profile and potentially pressurized situation. Jack's industry knowledge and entrepreneurial ability were the main reasons he was chosen for the role. He has a fairly senior team of five people. These people are all new to him and he has needed to build working relationships quickly. Each of his team has their own teams reporting to them. The overall project team is around 45 people.

Jack is married with a young family. He lives on his own during the week and travels home at weekends. This is a new situation for him and one that both he and his family are getting used to.

Initial objectives for coaching

Jack is interested in three areas:

1 His ability to manage performance, e.g. in terms of the ability to deliver. He admires anyone who can do this naturally:
   - 'I see people who are better at this than me.'
   - 'I don't feel strong in this area, I have trouble letting go sometimes.'

- 'It's especially difficult with such a senior team, we've got some strong characters.'

2 His ability to 'stay at the appropriate level', e.g. be the guardian of the vision and create leadership for others, rather than getting 'lost in the detail':
   - 'I need to manage my time better – that's an immediate opportunity.'

3 He'd like to find ways to foster better relationships, both within the team and with some of the suppliers.
   - 'Manufacturing is pretty cut-throat'.
   - 'This project is high profile so our approach must be different.'
   - 'The environmental conversation is an issue for everyone. We need to be collaborative.'

Jack's objectives for the project

→ 'I want the vision for the programme to be owned by the whole team – I want people to engage at an individual level, to feel that we're doing something worthwhile.'

→ 'That we stay aligned over time, i.e. what we're doing and how we're doing it.'

→ 'I want to feel that we're harmonizing our approaches; that people are really pulling together, supporting each other.'

→ 'That technically, we maintain quality. That we get the specifications side of the manufacturing process right. That's where we have the experience – I want to see that count.'

→ 'I'd like to see more creativity around some of our solutions; this is a new area for us, and we need to display a fresh approach.'

A need for a more consistent style

Jack acknowledged that his attitude towards the individuals in the team can vary. For example, if he believes in someone's ability from the outset, that person will get his commitment and support. That person will experience him as open, friendly and supportive. But if someone makes a poor first impression, he is likely to make assumptions based on their overall ability.

He may even withdraw support from them over time, simply by being less communicative or warm towards them.

This person's performance may then degrade, which may go unnoticed for a period, until Jack's attention is drawn to the situation. This person may have needed support and not been getting it, or concealing issues, which later cause difficult situations. Jack has recently had one such example, where a serious issue arose. 'The guy had been off doing his own thing – I just hadn't seen the mistakes being made.'

Through discussion, Jack decided that a more structured, consistent managing style would improve this situation over time, for example:

➡ Regular, structured group reporting sessions.

➡ Monitoring measures of performance more closely, e.g. delivery against plan.

➡ Regular, structured one-to-one meetings, based on coaching principles.

Jack explained that he has various styles of managing, dependent on the individual. Sometimes this works and sometimes it doesn't. For example, some people had regular one-to-ones with him, while others didn't. He anticipated this irregular contact with some people as one of the causes of his 'blind spots'.

Structuring time

Jack explained that he also wants to manage his time more effectively, in order to focus on the priority tasks. We quickly estimated how Jack spends his time, as shown in the table on the next page.

Jack saw opportunities to improve the allocation of his own time and also his team's time. For example, Jack wanted to spend less time being interrupted at his desk in ad hoc conversations. One way he thought this could be possible was to have regular, structured conversations with each of his team. He also saw benefits from involving the team more in some of his own activities, e.g. involving them during the early stages of generating ideas, sharing his workload, etc. One obvious area was to have the team take more responsibility for liaison with suppliers, once the team is more aware of the importance of that.

No.	Activity	Current %	Target
1	Reporting: preparing reports, technical data, presentations to the board, etc.	25	10
2	Internal meetings to discuss issues, progress, gain updates, etc. (wider team).	15	10
3	Supplier meetings: 'These are often just information update sessions; I need to delegate these more often'.	10	0–5
4	Dealing with electronic mail: 'I have to ignore some stuff'.	25–30	10
5	Informal discussions, e.g. being interrupted at his desk, random questions etc: 'I want to make this less acceptable to do'.	15–20	10
6	Planning/revising approaches: short–medium–term, long-term/vision: 'I need to make this less of a solitary task'.	15	20
7	Personal meetings with his team.	0	15–20

Jack decided that he wanted to spend time identifying what activities are needed for increasing performance across the team. Then he can work out how to focus more time on those activities.

Creating 'head space'

Jack initially explained he'd like more 'time to think'. When we explored this further, he realized that what he actually wanted was a feeling of 'free space' in his head, which is a slightly different idea. For example, if he felt the project was well organized, well structured, running well, he'd feel like he was 'on top of things'. Automatically that would mean that his thought processes would be clearer and he'd feel he had more time to consider things. He explained that he often felt 'on his back foot' and had a background concern of having forgotten something.

Conclusions

Jack valued the time spent talking about his situations and challenges. Together we agreed the initial focus of the coaching, and his objectives for it. He also agreed it would be useful to gather some feedback from his current and previous project team. Carla will gather this on his behalf. He would also be interested in seeking feedback on the project generally from some of his suppliers, but would like his own team to gather that.

Let's gather feedback

We agreed to interview some of Jack's colleagues to gain feedback about Jack's strengths and development needs. Jack will make requests of the following people:

1 Bob Bailey
2 Diane Cooper
3 Nigel Shelley

Jack will confirm contact details by e-mail (Carla will then interview them by telephone).

Actions

1 Jack to construct a 'list of priorities' and refocus his time against those priorities, e.g. meetings with his team.
2 Jack to contact the three people for Carla to interview and send contact details.
3 Jack to confirm how many coaching sessions he'd like and over what approximate time period.
4 Carla to send e-mail of actions agreed, plus book recommendations, e.g. *The 7 Habits of Highly Effective People* by Stephen Covey.
5 Carla to contact Jack's PA to schedule next session in approximately four weeks' time.

Toolkit summary   **Summary of a first session**

A first coaching session needs to build rapport, gather initial information and create a sense of direction for the future assignment. This
information and sense of direction will form the base on which further
conversations can build. It is not necessary to 'learn everything' about
the coachee or indeed 'solve all problems'. More important is that
trust and openness are developed between the coach and the coachee.
Remember that the process of conversation is a catalyst, as thoughts
and ideas continue to emerge for the coachee over time. So the simple
'laying out' of facts and objectives is often more valuable than we might
anticipate. The coach adds value by gently navigating through the
conversation, establishing background information, key goals for the
assignment, and then surfacing discussion on the coachee's areas of
interest. By the end of the session, the coach and the coachee should be
left with a clear sense of the approach being taken and the way forward.
Any follow-up needed by the coach, such as e-mailing key discussion
points, or arranging the next meeting, needs to be handled quickly and
professionally.

Building block 2.4 Feedback interview document

What is this?   A record of a conversation the coach has had on
                           behalf of the coachee.

What does it do?   Gathers feedback on the strengths and develop-
                           ment areas of a coachee.

                           Gathers perceptions of the coachee from people the
                           coachee has nominated for feedback.

                           Provides the coachee with additional sources
                           of reflection or observation that may help their
                           development.

                           Helps raise the self-awareness of the coachee.

When might I use it?   In the early stages of a coaching assignment, e.g.
                           after the first session, or indeed any time the
                           coachee feels the information is relevant/useful.

Collecting feedback on someone's behalf must be done sensitively and as openly as possible. Interviewees must be aware that the document will be attributed and they must have a chance to review and change the document before it is shared in the coaching session. The role of the coach is to collect the feedback in a way that is both efficient and effective. For example: interviewing people in a professional manner, recording comments in a way that distils the message clearly, and handling the approval process quickly. The coach can also 'coach' the interviewee to offer comments in an appropriate way (which generally people want to do). The other value the coach adds is in the delivery of the feedback. For example, helping the coachee to hear and digest the messages, before they decide what they want to do as a result of the feedback. Guidelines for interviewing people, writing the session up, and gaining approval to use the document are contained in Chapter 7, 'Coaching assignment: structure and process' (p. 185).

What follows is based on real examples adapted for this purpose.

> **Coachee name:** Simon Gibson
> **Input name:** Helena Phillips
> **Date of interview:** 17 March
> **Date approved for use:** 25 March

1 What is this person good at?

I think generally Simon brings skills to the role we really need, he's got relevant experience and qualifications and it shows. He's experienced in both building strong teams and managing projects; he's a professional. When things get awkward, e.g. we've got technical issues, Simon can usually contribute. He's also pretty objective and remains focused when things get stressful – I wish I could say that of more people around here. Plus he's a nice guy to have around generally – it's fair to say he's well liked.

2 What do you value most about them?

On reflection it's probably his ability to focus on solutions, rather than problems. We have some pretty difficult individuals here who like to apportion blame. Simon seems to stay out of all that, he automatically seeks the resolution, e.g. 'OK, that's how it is – so what can we do now?' I think I've come to really rely on him for that.

3 **What do they need to get better at?**

Generally I think I'd like to see Simon speaking up more, making a bigger impact. He tends to stay quiet sometimes. Like I said, he's often got a lot to add to the conversation, but can sometimes get 'drowned out' by the bigger personalities in the room. I don't know if it's a confidence thing, he seems pretty confident. I wonder if it's about avoiding conflict, not sure. In a fast-moving environment we need people to get in fast with views and opinions. It's just not a culture here where people seek out consensus, or listen patiently to quiet voices.

A smaller point is that he sometimes seems preoccupied with detail. In discussions it sometimes feels like he's 'over-explaining things'. Either he needs to find a way to communicate the key data more quickly, or else make more generalized points. Keep the conversation at an appropriate level. It's fine to tell us that the plan is going to be changed, but as an operational area we don't need always to understand the finer detail of what led us to that decision. We're more concerned about what's going to happen most of the time – if we want the detail I guess we can always ask. On matters of planning and scheduling, we trust his judgement – maybe he doesn't appreciate that?

4 **What do they need to do to be successful in their current situation or role?**

I think he's already doing a good job, so I would say that he's already fairly successful. I think if he wants to bring true value to the role he could use his position to act more as a 'bridge' between departments. For example, he sits between the customer-facing departments and the more technical functions. He's in an ideal position to mediate some of our issues, or facilitate discussions for us more. His ability to remain calm in a crisis (or a row) makes him ideal. But that's going to mean stepping forward more often into those situations, which may cause him discomfort.

5 **Do you have any other messages for this person?**

Just that I'm pleased to have been asked to do this. Simon is someone I'm incredibly supportive of, we really value his contribution. If there's any of this feedback he wants to discuss with me, I'd be glad to – I'll even buy the coffee!

Toolkit summary **Feedback interview document**

Gathering constructive feedback can be a valuable way to support the coaching process. The additional perspectives raised, or insights offered, are often new information for the coachee. The information will often create both useful discussion and additional development goals for the coachee. It's important that the coach appreciates the principles of gathering the feedback and the ground rules for recording, approval and delivery. A well-prepared coach will add value to the process and improve the benefits of the process for the coachee.

Index